EQUINE BIOMECHANICS
FOR RIDERS

EQUINE BIOMECHANICS FOR RIDERS

The Key to Balanced Riding

KARIN BLIGNAULT

J.A. ALLEN · LONDON

*In memory of my dear and supportive friends, Judith Moxon
and Marcelle Smallberger.*

© Karin Blignault, 2009
First published in Great Britain 2009
Reprinted 2012
Reprinted 2015

ISBN 978 0 85131 953 7

J.A. Allen
Clerkenwell House
Clerkenwell Green
London EC1R OHT

www.allenbooks.co.uk

J.A. Allen is an imprint of Robert Hale Limited

A catalogue record for this book is available from the British Library

Edited by Martin Diggle
Designed and typeset by Paul Saunders
Illustrations by Maggie Raynor based on drawings by the author

Printed in India

Author's note

I would like to apologise to those riders whose photographs show them
or their horse in a less-than-perfect moment. These images have been
included purely for the good of the horse.

Contents

Foreword

In the past, riding at a high level was considered to be an art because only a few élite practitioners could manage the complex biomechanical interaction and communication between the rider and the horse. Through practice and experience they reached the highest level of skill and some of them transmitted their experience by teaching and writing books. It was these influences which formed the basis for the different riding schools in Europe. This was a time of empirical and subjective knowledge of horses and their functions.

From around the nineteenth century onward, equine sciences such as exercise physiology, biomechanics, sport medicine and ethology began to add to our knowledge about how the horse functions by providing objective measurements of the biological responses to exercise. This is a process that continues at an accelerating rate today. Consequently, riding education and training have improved because the teachers can better explain how the horse and rider should work with a minimum of stress and a maximum of efficiency. For example, equine locomotion studies have assisted in defining an accurate terminology to describe all the gait characteristics that are measured by gait analysis systems such as image analysis, force plates and accelerometers. One aspect of such studies is that better knowledge of equine motion should help riders to avoid uncomfortable exercises which lead to horse and/or rider injuries.

Equine ethology studies provide interesting observations for improving horse-rider communication, which is the key of riding performance. The horse is a very sensitive animal and can move very efficiently if the rider can stimulate the required motion at the right time and the right way. The seat and limb movements of the rider on his back should be harmonious stimuli for the horse motion (isopraxia). With better horse-rider communication, the horse's performance could be greatly improved and equestrian practice should be safer for both parties.

For all these reasons, I would like to congratulate Karin Blignault on her book which is a very good rider's digest of applied equine biomechanics. This book can be devoted to the pleasure of the horse in motion. Good reading and riding.

Eric Barrey DVM PhD
(Genomics and exercise physiology research
director, and biomechanics consultant)

Acknowledgements

I am indebted to my father who gave me the opportunity to study Occupational Therapy. Without this knowledge I would not have been able to make the connection to and compare human biomechanics with equine movement.

I would like to thank Caroline Burt, Cassandra Campbell and Lesley Gowers for each one's unique involvement with the development of this book. I particularly thank Martin Diggle, not only for the editing, but also for making me think more deeply about equine biomechanics and for livening up my day with his wonderful sense of humour. Thanks too to proof reader, Jane Lake.

I am indebted to Prof Dr Hannes Loots for reading the manuscript in the early stages and giving me advice on modern biomechanical concepts.

I am grateful to Dr Eric Barrey for his assistance in acquiring research information and honoured that he agreed to write the foreword.

Physiotherapists, Patrick Thomas and Claire Waumsley are constant sounding boards and advisors to me on neuro-muscular function and biomechanics. I thank them for their generosity in the sharing of knowledge.

I owe a great debt to my friend and editor of HQ Magazine, Johann Theron, for his endless patience with the majority of the photographs. Thank you also to Andrea Lindenberg for contributing the photographs 4.7, 7.1a, 9.3, 9.4, 10.5, and 11.3, to Tessa Moxon for the photographs numbered 2.4, 2.7, 3.1, 3.2, 5.1, 9.2 and 11.1, and to Claire Lilley for photograph 1.6.

I also thank Romy Chames for the many hours she put into the illustrations and Maggie Raynor for her expert alterations to my drawings.

Thank you to my friends, Mignon, Anna and Karin for their help, input and the loan of books, and also to my pupils Jess, Sarah and Emma-Kate for their patience with the photographs.

My husband André deserves mention for his help with my word-finding problem and his unquestioned acceptance of the household chaos so that I can have time to write.

Lastly, thank you to designer, Paul Saunders who has put the book together to turn it into a thing of beauty so that opening the final product feels like opening a special Christmas gift.

Introduction

The great French master, General L'Hotte, said in the nineteenth century that 'science has developed far faster than the art of riding'.[1] Today, a century and a half later, there has not been significant development in the art of riding. In fact, it has been encouraged to remain static by the emphasis on 'classical'. We have split the atom, developed computer chips the size of pinheads, trains which run at over 500 km per hour and keyhole surgery, yet after approximately 6,000 years, most of us have not mastered the sophisticated skill/art of riding. There is still considerable confusion as to how we should communicate with the horse. This is most probably because of the lack of scientific research in how the horse understands the rider. This is also the reason why, over the centuries, all kinds of gadgets, which force the horse into some position or other (especially to 'yield'), have developed out of proportion to their necessity. The fact is, if a horse does not react correctly after a few minutes of attempted correction by the rider, then he has either misunderstood or is in discomfort. The rider should then try a different method or seek the help of a veterinarian or equine physiotherapist.

Science, specifically sports science, neuro-muscular and exercise physiology, has developed with enormous strides during the previous and present century. Although still in its infancy, equine sport science teaches us how a horse's body and mind function. Through an understanding of this natural science, together with literature left to us by the classical masters, training horses, without the dependence on gadgets, becomes

1 Nelson, H., Alexis-François L'Hotte *The Quest for Lightness in Equitation*, J.A. Allen (London) 1997.

1

extremely easy and logical. Knowledge of equine biomechanics removes mystique and turns training horses and teaching riding into a completely logical process.

Sports science is the science behind the development of new and improved training techniques in sport today. It is the reason why sporting development is on a fast track. Sports science comprises exercise physiology, neuroscience, skeletal-muscular physiology, dietary aspects, sport psychology, kinetics and biomechanics of the athlete. The study of equine biomechanics can do for riding what the study of human biomechanics has done for human athletic training. There is enormous value for riders and trainers in gaining knowledge of biomechanics and neuro-muscular behaviour, and applying it. Correctly applied, it leads to accelerated learning of new skills in equestrian sport, for both the horse and the rider, because it is based on the laws of nature. Thus neuro-science will help the rider to understand how a horse moves and how to move a horse. It is especially helpful to know how the horse can be manoeuvred/positioned correctly to enable him to understand and respond appropriately to the so-called 'aids'. It also gives the rider insight into the horse's well-being and soundness. Most importantly, riders learn empathy for the horse because of an understanding of the effects of their instructions on the horse.

I should mention at this stage my reason for using the phrase so-called 'aids' with the word 'aids' in quotation marks. I have done this because many novice riders interpret the word as meaning 'automatic signals' – a magical recipe that will induce the horse to respond correctly. Novice riders often ask, 'What are the aids for piaffe?', 'What are the aids for a flying change?', etc., the implication being that simply placing one's legs in a certain spot, or producing some specific influence with the reins will immediately elicit the required effect. Horses are too often punished for misunderstanding these signals: riders often complain that they 'are giving the correct aids, but the horse won't respond'. We have a responsibility towards the horse to communicate in a way which he can understand. *Genuine* aids – communications which the horse understands – do this, and eventually become mere signals which maintain their efficacy. It is at this stage, when the horse also knows the entire preamble to the command, that the aids become almost invisible. (This process can be compared to teaching a rider a new concept, such as 'shoulder-in'. First, one has to explain what shoulder-in is, and why it is necessary, but once the rider has associated the word with the explanation, the word alone is all that is required for understanding.) The aids we use today developed over many centuries because they position/manoeuvre the horse in a way that facilitates a correct reaction. With a novice horse, it is not simply a question of 'pushing the correct buttons.'

Wars break out, friendships are lost and marriages disintegrate because of lack of appropriate communication. Similarly, most of the resistances in horses are caused by lack of constructive communication between rider and horse. The main reason for this is that humans are not that proficient at non-verbal communication. How can we expect horses to understand the human's inadequate ability to communicate non-verbally? (The great and gifted riders of the world do have exceptional ability in this field, but only a few show up in each century. These people include all the great names in the literature of the previous centuries, but I would emphasise the fact that there were not that many of them if we consider that the horse was in common use until the middle of the twentieth century). Unfortunately, these riding masters were not always fully aware of the exact nature of the relationship between their communications and the horse's biomechanical reactions. They therefore passed on a legacy of verbal instructions which were not always based on scientific fact, and may not necessarily have been correct. These were the original errors on which many of the riding instructions and explanations of today are based (some of these are discussed in Chapter 7).

It is, in reality, our duty to learn how to communicate effectively with our equine partner, because he owes us nothing. By understanding how equine biomechanics works, and how to use this knowledge to influence horses, most of the misunderstanding between horse and rider becomes avoidable. Ninety-nine per cent of schooling problems are solvable through knowledge of equine and human sports biomechanics and equine-human communication.

I would like to give a recent personal example of how the knowledge of biomechanics helped my own communication with my mare. I had been struggling with the piaffe with her for a very long time and could not understand why she was so 'stubborn' about doing it. I had taught this movement to many horses in a time frame ranging from one to three days, yet my mare was taking years to accept it. I became extraordinarily frustrated. At some point I realized that the piaffe is not difficult because of lack of power; it is difficult because of the effect it has on the horse's equilibrium. Once I understood that my mare does not like her stability challenged, I found the way by which to solve the problem. Applying this knowledge of the biomechanics of the piaffe, my mare understood in five minutes and got her piaffe in three days. [The explanation is on page 246].

So, we should endeavour to perceive the world through the eyes, ears and body of the horse. We have to imagine how it feels to be a horse, especially what it must feel like to be constantly vigilant to possibilities of danger. We have to imagine how we, as horses, would perceive the rider's 'aids'. We also have to be extremely aware of how our actions affect the horse's balance. Balance in every aspect of life as well as riding is extremely important. Loss of mental or physical balance leads to friction and degeneration. It is no wonder that the development of rhythm and balance are the first steps in the training format.

This book aims to investigate the horse's natural methods of performing movements and to compare these with the movements he performs in dressage and jumping. It will further highlight the biomechanical difficulties the horse encounters in his efforts to please the rider, and give suggestions to riders and trainers on how to overcome these difficulties. It further gives judges pointers on how to recognize these problems.

The biomechanical misconceptions and related trends are analysed using biomechanical principles. Many misconceptions developed because dressage grew as an art form and not as an exact science and developed in the royal courts and in the cavalry, where soldiers were taught to react and obey rather than to ponder and analyse. All acquired knowledge, ideas and principles, should be re-examined from time to time – this is the path of progress – but riding has not undergone much of this re-examination to date. Dressage can be practised as an art or as a sport. As a sport, it is a competitive undertaking and, as such, it should undergo the scrutiny of science. As an art, it is exhibited and, as with other art forms, is subject to individual interpretation and evaluation.

The following pages re-examine the traditional ideas of classical riding. The theories expressed in this book are based on sound biomechanical principles, together with many hours of detailed observation of many horses by the author. Research is quoted where appropriate.

The terms 'push' and 'pressure' are used regularly in this book because novice, female and child riders generally need a mental picture of pushing for their motor control to be effective in their communication with the horse, especially a green horse. Whereas mens' muscles are automatically stronger and more effective. Correctly trained horses need only light and invisible aids to perform all the dressage movements, but this represents the finished product of both horse and rider.

The term 'take and give' is used freely throughout this book. It is, however, one term encompassing a range of hand and finger squeezing on the reins, varying from firm pressure to light vibrations. The action is always accompanied by the release of pressure the instant the horse yields.

This is not a book for teaching riding, neither is it a complete guide to schooling horses. A balanced and poised riding seat is assumed. An earlier book of mine, *Successful Schooling*, was written for the purpose of schooling and a forthcoming book will teach the rider how to develop a balanced and poised seat.

1

Definitions of Biomechanical Concepts

Biomechanics is the mechanics of living systems and differs from the mechanics of inanimate objects. The latter concept concerns the effect of a force on an inanimate object. In biomechanics, this pure mechanical functioning is modified by the effect of gravity on muscular action, the nerves, voluntary muscle control, automatic and learned patterns of movement, tendons, fascia and especially by motivation (intent) and thought processes (see Figure 1.1b). For example, in terms of *pure* mechanics the rider has to follow certain rules of riding such as, the hand should never cross the midline of the horse's withers. However, in *biomechanical* terms we would like the horse to understand what every predetermined action of the rider means and if, when horse or rider is learning, initial crossing the withers gets the message across to the horse, so be it. This deviation from the aesthetic is more advantageous to the horse's well-being than inadequate communication based on mechanics, which confuses him. Once the rider's co-ordination and communication with the horse become more effective, this movement becomes an invisible tightening of the rein towards the withers (the ultimate aim being to ride with invisible aids).

The study of equine biomechanics will lead to improved performance and accelerated learning of new skills by the horse. Through equine biomechanical analysis, riders will learn to understand the horse's physical requirements for the movement he has to perform. It will highlight the horse's limitations when performing certain movements, and will thus teach the rider to make requests in such a manner that the horse does not lose balance in his attempt to comply. Knowledge of biomechanics determines which actions will improve both the horse's and rider's performance but, most importantly, it distinguishes fact from misconception about equine movement. Thus knowledge of equine biomechanics plays an important role in the prevention of injury as well as in rehabilitation.

Figure 1.1a. In mechanics, the downward force on the crowbar lifts the weight. When the force is released, the weight drops.

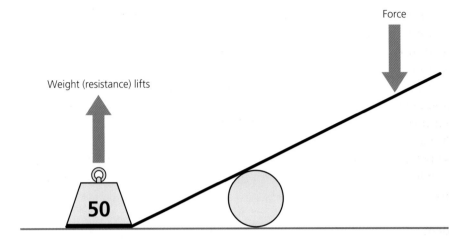

Force

Weight (resistance) lifts

50

Figure 1.1b. In biomechanics, muscular contraction lifts and lowers the weight and the process is controlled by the central nervous system.

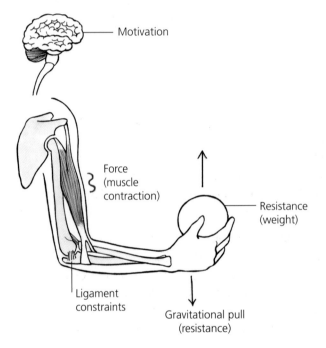

Motivation

Force (muscle contraction)

Resistance (weight)

Ligament constraints

Gravitational pull (resistance)

Gravity and the Horse's Muscles

According to Newton's Theory of Universal Gravitation, the force of gravity acting between Earth and any other object is directly proportional to the mass of the object and the mass of Earth, and all objects attract each other with a gravitational force. The gravitational force between two objects such as horse and rider is negligible, but the effect of the earth's gravitational force on both horse and rider is significant for all aspects of riding.

Gravity forms an outside force on the body and it is extraordinary powerful. Our human muscles have to maintain our upright position against its force. However, without gravity and the constant resistance of its force against these muscles, we are weightless and extremely weak. Furthermore, the bigger the mass of the body, the more gravity will pull on it and gravity thus has an enormous effect on the muscles and on the ground reaction force (GRF – see Glossary) of the 500–600 kg (1,100–1,320 lb) horse. (The exception to this scenario is that, when a body is in water, the gravitational effect on muscle action is reduced by about 90 per cent. That is why swimming is such good remedial exercise for horses recovering from muscle or tendon injuries.)

The way in which the effect of gravity changes muscle behaviour depends on the position of the relevant body part in relation to the gravitational force. When moving against gravity the muscle fibres contract differently from when moving in the direction of gravity. The muscle's action then becomes opposite to its normal function. The following exercises illustrate the effect of gravity on the muscles.

EXERCISES

1. Lift and hold both arms horizontally at your sides and measure the length of time you are able to maintain this position. Now lie on your back with your arms in the same position. Note that the muscles do not tire at all. This is because, in this position, the deltoid muscles (the ones on your shoulders that hold up your arms) are lined up parallel to the surface of the Earth. Thus their contraction is not against gravitational resistance.

2. Place your hands on the back of a chair. Lean forwards, placing your weight on your hands and arms. Now alternate active hollowing of your back and rounding it. Your back muscles will contract when you hollow your back. Your abdominal muscles will contract when you round your back. Your back muscles do not contract when you simply maintain this flexed position with your arms taking the weight because gravity does not resist their action in this position.

3. Maintain the same position, but lift your hands from the chair. Feel how your back muscles tighten to maintain this flexed position and how tiring this is. The force of gravity is pulling on your upper body and therefore your back muscles have to contract against this force.

This same principle applies to the horse's muscles. When at least one foreleg together with one hind leg are in stance, the gravitational resistance to the actions of the back muscles is negligible (see Figure 1.5a). However, when both forefeet are in suspension and one or both hind legs are in

Deltoid muscle

Gravitational
pull

Figure 1.2a, b.
Exercise 1 – see text.

a

b

Figure 1.3a, b.
Exercise 2 – see text.

a

b

Figure 1.4.
Exercise 3 – see text.

stance, such as in canter, the force of gravity will pull the horse's forehand down and his back muscles will contract against this force (see Figure 1.5b). The opposite also applies to forelimb stance with hind limbs in suspension, such as when a horse kicks out with both hind limbs. This fact helps to diagnose back and hind leg muscle strain (see The 'on the bit' walk to canter in Chapter 10).

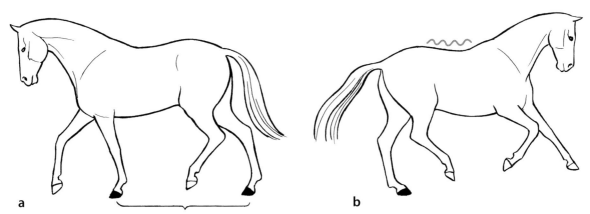

a   b

The Centre of Gravity and the Horse's Movement

The centre of gravity or centre of mass is the point around which all the body parts and the entire mass are arranged in perfect balance. (A specific mathematical formula can equate the exact position of the centre of gravity.) As soon as one part, such as a leg, the head or the ribcage, moves, the centre of gravity changes position. Thus it changes continuously as parts of the body move.

It is important for riders to know how the horse's movements affect his balance and his stability and an understanding of the centre of gravity is essential for this purpose. When the horse moves his neck forwards, his centre of gravity moves forwards. When he lifts his neck, his centre of gravity moves backwards. When he moves his shoulders, head and neck to the right, his centre of gravity moves to the right and similarly to the left (see Figure 1.6e). The more the horse's hindquarters move underneath him, the further back the centre of gravity moves. As soon as a body part moves, the horse's centre of gravity moves and he thus has to rearrange his other body parts around the new position in order to maintain balance. This is a continuous and automatic process. During canter the centre of gravity moves significantly forwards and backwards at each stride.

Figure 1.5a. At the trot the horse's back muscles are supported by one fore and one hind limb, therefore back muscle action is moderate.

Figure 1.5b. During canter there is no forelimb support. The back muscles therefore contract against gravitational resistance.

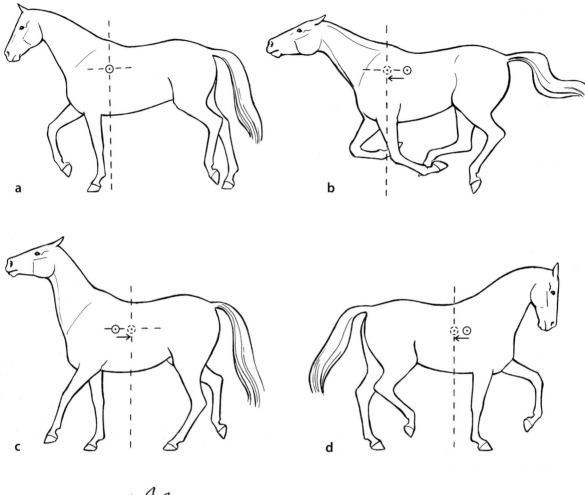

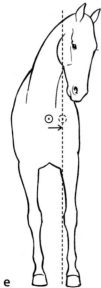

Figure 1.6a. The approximate area of the horse's centre of gravity.

Figure 1.6b. The centre of gravity moves forward when the horse moves his head and neck forwards.

Figure 1.6c. The centre of gravity moves backwards when the horse lifts his neck.

Figure 1.6d. When the horse moves his hindquarters further underneath his body, his centre of gravity moves backwards and his head and neck raise. A fully engaged horse thus becomes completely balanced and in self-carriage.

Figure 1.6e. When the horse moves his shoulders, head and neck to the side, his centre of gravity also moves to the same side.

The Gravity Line and the Horse's Balance

The *gravity line* is the imaginary vertical line dissecting an object. Its position changes together with the changes of the centre of gravity. The *base of support* of an object is the area within the lines which connect the outer perimeter of each point of support. In the case of the horse, it would be within the lines connecting the outside of each hoof. The base of support of the horse changes at each stride and in each gait.

When the gravity line is close to the centre of the base of support, the object will be in stable equilibrium (good balance). When the gravity line is close to the limits of the base of support, the object will be in unstable equilibrium. It is extremely difficult for the horse to balance on two lateral feet in stance because the gravity line is beyond the perimeter of his base of support, his base will be narrow and his centre of gravity too high. Although, when he kicks back, he can lift both his hind legs, he cannot maintain this position, and he can only balance on two hind legs when his gravity line is close to the centre of his base of support, as in levade. In rearing, the balance is very precarious because the gravity line is beyond the horse's (small) base of support and the centre of gravity is very high.

It is extremely difficult for the horse to hold these positions when his gravity line does not dissect his base of support. When the horse is asked to balance in such unstable equilibrium, he has to use superior muscle power to counter this unbalanced weight distribution.

Photo 1.1a. *above* In the levade the flexion of the hind limbs lowers the centre of gravity and the gravity line dissects the base of support of both horse and rider.

Photo 1.1b. Balance in rearing is very precarious for the reasons explained in the text.

Balance, Stability, Equilibrium and Agility

Agility is the capacity of an animal to return to a state of equilibrium or to its original position (regain balance) rapidly after a disturbance of balance. In other words, it is the ability to move the centre of mass efficiently outside the base of support and then back again, such as in jumping. *Stability* is the ability to maintain the mass within the base of support and maintain it in equilibrium, and as such is a key aim in dressage. The horse's stability is constantly challenged while he is ridden because the effects of gravity are always in operation. When the rider does not continuously prepare and explain the next step to the horse, he is almost always 'caught by surprise' because the rider is requesting the horse to use techniques which are not quite natural to him. It is a common occurrence amongst riders to ask for changes of direction, speed or gait without warning or preparation. It is, however, the rider's responsibility to assist the horse in the maintenance of his balance: preparation is essential for these movements and transitions.

Static and dynamic balance

Static balance is balance in stance. The horse has exceptional static balance because of the size of the base of support and his considerable weight.

Dynamic balance is balance in motion or balance on top of a moving object. When the base of support is small, it is easier to maintain equilibrium whilst moving than whilst stationary. Horses naturally have good dynamic balance but this, unfortunately, is often disturbed by rider interference during training.

EXPERIMENT

Balance on the toes of one foot and notice how you maintain balance, after a minute or two, with small hops.

Forward momentum, in faster gaits, allows horses to balance effectively with fewer legs in stance: momentum allows for faster recovery of balance because the limbs are in movement. The slower the speed, the greater the need for a large base of support and inner muscle stability. At faster speeds, however, balance is more easily disturbed by external forces and this is where agility plays a major role in regaining balance. The rider's equilibrium is also more easily lost at the faster gaits: riders usually do not fall off a standing or walking horse.

Photo 1.2. When grazing the horse generally places one forelimb forward to enlarge his base of support. His centre of gravity thus stays well within the perimeter of his base of support.

Dynamic balance is closely related to rhythm. When balance is lost, rhythm is lost; also, loss of rhythm usually disturbs balance. Horses with great innate rhythm do not lose balance easily. Dressage and jumping are sports in which balance and rhythm are of great importance. Only a balanced horse can work in a consistent rhythm.

Factors affecting the horse's stability

1. *The weight of the object.* The heavier the object, the more stable and the more difficult it is to displace or move. The lighter the object the easier it is to topple. The heavier and larger the horse, the more difficult it is to manoeuvre him laterally. The large mass also causes increased inertia (see Glossary). Larger horses are therefore, usually less agile than small horses and take more power from the rider to move and manoeuvre during the earlier stages of training. (With correct training, horses become sensitive to the aids and the need for more powerful riding disappears.)

2. *The size of the base of support.* The bigger the base of support, the better the stability and balance. The smaller the base of support, the less stable the body. When the horse halts, his base of support is very large, giving him great stability. At the trot the base is the circumference around the two diagonal feet. At the canter it changes with every beat from the very small one foot stance phase to the triple stance phase. During piaffe the base of support is relatively small. The horse's base of

support covers the area of his entire body except for his head and neck. This fact is significant when doing biomechanical analysis of the horse's movement. A horse who is broader through the shoulders and hips has better stability than a tall narrow horse, since the latter's base of support is smaller.

3. *The height of the centre of gravity.* The closer the centre of gravity is to the ground, the more stable the object and the more difficult it is (the more force is required) to displace or topple it. This is because more weight will be concentrated close to the base. Lying down is thus the most stable position for man and beast. The higher the centre of gravity, the less stability it has and it topples with less effort. In the latter cases, more effort is also needed to maintain stability. The tall horse with long, thin legs has a high centre of gravity as compared to a short-legged pony. Ponies, in general, do not seem to lose their balance in fast jump-offs to the extent of larger horses.

4. *The relation of the gravity line to the base of support.* As mentioned earlier, the nearer the gravity line is to the centre of the base, the greater the stability of the object. Therefore it is important to maintain or re-gain this position as soon as possible when riding either dressage or

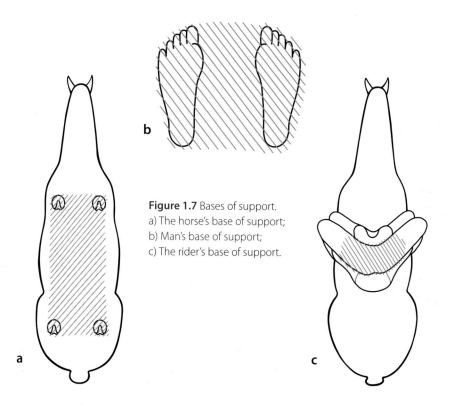

Figure 1.7 Bases of support.
a) The horse's base of support;
b) Man's base of support;
c) The rider's base of support.

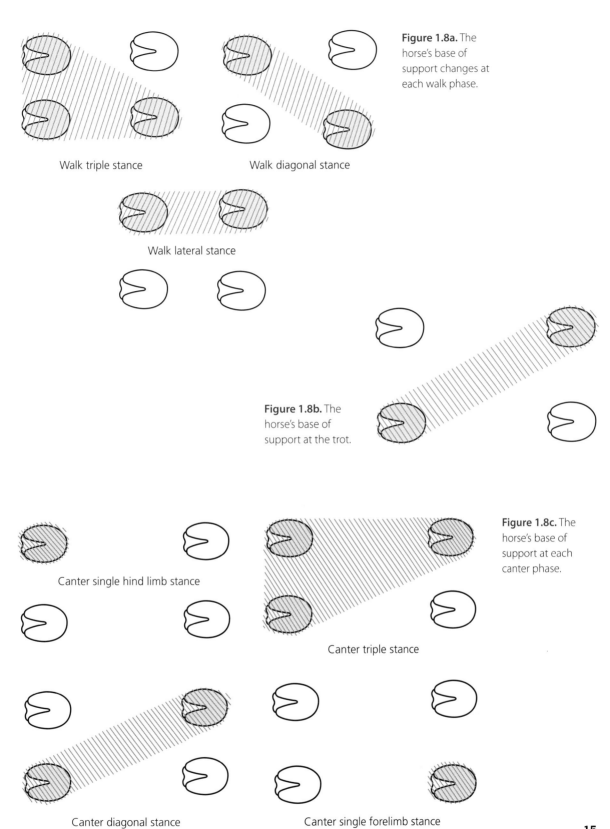

Figure 1.8a. The horse's base of support changes at each walk phase.

Walk triple stance

Walk diagonal stance

Walk lateral stance

Figure 1.8b. The horse's base of support at the trot.

Figure 1.8c. The horse's base of support at each canter phase.

Canter single hind limb stance

Canter triple stance

Canter diagonal stance

Canter single forelimb stance

jumping. When the horse is engaged and in the 'on the bit' position, his gravity line is closer to the centre of his base of support (see Figure 1.6d, page 10).

5. *Friction of the surface*. The greater the friction on the surface, the better the balance. Therefore, the horse is more likely to slip on wet grass than on gravelly sand or rubber chips.

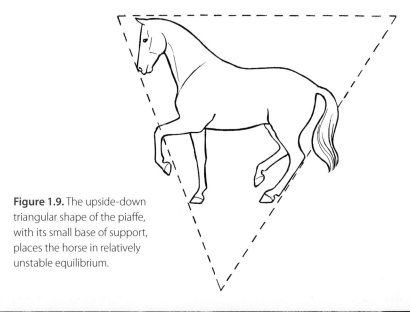

Figure 1.9. The upside-down triangular shape of the piaffe, with its small base of support, places the horse in relatively unstable equilibrium.

Photo 1.3. An American Saddlebred in stretch. This triangular shape with the horse's body length slightly shorter than its large base of support ensures great stability.

6. *Segmentation.* Maximum stability is ensured when the centres of gravity of all the segments (particles) lie in a vertical line, which is centred over the base of support. Thus the horse's balance is better when the rider's centre of gravity and gravity line are in a vertical line with the horse's centre of gravity and gravity line over his base of support. (This is an important consideration when designing saddles.) When a horse is in his natural balance with 60 per cent of his weight on his forehand, the rider sits behind his centre of gravity. This position of the rider moves the horse's centre of gravity further back and, as the horse becomes more engaged and his forehand lifts, his centre of gravity moves back further still and more underneath the rider's seat. The horse, however, changes his centre of gravity at each gait and through each transition. It is therefore impossible for the rider to maintain a constant position over the horse's centre of gravity. Dressage saddles should therefore be positioned so that the rider's and horse's gravity lines are in alignment when the horse is correctly collected.

7. *The effect of speed on balance.* Balance is maintained and regained by movement, although it is disturbed more easily during fast movement. When a horse is too forward-going, he often moves himself out of a balanced trot or canter. However, as explained earlier, balance is regained with greater ease during movement because the limbs are already in motion and ready to ground. Here, superior agility is of great help.

(A bicycle will fall over when it does not move, but does not fall over when moving fast, even when at an angle. Attempt to maintain a motionless bicycle in balance. You do this with continuous small forward and back movements of the pedals.)

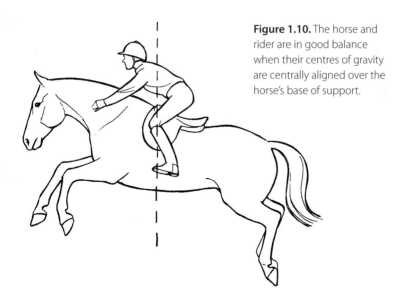

Figure 1.10. The horse and rider are in good balance when their centres of gravity are centrally aligned over the horse's base of support.

The slower the gait, the more feet have to be in stance to increase the size of the base of support. *It is easier to hop on one leg than to balance on one leg.* During the walk the horse has either two or three legs in stance simultaneously. During trot, two legs are in stance with a moment of no support (suspension) in between the strides. At the canter the support ranges from no legs in stance (suspension) through one, two and three legs in stance. The relatively small base of support during movement is probably the reason why the piaffe has almost no suspension time.

Showjumping horses need stability when landing and turning, but these are the super athletes, who also need great agility and longitudinal flexibility to perform. Horses with more flexibility and agility can regain their balance more efficiently, whereas horses with less flexibility generally have more stability and do not push themselves out of equilibrium. Horses used in haute école, such as the Spanish and Portuguese horses, need great stability and are indeed built for it. The 'body-builder' type of horse often has more stability and less flexibility. They generally have higher muscle tone and shorter, more defined muscles. These horses generally halt square naturally, but do not have the extraordinary free and loose movement of the low muscle-toned horse. They are easier to ride than the latter and have a steadier head carriage. Their transitions are easier with less loss of balance. Horses with less athleticism and agility tend to contain themselves more and are therefore more stable.

The extremely flexible horses with loose ligaments, low muscle tone and longer, more supple muscles do not always maintain regular rhythm and balance. (This is of no concern to the horse, only to the rider). Some, especially the very forward-thinking horses, tend to lift their necks in a balance reaction or lose rhythm in the transitions, especially during downward transitions. This also applies to transitions from large movements to small movements and to changes of direction. However, they have large ranges of movement and are generally sought-after dressage horses.

Some very flexible horses often sprawl in the halt or take strange halt stances when they halt naturally because they have the confidence that it won't disturb their equilibrium. This, however, does not apply to all the low-toned horses. It depends on their 'use' of body. Some literally 'hang' on their ligaments when standing free and 'pull themselves together' while being ridden.

The larger and slower the movements, the more challenging they are to stability. The rider has to focus on exercises to enhance stability, increasing both muscle tone and proprioceptive skill (see Proprioception in Glossary), with this type of horse. These would be small-range strengthening and engagement exercises which increase muscle tone on a preliminary basis.

Photo 1.4a. The low muscle toned horse 'hanging on her ligaments'. This is this particular horse's normal natural stance.

Photo 1.4b. The same horse 'pulling herself up' with attitude.

Very agile horses also tend to be less careful about disturbing their equilibrium because their agility will help them to maintain it. The modern dressage horse needs great flexibility, which is important for the extended trot, flying changes and passage. He also needs superior strength and great stability, for piaffe and canter pirouettes. It is the rare example who has superior flexibility combined with superior strength and balance. Such horses are the dressage superstars, for example Blue Hors Matine.

▶ RIDING AND TEACHING APPLICATIONS

1. Without the rider, the horse has great balance and stability. When he moves too fast or on the forehand it does not bother him because he is in total control of his body. The rider however, disturbs the horse's

Photo 1.5. An extremely agile and balanced horse has little need to maintain his centre of gravity precisely over his base of support.

Photo 1.6. Blue Hors Matine.

balance when interfering with his automatic reactions or not preparing him for the movement. In equitation, riders do not want the horse to be on the forehand. It is therefore their responsibility to slow the horse down, prepare him for all movements and bring his hindquarters more underneath.

2. Large horses are more difficult to manoeuvre. Therefore small riders should preferably ride small horses. Many riders are over-horsed because this is the fashion today.

3. It is important that the saddle places the rider as closely as practical in line with the horse's centre of gravity. As this line changes at each step, it is impossible for the rider's centre of gravity *always* to be in line with the horse's centre of gravity.

4. Very forward-thinking horses have to be balanced continually with balancing half-halts.

Balance reactions

As explained earlier, balance is disturbed when the gravity line moves beyond the perimeter of the base of support. When this happens all animals react automatically to maintain or regain balance. The body will rearrange itself automatically around its centre of gravity to prevent falling. Neither horse nor human has to think actively about this. Let us investigate a few of these automatic reactions to the loss of balance.

1. When we fall, we throw our arms forwards and lift our heads in extension to prevent falling on our faces. This is automatic. The horse 'plants' his forelegs and lifts his neck in extension in the same manner when he loses balance.

2. We run forwards when we are pushed, to prevent falling. The horse runs with small faster steps when the rider pushes him forwards out of balance and onto his forehand if he has not yet developed the capacity to carry his weight on his hindquarters.

3. We step sideways when we are pushed from the side. The horse does a leg-yield or a few steps of the turn on the forehand automatically when pushed sideways behind the centre of gravity.

4. When we are pushed backwards on the chest, we will usually react in one or two different ways. If the push is gradual, we will lean forwards against it, but if it is sudden and above the centre of gravity, we will hollow our backs, lift up our arms and step backwards. The horse will react in the same manner. His forward push into gradual pressure is an

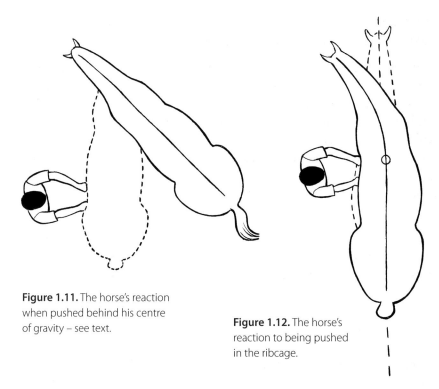

Figure 1.11. The horse's reaction when pushed behind his centre of gravity – see text.

Figure 1.12. The horse's reaction to being pushed in the ribcage.

example of the saying 'horses move into pressure'. However, when the push is sharp or sudden, horses will lift their heads, hollow their backs and retract their legs.

5. When we plant our feet slightly apart and are pushed sideways at the waist, it will bulge to the side and our shoulders and head will move in the opposite direction. The horse will react in the same manner to pushing on the ribcage. He will move his head, neck and tail to the inside to compensate for the ribcage tilting to the outside.

▶ RIDING AND TEACHING APPLICATIONS

1. Riders should have knowledge of all these automatic balance reactions and the effect they have on the horse when they make sudden requests from the horse.

2. The reaction of both horse and rider to loss of balance, is rigidity: they tighten muscles to regain balance. In the horse this starts in the neck and thus affects the rest of the body. If the rider can inhibit this rigidity in the neck, the horse will stay soft through his back and maintain balance through the movements and transitions. This roundness is simply maintained with timely 'take and give' requests. However, when the loss of balance is monumental – the horse actually tripping or being in danger

of falling – 'take and give' is of little use. In such cases the horse will need freedom of his head and neck to regain balance.

3. From the ground, push the horse's ribcage over with your hand. It will bulge out on the other side. Notice how the horse's neck will move towards you, his inside fore and hind legs will abduct (open) and his hindquarters will move towards you. If you move in behind him you will notice the dock of his tail moving to the side of the pressure. Therefore, when riding, the more the rider pushes with the inside leg on the girth to tilt the ribcage, the less hand will be needed to request an inside bend through the turns and circles.

4. Exercises focusing on enhancing stability, increasing both muscle tone and proprioceptive skills are important for extremely flexible horses. These are primarily small-range strengthening and engagement exercises such as transitions and little steps at the trot.

'Force' in Equine Communication

We communicate with and position the horse by physically manoeuvring him with an external force. A force, in biomechanical terms, is a push or a pull. These 'pushes' and 'pulls' are the large movements we use to manoeuvre a horse's body when we start to train him. These eventually become light pressure of the legs and/or seat and invisible squeezes on the reins.

'Muscles alone are incapable of producing changes in the motion of the body's centre of mass.'[1] The muscles can move the limbs and the neck, but cannot move the horse's body without external forces acting on it. Thus the horse (or any other living organism) can only move his mass if he can pull or push against an external object. In riding, the rider and the ground are the external forces/objects acting on the horse. (The object of dressage is that the horse and rider form a harmonious partnership/unit and this develops at every stage of training when the communication between horse and rider becomes automatic. However, when learning new movements, and from a biomechanical viewpoint, the rider may sometimes represent an external force.) The ground is the primary object against which the horse pushes with his legs in the stance phase in order to move. The rider may also act as a motivating force to produce and influence this movement. For example, when teaching lateral movements, we disturb the

---

1 P.M. McGinnis, *Biomechanics of Sport and Exercise* (Champaign, USA, Human Kinetics, 1999).

horse's balance for lateral displacement by an external force, the leg. He then moves his legs sideways by pushing against the ground. To move the whole object, the centre of gravity has to be moved. The rider's leg position is important because it has to be in the correct position on the horse's body, to move his centre of gravity laterally.

According to Newton's First Theory of Motion, *every body continues in its state of rest, or of uniform motion in a straight line, unless it is compelled to change that state by forces impressed upon it.* This means that if no external force is acting on a body, it will remain in its state of rest. It also means that if a body is already in motion it will continue moving in a straight line and at the same speed unless an external force acts on it. In an equestrian context, these forces include the horse's own muscle actions when his legs push against the ground. It also includes influences of the rider, such as leg pressure pushing the horse to move laterally.

According to Newton's Second Theory of Motion, *the change of motion of an object is proportional to the force impressed and is made in the direction of the straight line in which the force is impressed.* This means that if you push your horse with your leg, he will move in a straight line in the same direction as the push unless his motivation opposes it (resistance). This motivation is one of the factors which change the principle from one of pure mechanics to biomechanics.

EXERCISES

1. From the ground, push against the horse's shoulders. His shoulders will move sideways in a straight line away from the 'force' provided that he does not evade the pressure.

2. Push the horse's hindquarters. His hindquarters will move sideways away from the 'force' provided that he does not attempt to evade.

▶ RIDING AND TEACHING APPLICATIONS

1. An outside force has to be fairly strong to effect a change if the horse does not understand the concept. A slight weight change will not affect the direction of the movement unless it is meaningful to the horse (see Chapter 9). An example of this is when the rider teaches the horse the concept of the flying change, particularly with older horses. With some of these horses the aids often have to be exaggerated with significant lateral balance disturbances – almost 'throwing' the horse off balance to the new side.

2. The direction of the outside force will determine the direction of the horse's movements. This is significant when we train the horse in piaffe.

During piaffe the direction of the force against the ground is upward. His hind legs therefore have to be more under his body. By contrast, during extended trot, the direction of the force is forward.

3. During half-pass the direction of the rider's leg pressure determines the angle of the hindquarter movement.

4. In shoulder-in, the direction of the leg pressure is important in ensuring that impulsion is not lost. Many horses stop moving forwards in the shoulder-in when the rider is first learning how to coordinate the exercise. One of the reasons is that the rider is pushing in the wrong direction, but trainers often find that a verbal explanation concerning direction does not seem to get the concept across. They may find it helps to stand on the outside of the school in a diagonal line to the horse and rider (approximately 30 degrees to the track) then ask the rider to push in their direction. The horse will immediately have more impulsion and the shoulder-in angle will be corrected (see Figure 1.13).

5. According to Newton's Third Theory of Motion, *to every action there is always opposed an equal reaction.* If one object exerts force on another object, the second object will exert the same force in the opposite direction. Thus when a rider pulls on the horse's mouth via the reins, the horse will pull back with equal force, and vice versa. This sets up the pulling and hanging pattern in the horse's contact with the rider's hands. The more the rider pulls or hangs, the more the horse will pull or hang in the opposite direction.

   a. Prevent this 'tug of war' by teaching the horse to yield to soft squeezing on the reins, ensuring immediate release of pressure as the horse yields – 'take and give'.

   b. Balance the horse with many half-halts followed by rein releases to ensure that he does not place too much weight on his forehand and thus set up this pulling relationship.

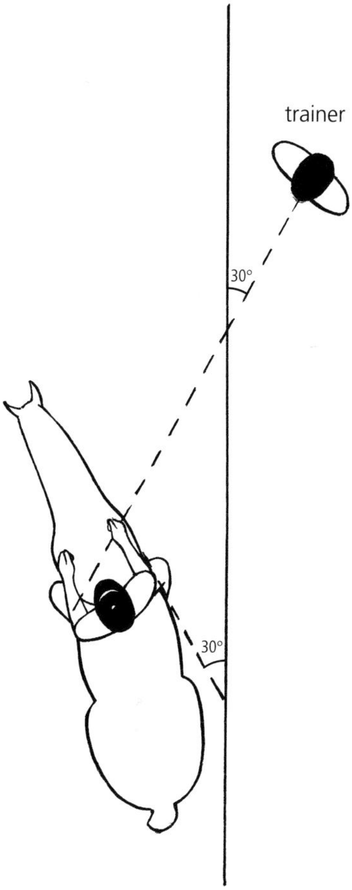

Figure 1.13. The rider 'pushing' towards the instructor standing outside the arena – see text.

Patterns of Movement

The body works as a unit or system in patterns of movement which move the body as a whole. Movement in one part will thus have an effect on the other parts. A few automatic, coordinated, movement patterns are established before birth. These patterns are governed by the brain and they include what English riding calls the three basic gaits of walk, trot and canter patterns in the horse. The flexor pattern, the extensor pattern, lateral flexion patterns and the 'pull' and 'push' patterns are the basic patterns of movement in all animals. The brain and body have an added ability to develop new movement patterns throughout life. Some of the patterns which we use in dressage movements are not developed before birth, but are developed by changing the normal automatic pattern when the horse learns new skills. These are learned patterns and they mix flexor with extensor patterns. This is easy for man to do, but difficult for a quadruped. The leg-yield, for example, is an automatic pattern, but the half-pass, travers, the perfect rein-back (in a round frame) and to some extent the shoulder-in are 'man-made' learned patterns. The brain and body have to build and store the new man-made patterns while 'neutralizing' the natural automatic patterns.

Another example of a mixed pattern is the flight pattern during jumping when the head, neck and back bascule in the flexion pattern, but the pelvic area extends.

A variety of gait patterns of movement exist in nature and certain equine breeds and some individual horses have a propensity towards the development of these patterns. Certain animals can pace, tölt, rack, aubin (the hind legs trot while the forelimbs gallop) and traquenard (the forelegs trot and the hind legs gallop). One can see these forms of movement in nature but, when required under saddle, they have been further developed. In modern-day dressage however, we train the horse in the three gaits of walk, trot and canter.

Automatic patterns of movement

Automatic reactions controlled by the brain involve the entire body. All animals, including the human kind, have these same reactions. Understanding these reactions is an extremely important biomechanical concept in the training of the horse. Together with the balance reaction, automatic patterns are the main reason why we are able to train the horse with ease and why he can respond to our instructions. The aids we use today developed through the centuries because of the influence they have on these reactions.

The flexor pattern

This is the 'on the bit' pattern of movement. It is initiated by flexion of the head. It leads to contraction of all the bottom line muscles and engagement of the hindquarters. It can, however, be encouraged by abdominal flexion or hindquarter flexion, but this does not always lead to a total flexor pattern because of the extreme elasticity of the nuchal ligament (see page

57). When the horse bends his head down, his neck flexors will contract and flex his neck, followed by contraction of his abdominal flexors, then by hip flexion and stifle flexion, hock flexion and finally fetlock flexion. This brings the horse's hind legs more underneath his body. The foreleg pattern is flexion of the elbow and fetlock. Tightness in the horse's neck inhibits the flexor pattern and the horse's ability to engage his hind legs.

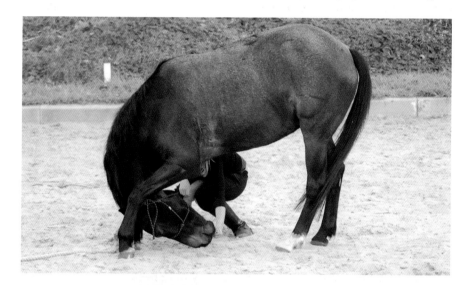

Photo 1.7. The flexor pattern in both horse and girl! Note the hip flexion in the horse, which is so necessary for engagement of the hindquarters.

Photo 1.8. The fully engaged hindquarters in the sliding halt do not lead to the round flexor pattern in the neck. Note the muscle definition in the quadriceps femoris muscles.

The flexor pattern starts at the point of full extension and ends in the fully flexed position. Therefore, a horse may appear to be in an extended pattern while it is his flexor muscles which are in contraction.

The extensor pattern

This is the pattern which hollows the horse's top line. It is also initiated by the head and neck and leads to the contraction of all the top line muscles and extension of the hip joint. The head and neck extend, followed by hollowing of the back, extension of the hips, stifle, hock and fetlock. The foreleg straightens and the knee and fetlock extends. It is the opposite of engagement.

The extensor muscles of the head, neck and back all work as a unit. The longissimus muscles form a unit from the head right down to the sacrum and the pelvic bone. Their attachments criss-cross over each other and over the vertebrae. They are all connected by fascia, therefore, when the front extends, the whole back will extend (as when the horse steps naturally into canter). When the back end extends, the whole front usually extends (as when the horse kicks up with his hind legs). Research has shown that the extensor pattern restricts back mobility.[2]

The extensor pattern starts from full flexion and continues to the fully extended and hollow position. A horse may thus appear to be in a correct flexor pattern, but in fact be using the incorrect muscles. Only the rider will know this through the tightening feel on the reins.

Photo 1.9. The extensor pattern straightens the hips thus working against engagement.

2 C. Gómez, M. Rhodin, L. Roepstorff, M. Weishaupt, M. and R. van Weeren, 'A high head and neck position reduces back movement in dressage horses compared to a natural position' (research paper presented at the International Conference on Equine Exercise Physiology, Fontainebleau, 2006).

When a horse with a high neck carriage is blocked by the rider's hands, he may look as though he is 'on the bit' with roundness at his poll, but he will be hollow at the base of his neck and in his back. The giveaway sign is the little hollow area (dip) in front of the horse's withers, together with the defined muscles at the top of the neck. This muscle definition is caused by the simultaneous contraction of the top line muscles and the stretch of the muscles which allow the head to 'nod' in the 'on the bit' position. It is often seen in jumping horses. When a horse is ridden correctly it disappears instantly (see 'The hollow in front of the withers is a conformation fault' in Chapter 7).

Young horses and horses lacking condition have this hollow area but in these cases it is not connected to pulling hands. It disappears as soon as the horse matures and puts on condition.

Lateral flexion pattern

When we ask the horse to move his head and bend his neck laterally, the muscles on that side will all contract. The head bends to the side, followed by the neck. This is followed by contraction of the side muscles with the consequent tilting of the ribcage to the opposite side. This pattern generally goes together with abduction (opening) of the inside foreleg and adduction (closing) of the outside legs. To maintain balance in this pattern at the halt, the horse generally places more weight on his inside foreleg and his outside hind leg. In leg-yield and shoulder-in, however, the horse places

Photo 1.10. This horse lacks the layer of fat above his nuchal ligament, especially in the dip in front of the withers. The hollow area usually disappears when it fills with fat as the horse puts on condition.

more weight on his outside legs. In half-pass, travers, renvers and the pirouettes, the horse has to learn an unnatural balance adjustment (see Half-pass in Chapter 11).

▶ RIDING AND TEACHING APPLICATIONS

1. The body parts of a horse are not separate entities, but are 'interacting components of a self organizing system'.[3] Therefore, when the rider moves one part of the horse, this will affect the rest of the horse. The rider has to learn how single actions affect the whole of the horse.

2. It is important to note that extension of the spine starts from the position of full flexion and ends in complete hollowness. Thus, a horse may appear to be in a round 'on the bit' frame when he is actually contracting the incorrect extensor or hollowing muscles. A feeling other than lightness in the hand is an indication that the horse is moving into an extension pattern. As soon as the rider detects a slight tightening on the rein, the fingers should close to establish the flexor pattern again and release as the horse yields.

3. Similarly, flexion of the spine starts from full extension – the hollow frame – to the complete round frame. The feeling during this whole process is of softness as the horse yields towards the rider's hands.

4. A rider who understands these automatic reactions can use them to advantage to manoeuvre a horse to do any movement the first time it is requested *provided* the horse has developed enough power to do so. In the same way, a rider can also inhibit unwanted actions while teaching the horse new movements such as the walk pirouettes, shoulder-in and travers.

5. When the horse brakes with his forelegs, he does so naturally in the extensor pattern. It is thus difficult for him to do downward transitions without lifting his head and neck. Therefore, great care should be taken to assist the horse in maintaining the round flexor frame in downward transitions.

6. The little hollow area in front of the withers is an example of a mixed pattern of movement. The 'on the bit' head position and the first few cervical vertebrae are in the flexion pattern, but the base of the neck is in the hollow extensor pattern, thus giving the 'swan neck' effect. The horse thus 'shortens' his neck in an attempt to move away from uncomfortable bit pressure. Correct this hollow area in front of a horse's

---

3 J.M. Loots, 'Classical horse riding: a systems theory approach' (doctoral thesis 2006).

withers with 'take and give' (pressure – release) actions on the reins and *not* by pulling or holding him in the 'on the bit' position.

7. The lateral flexion pattern is initiated with 'take and give' on the inside rein and not with a *pull* on the inside rein. A constant pull on the inside rein will enact Newton's law of equal and opposite force. Muscles on the opposite side of the neck will contract, giving rise to the *false bend*. This tightens the horse's neck and spine and will move his hindquarters out of the circle. This is the reason for never having a constant pull or pressure on the inside rein. The horse must bend his own neck to elicit lateral flexion. The rider's inside leg, which pushes the ribcage over, ensures more lateral flexion. See 'Riding from the inside leg to the outside rein' in Chapter 4.

8. When a horse is positioned correctly through manoeuvring his balance reactions and automatic patterns of movement then you can use any 'aid' together with intent to coerce him to canter on the correct lead.

9. The round frame is initiated by rounding the horse's head and neck first. Encouraging the round frame from the hindquarters will round the horse's back, but not necessarily his neck unless there is some restriction (on the reins) preventing him from lifting his head.

▶ JUDGING SIGNIFICANCE

1. The little hollow area in front of the withers is a sure sign that the horse is not in a correct contact. It is usually a training and riding error, but some highly strung horses may go into this position when they are tense. If the horse is clearly not tense, this posture should be penalized in the 'correct use of aids' section of the dressage test.

2. When the horse's neck is hollow, the judge can assume that his back is also hollow as a consequence of the extensor pattern.

3. A horse may appear to be in the correct flexor 'on the bit' frame, but in fact be contracting his extensor muscles. The contact will be tight, but judges often cannot perceive this tightness. Thus it is important to look for the signs of tightness in the rider's arms and hands as well as in the horse's expression.

Co-contraction of the head and neck

When the flexor muscles and extensor muscles of the neck all contract simultaneously, the neck becomes rigid. This reaction is clearly illustrated when a horse is tense in the fright/flight mode. It leads to the spine and body also becoming rigid. When the horse's neck is rigid, his hind legs will not follow in the tracks of his forelegs in a circle. This is often referred to as the horse not being straight, but in fact, the horse is literally *too* straight and cannot 'bend' around the circle. This co-contraction inhibits bend throughout the body and prevents the lateral flexion pattern. It affects all the lateral movements, especially the shoulder-in, the half-pass and the walk pirouette. We can inhibit this co-contraction by asking the horse to bend his own neck through the great classical principle of 'take and give'. When he bends his own neck, the rest of his lateral spinal muscles will 'yield' in the curve and the horse will become 'straight'.

▶ RIDING AND TEACHING APPLICATIONS

1. A rigid neck will lead to the horse's hindquarters swinging out in circles, spirals, in shoulder-in and in the walk and canter pirouettes. The horse's hind legs will also become 'stuck' in the pirouette. The rider should ensure that the rigidity is inhibited with continuous invisible 'take

and give' (vibrating) on the inside rein during these movements. Co-contraction is inhibited when the horse bends his own neck. When the horse yields perfectly to the inside rein, the quarters will not fall out in the shoulder-in, neither will the quarters fall out when riding a spiral and the rider's outside leg will not be needed to prevent this. In fact, if the quarters need *pushing in* during these movements, the horse is not yielding sufficiently to inside rein pressure.

2. Co-contraction inhibits the horse's ability to engage his hind legs. It prevents flexion of the head and neck. This is the reason why running reins and the deep and round method were developed. Riders who do not have the skill to inhibit co-contraction of the horse's neck resort to these methods.

3. When the rider allows the horse to hold his neck rigid, the flying changes will be crooked and the quarters will swing. When the horse yields instantly and perfectly to light pressure on the reins his flying changes will be straight.

4. If the horse tightens his neck in a balance reaction during the counter-canter, he will break into a trot or do an 'unauthorized' flying change because of the influence of this co-contraction throughout his body.

▶ JUDGING SIGNIFICANCE

1. When the horse's hindquarters do not follow the tracks of the forelimbs in turns and circles, the horse is not yielding to pressure on the inside rein and the rider is using incorrect training techniques.

2. Swinging hindquarters during the flying changes usually means that the horse's neck muscles are in co-contraction or he is not yielding to inside rein pressure. This should be penalized under the 'correct use of aids' section of the test as well as in the suppleness of the back section.

3. When the horse's hindquarters 'stick' in the walk pirouette, the horse has tightened his neck and has either become hollow or does not yield to inside rein pressure.

Learned patterns

Humans have to learn new patterns for each new sport or activity such as playing the piano, gymnastic tumbles – and especially in learning to ride lateral movements. At first this new coordination pattern is slow, but with practice it becomes automatic. When learning a new movement, it is the extraneous movements (associated movements or parasitic movements), which have to be inhibited to allow only the actions relevant for the movement. This is the reason why it is so difficult to learn a new activity and why it should be done slowly until all the extraneous movements have disappeared. The horse, too, has to learn new movement patterns such as the travers and pirouette.

EXERCISE

Cut material with your left hand (or non-dominant hand) and note how your mouth, tongue and right (other) hand 'attempt' to assist. These are the extraneous associated movements. With practice, all these little 'helpers' disappear and leave only the most economic muscle usage for the job.

▶ RIDING AND TEACHING APPLICATIONS

The half-pass, travers, renvers and pirouette are more difficult than the shoulder-in and leg-yield for the horse to learn because his natural lateral flexor pattern is altered. When he is bent away from the direction of movement as in leg yield and shoulder-in, his centre of gravity remains close to the centre of his base of support. During the half-pass, travers, walk pirouette and canter pirouette, the bend is in the direction of the movement. The action of the horse bending his head and neck brings his centre of gravity close to or outside the perimeter of his base of support and thus disturbs his natural balance. When the rider asks him to take lateral steps, placing his weight on his inside legs, he will attempt to maintain balance by straightening his neck or bending it in the opposite direction. Therefore, the rider has to 'flip' his ribcage to the outside, thereby maintaining his centre of gravity within the perimeter of his base of support in order to help him maintain balance. This is especially important during half-pass and canter pirouette, which should be taught very sympathetically and slowly.

Dominance

Horses, like humans, have a dominant and non-dominant side. Young horses however are usually equally supple and straight on both sides because their dominance has not yet been fully established. (In humans this is only fully established by the age of five.)

The horse (if ridden for an hour a day) has twenty-three hours a day in which he uses his dominant side muscles more than his non-dominant side. Horses thus become more one-sided as they mature and horses who have had to take long breaks during training rapidly become one-sided.

The rider usually rides for only about an hour a day and this is not enough to maintain the horse's ambidexterity – equal strength and suppleness on both sides.

▶ RIDING AND TEACHING APPLICATIONS

1. It is important to maintain equal suppleness and strength in the horse. It may therefore be necessary to work the weak side more than the strong side. This is easily done if the rider is disciplined enough to always start the work on the weak side. (It seems to be a common rider habit to work one side, change rein, work the other side and then go back to the first side again.)

2. All new work should, however, be taught on the 'good' side first.

3. Use discretion because young horses may develop an aversion to the work if it is always started on their side of discomfort.

4. This dominance is very noticeable during transitions on the 'stiff' side. Horses usually change their bend very slightly towards the dominant outside during upward and downward transitions. Correct this by over-emphasizing the inside bend on the stiff side with a strong inside leg flipping the ribcage to the outside, and clear 'take and give' on the inside rein. This will ensure that the horse maintains his own inside bend throughout the transitions.

5. Place the horse in a slight shoulder-fore position during the transitions on his 'stiff' side.

6. The horse usually has his dominant foot forward when grazing. This stretches all the tendons on the dominant side. The tendons on the non-dominant side shrink and often lead to a contracted 'box' foot. It is thus important to maintain the suppleness on this leg especially when a horse has a contracted foot.

2

Basic Functional Anatomy

Basic Skeletal Functions

The skeleton is a framework of rigid bones and cartilages connected to each other at joints, which define specific movement planes. It has 'the all important function of providing attachments for the muscles and levers for movement of the body'.[1] It also covers and protects the vital organs of the body such as the brain, the spinal cord, the heart and lungs. It grows marrow for the endless blood supply needed by the body and it stores substances such as calcium and phosphorus to supply when the body is in need.

A joint is the point of articulation where two or more bones meet. Its functions are to join bones together, to define the axis and movement planes between them and to allow movement. Joints are bound together by strong ligaments which give stability and determine the range of movement.

Movement

Movement planes

Movement planes describe the direction of movement. The limbs move parallel to these planes. Movement planes divide the body in stance through the centre of gravity.

The sagittal plane cuts the body in half through the centre of gravity

---

1 R.D. Lockhart, G.F. Hamilton and F.W. Fyfe, *Anatomy of the Human Body* (London, Faber and Faber Ltd., 1959).

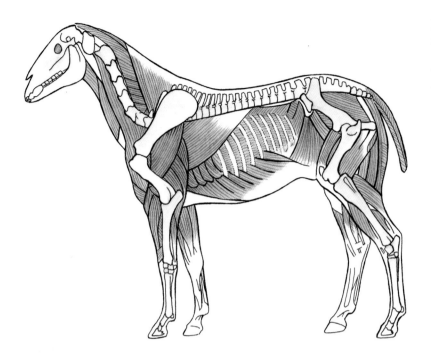

Figure 2.1. The horse's skeleton superimposed over the muscles. Note the low position of the neck vertebrae under the brachio-cephalic muscle. This may create the impression of over-development of this muscle.

from the front to the back. Movement in this plane is forwards and backwards as well as the vertical lift, as in piaffe.

The lateral plane cuts the body in half through the centre of gravity from side to side. Movement in this plane is lateral (from side to side).

The horizontal or transverse plane cuts the body horizontally through the centre of gravity. The movement in this plane is rotational.

These three planes meet at the centre of gravity.

Movement of the spinal column

The head and cervical vertebrae

The horse's long neck, with its seven vertebrae, can move in the sagittal, lateral and transverse planes. It is the most mobile part of the horse's skeleton and horses use it liberally for balance and for reaching in all directions. The horse's head can nod and it can also swivel/rotate. The joint between the head and the first vertebra, the atlas, allows the horse to nod his head and also allows a small degree of rotation.[2] There is a restriction to the nodding and this is the limit of the 'on the bit' position. The limit is usually when the horse's nose is on a vertical line when the poll is the highest point. The first two vertebrae (the poll) do not allow flexion, therefore in the 'on

---

2 Dr Gail Williams, article in *Your Horse*, June 2000.

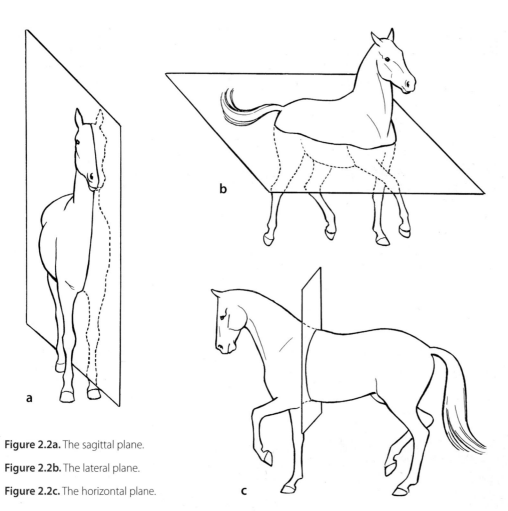

Figure 2.2a. The sagittal plane.

Figure 2.2b. The lateral plane.

Figure 2.2c. The horizontal plane.

the bit' position, the head is at a 90° angle to the poll. This is important when considering the 'long and low' position or even the slightly lower novice outline. In these positions the horse's head will thus be behind the vertical, but still flexing within the parameters of the ±90° angle, when he is yielding to the rein. That is to say, this is still biomechanically the same head and neck angle as the 'on the bit' position (see photos 2.1 a and b).

Considering the expectation that the horse's head should not be behind the vertical, it may be difficult for the horse to understand that the angle (or rounded position) should now be more than 90° if the rider maintains the contact. By yielding the reins, the rider can however encourage the horse to increase this angle.

As soon as the limit of this joint range is reached and the rider continues to ask for more roundness, the horse will flex the neck from the third to the seventh cervical vertebrae, or lower, at the cervico-thoracic joint. His neck will thus become lower and rounder. The neck vertebrae can flex until

Photo 2.1a. The 'on the bit' position showing the 90° nod between the poll and the head.

Photo 2.1b. The long and low frame with the nose behind the vertical, yet a larger than 90° angle.

the horse's nose can touch his chest. This constitutes the 'deep and round' method of riding. Maintaining joints in their outer ranges of movement can destabilize them and lead to inflammation and pain. Although research has shown that this position increases the mobility of the spine, the spine is designed to be fairly rigid to support the horse's great mass. Arguably, too much movement may cause back problems, especially with prolonged maintenance of this position (see 'Deep and round' in Chapter 8).

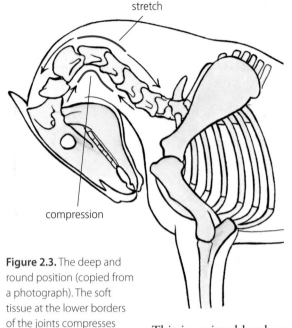

stretch

compression

Figure 2.3. The deep and round position (copied from a photograph). The soft tissue at the lower borders of the joints compresses while the soft tissue at the upper borders stretches.

The wings of the atlas can be palpated on either side at the top of the horse's neck. It is important that there is enough distance between the wing of the atlas and the posterior ridge of the jaw to allow the 'on the bit' position. However, this is only a problem when the two bones actually touch. Provided that the space is even as small as the width of one finger, the horse can still remain in the 'on the bit' position with ease. Riders/trainers often blame a horse's difficulty in remaining in the 'on the bit' position on this physical relationship, but it is rarely the true cause of the problem.

The joint between the atlas and axis, the second cervical vertebra, allows the horse to 'swivel'/rotate his neck in the transverse plane (from side to side) so that his nose can point sideways without the rest of his neck bending. This is assisted by the small rotational ability of the skull on the first vertebra. This tilt becomes obvious when the horse compensates for stiffness in another part of his neck.

The next five cervical vertebrae allow the horse to bend his neck up, down and from side to side. The nuchal ligament, which is attached to the occipital tuberocity and the fourth thoracic vertebra, supports the horse's head and the cervical vertebrae (see Figure 2.19, page 59).

Photo 2.2a. A horse with a 1 cm (½ in) space between his jawbone and the wing of the atlas.

Photo 2.2b. The same horse in the 'on the bit' position with ease.

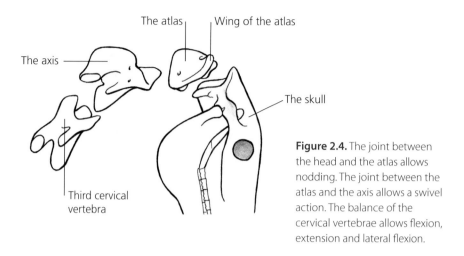

The axis

The atlas

Wing of the atlas

The skull

Third cervical vertebra

Figure 2.4. The joint between the head and the atlas allows nodding. The joint between the atlas and the axis allows a swivel action. The balance of the cervical vertebrae allows flexion, extension and lateral flexion.

The thoracic vertebrae

The horse's back (thoracic, lumbar and sacral vertebrae) is designed for rigidity rather than flexibility to contain the weight of his heavy visceral mass, to provide stable attachment for the limbs and to transfer propulsion from the hindquarters forward. Because of the attachment of the ribs and position of the facets/joints the eighteen thoracic vertebrae have a maximum of only a few millimetres of movement, during the full outer range of movement when the horse touches his rump with his nose. The movement in the thoracic spine is probably only to give a cushioning effect for the viscera when the horse moves. The intervertebral discs are extremely thin because the horizontal spine does not need as much cushioning as the vertical human spine. The thoracic spine, back to the sacrum, is relatively rigid, but the junctions between the different sections of the spine, allow more movement. There is less powerful muscular support at these junctions.[3] The hollowing we see when the horse draws his neck back is largely situated between the last cervical vertebra and the first thoracic vertebra.

The lumbar vertebrae and the sacrum

There are normally six lumbar vertebrae. The last three are fused together by the mamillo-articular processes. Movement in all directions is extremely limited between these vertebrae. The most flexion in the horse's body below the neck occurs between the last lumbar vertebra and the sacrum (lumbo-sacral joint). (The thoraco-lumbar joint between the last thoracic vertebra and the first lumbar vertebra also shows some flexion

---

3 S. Wyche, *The Anatomy of Riding*, (Marlborough, Wiltshire, The Crowood Press, 2004).

mobility.) This lumbo-sacral joint shows moderate ability for flexion and extension, which has a significant effect on the athletic ability of the horse. It is the joint which allows the pelvis to tilt and thereby place the hind-quarters further forward in engagement. Constant flexion of this joint, however places strain on the horse's back. Thus it is important that work at collected gaits should be interspersed with rest periods and stretching to alleviate the strain.

The five vertebrae of the sacrum itself are fused together. Therefore there is no movement in this area. The sacrum's main purpose is to be an anchor for muscles, ligaments and the pelvis.

The pelvis rests on top of the sacrum and is joined to it by the tough sacro-iliac ligaments. The sacro-iliac joint is not a joint in the true sense of the word, being almost immobile until the connective tissue tears. The fact that in the horse it is not fused with the sacrum (as it is in humans) could mean that the ligaments have some shock absorption function. The sacro-tuberal ligament connects the underside of the sacrum to the pelvis. Although powerful muscles protect this joint when the horse slips or falls, it is a common area of soft tissue injury. These ligaments are injured through play, slipping and sudden powerful movements in sport when the balance in the stabilizing muscles is disturbed. The prognosis for recovery is good, but the horse is often left with an asymmetrical bump on top of the joint and asymmetry in the pelvic action.

▶ RIDING AND TEACHING APPLICATIONS

1. Bilateral or unilateral bumps on top of the pelvic spine may be a tell-tale sign of weakness in this area. Asymmetry in this area, when one side of the pelvis rises higher than the other during trot or walk, may be an indication of some weakness and is often a sign of previous injury to the sacro-iliac ligaments. Therefore it should be checked by a veterinarian.

2. A problem in this joint may lead to difficulty changing the lead of the hind leg during flying changes.

3. It could also lead to difficulties with canter pirouette as well as with half-passes, particularly on one rein.

4. Many jumping horses are, however, very successful after rehabilitation despite having torn this ligament.

▶ JUDGING SIGNIFICANCE

1. When the head is in full flexion on the atlas, the horse's nose will be in a vertical line when his neck is in a high, collected frame. When he maintains this full flexion, but his neck is carried in a novice or long outline,

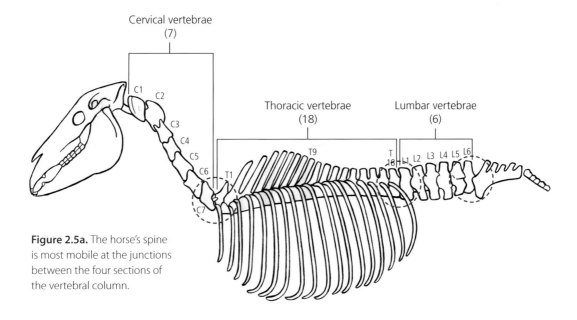

Figure 2.5a. The horse's spine is most mobile at the junctions between the four sections of the vertebral column.

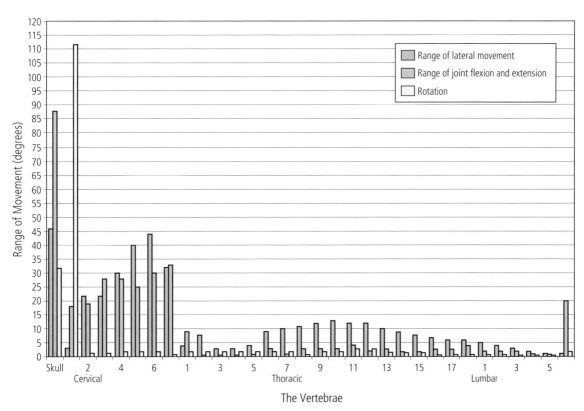

Figure 2.5b. Spinal movement in degrees. The vertebral column allows limited movement in the three movement planes described earlier in this chapter. The graph shows the movement ability from full flexion to full extension and the total lateral flexion from one side through to the other. This means that only half the movement occurs during full lateral flexion when the horse touches his hip with his nose. Thus, when the lateral bend is only around, say, the circumference of an 8 m circle, the bend in the spine further back than the neck will be negligible.

Photo 2.3 Even when the horse is in the end range of lateral bend, the thoracic and lumbar spine shows negligible movement.

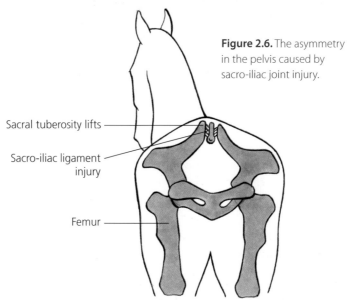

Sacral tuberosity lifts

Sacro-iliac ligament injury

Femur

Figure 2.6. The asymmetry in the pelvis caused by sacro-iliac joint injury.

his nose will be behind the vertical. This does not mean, however, that the horse is 'behind the bit', evading it or 'sucking back'. The position is biomechanically correct provided the angle between the head and poll is 90°, he is yielding correctly to the rider's hands and is not evading the contact defensively. However, if this position is a consequence of the horse being pulled in or 'hanging on the reins', it should be penalised appropriately.

2. Since the horse's thoracic and lumbar spines have very limited lateral bend, the horse cannot be expected to bend uniformly through his spine

in line with the shape of the circle. The total curve is understood to be approximately 30°; only three cervical joints in the spine allow a 30° bend. The rest of the spine allows ranges of 0° to 10° only (see Misconceptions about bending and circling in Chapter 7).[4]

3. A horse with a long back may not appear to be as engaged as a short-backed horse. This is an optical illusion. The long-backed horse is as capable of moving his hindquarters further underneath his body as a short-backed horse, but his hind legs will not reach as close to his forelegs. Therefore overtracking or tracking up is not a good sign of engagement in these horses.

Characteristics of Bone

1. Bone grows thicker, denser and stronger through weight-bearing and high-impact loading. In the horse, high-impact, short periods of loading, such as trotting on a hard surface or jumping, increases bone mass. Research has found that 'young horses subjected to high levels of exercise did not show as high an incidence of osteochondrosis (OCD, commonly referred to as joint mice) as the control group given lower levels of exercise.'[5] Research has also shown, however, that excessive repetitive exercise over long sessions can cause fatigue damage to bones and joints.[6] Endless trotting in endurance races is one example of this kind of repetitive exercise. This damage is known as repetitive strain injury (RSI). Excessive and too repetitive high-impact training can affect the shock-absorbing qualities of bone, which becomes dense immediately under the articular surface. This leads to a diminished shock absorption capacity of cartilage, and arthritis (degenerative joint disease/ringbone) affecting the carpal bones. 'The adaptive response of bone requires a gradual increase in mechanical demand.'[7]

2. Bone will grow in the areas on which the muscles and tendons pull. For example, swimmers develop broad shoulders as a result of the shoulder muscle attachments pulling on the bone. Although they lose a fair amount of muscle when their competition life stops, the broad shoulders remain for life. Thus foals need large paddocks for exercise in order to develop strong, dense bone.

---

4 Dr Gail Williams, article in *Your Horse*, June 2000.

5 A.E. Goodship and H.L. Birch, 'Exercise effects on the skeletal tissues' as quoted in W. Back and H.M. Clayton *Equine Locomotion* (London, Harcourt Publishers Ltd., 2001).

6 Ibid.

7 Ibid.

3. Bones continue to grow after birth and they stop growing in sequence starting at the carpal bones from six months of age. By the age of two and a half, the horse's legs have reached their mature length. The spine and pelvis are the last to mature between the ages of six and seven, depending on the size of the horse. This is why it is relatively easy to predict the adult size of the horse after two years of age.

▶ RIDING AND TEACHING APPLICATIONS

1. Although many studies have confirmed these findings and it is clear that developing bones and joints need exercise, it is still not clear as to *how much* exercise, in terms of loading and time, is needed for optimal bone and cartilage development. Thus it appears essential that all young horses should have moderate exercise regularly for short periods to develop and maintain strong bones. Increase in exercise intensity should be gradual and diverse to prevent fatigue damage. The philosophy of leaving a horse until the age of four before giving him regular work is based on incomplete knowledge of physiology.

2. There are two methods for predicting the size of a horse from the age of two years.
   a. Using a tape measure or a piece of string, place one end on the ergot at the back of the front fetlock and measure from here to the point of the elbow. Double up the tape/string from the point of the elbow towards the horse's withers. The height of the string above the withers is usually the lowest height he will reach.

Photo 2.4. Foals exercising freely develop their bones and muscles.

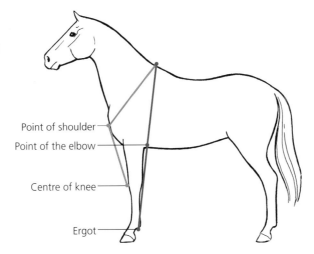

Figure 2.7. Predicting the eventual size of a horse.

Point of shoulder

Point of the elbow

Centre of knee

Ergot

b. Measure from the centre of the knee to the point of the shoulder. Then take the beginning of the tape up to the withers. This will measure to the approximate same spot as in (a).

Muscles and Associated Tissues

The shape and size of the superficial muscles define the outer shape of the horse. Muscles differ in shape, tone and texture from horse to horse. This is most evident when we compare the necks of a few horses. Some necks are thick and well-muscled while others are long and elegant. Although muscles become larger when exercised, this exercise cannot change the predetermined shape of the muscle. Therefore, one neck cannot be made to look exactly like another. The shape of the fascia (see below) determines the shape of each individual muscle as well as the shape of groups of muscles bound together. That is the reason why some horses will never have beautifully shaped necks or hindquarters, no matter how hard the rider works at developing the muscles. Compare this with the different shapes of human legs. No amount of exercise can turn unshapely legs into perfectly shaped legs.

Fascia

Fascia forms part of the connective tissue in the body and is a shaped packing medium – a body stocking. If all the insides of the body were removed from the fascia, you would be left with a complete outline of everything in the body.

Fascia has a superficial and a deep layer. The deep fascia is dense and tough and surrounds each muscle in a sheath. It also surrounds each

Photo 2.5a. This neck has a thick layer of fat above the nuchal ligament.

Photo 2.5b. No amount of exercise will turn this horse's neck into the same shape as the horse in 2.5a. The fat layer above the nuchal ligament has to increase, but the horse's particular physiology does not allow this.

muscle fibre and ties the muscle groups together, 'holding' the whole muscle structure in one large bag. It facilitates the gliding of the adjacent structures such as blood vessels, nerves and bones. 'It forms a soft bed for each of its embedded structures.'[8]

The quality, nature and consistency of the fascia is different depending on which organ it covers. Where it covers tendon, it is called the tendon sheath; where it covers muscle it is called the muscle sheath and when it covers bone it is called the periosteum.

---

8 R.D. Lockhart, G.F. Hamilton and F.W. Fyfe, *Anatomy of the Human Body* (London, Faber and Faber Ltd., 1959).

The fascia connections and binding facilitate the chain reaction of muscles and makes the muscle system of the animal work as a unit. It makes the muscle action in front affect the back and makes the action of the back affect the front. The action in the middle affects both ends.

The tensegrity (see Glossary) between muscles, fascia and bones ensures that the whole musculo-skeletal system works in balance to protect the horse's body against injury. However, injury in one part of the body weakens the tensegrity and will therefore affect other parts. For example, pain in the shoulder muscles on the horse's right side often leads to painful hind limb muscles on the horse's left side.

General Functions of Muscles

The basic function of the voluntary muscles is to move or stabilize the bones which they connect, because bones cannot move by themselves. Thus muscle activity brings bones closer together or further apart to produce movement. It also stabilizes the joints to maintain a position. The fibrous tendon at each end of the muscle body connects the muscle to the bone.

In simple terms, muscles are generally arranged in opposing groups, the movers and the antagonists. This ensures smooth movement. When the mover contracts, the antagonist will relax unless the muscles are in co-contraction. The muscles move the bones in combinations of four directions. *Flexion* closes the joint while *extension* opens the joint. *Adduction* moves the bone closer to the body while *abduction* moves it away from the

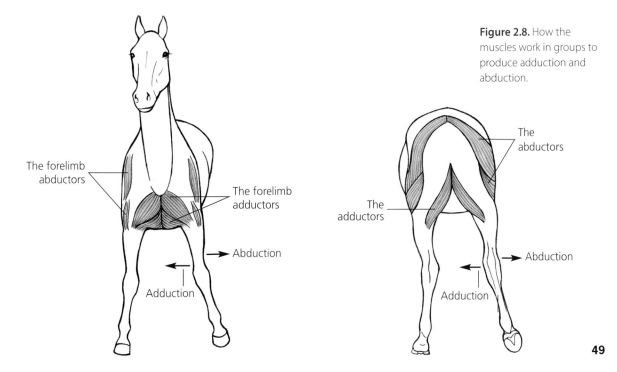

Figure 2.8. How the muscles work in groups to produce adduction and abduction.

The forelimb abductors

The forelimb adductors

The abductors

The adductors

Abduction

Adduction

Abduction

Adduction

49

body. A combination of these functions will produce circular movement, although this is restricted in the horse. In real terms, muscles work in co-ordinative structures in whole patterns of movement: muscles never work in isolation.

The muscles have two different types of contraction. In *concentric contraction* the muscles shorten to move one bone closer to another. In *eccentric contraction* the muscles work 'backwards' against the effect of gravity. This is a coordinated gradual releasing of the muscle contraction as when, for example, a person lowers a weight slowly. It is the type of contraction in the horse's hindquarter muscles during the canter when the forehand moves towards the ground after the lift. The weight of the horse's body is lowered slowly against gravitational forces. This contraction is often more measured than concentric contraction. (This form of contraction is often referred to in biomechanics as 'lengthening' contraction, a form of words that may be puzzling to laypeople. In fact, in many instances, the muscle does not actually lengthen.)

Muscles can contract without a significant change in movement of the limb. The horse can thus appear to have an inside bend, but the opposite muscles may be in contraction. This results in a strong contact on the inside rein – the false bend (see that heading in Chapter 4).

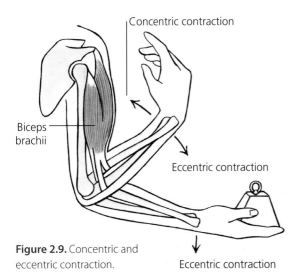

Figure 2.9. Concentric and eccentric contraction.

Concentric contraction

Biceps brachii

Eccentric contraction

Eccentric contraction

Specific Functions of Muscle Groups

Overview

In general the horse's muscles below the vertebral column flex the body from the head to the tail when contracting bilaterally. The muscles above the vertebral column, the top line muscles, extend it and thus hollow it from head to tail when contracting bilaterally. The flexor muscles close the joints, while the extensor muscles open the joints. Although muscles have individually defined movement, they generally work together in functional groups (coordinative structures) and in chains as a result of the fascia connections. The flexor and extensor groups also work in synergy to prevent injury.

The horse uses his left side muscles to bend to the left and his right side muscles to bend to the right in unilateral contraction.

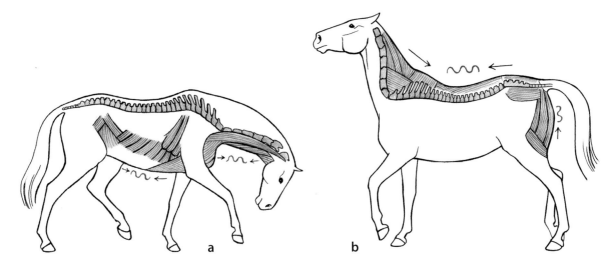

Figure 2.10a. The rounding muscles of the flexor pattern

Figure 2.10b. The hollowing muscles of the extensor pattern.

The neck muscles

The neck muscles below the spine flex the neck down against the very strong nuchal ligament. A common misconception has existed for many years that the top line muscles develop as a result of the horse working in a round frame. This 'cause and effect' is an impossibility because of the action of the nuchal ligament, which stretches from the head to the withers and supports the horse's head and neck. The muscles below the spine have to contract against this strong ligament to flex the horse's neck down and round. Most of the neck muscles above the spine have the main function of supporting the neck vertebrae in a 'sling'. They only develop in bulk when the horse bends his head and neck laterally from side to side when maintaining an inside bend in dressage. It is notable how often hacking and jumping horses lack the developed neck of the dressage horse. Horses in the first two categories do not generally practise much bending. Two examples of neck muscle action above and below the spine demonstrate how this works.

1. The splenius muscle above the spine stabilizes the neck for the brachio-cephalicus muscle to pull the forelimb forwards. It also assists the nuchal ligament to maintain the stretched out neck position against gravity. It supports mainly in isometric contraction, in which it does not shorten. In active contraction it hollows the horse's neck and in unilateral contraction it bends the neck sideways. In its first role it does not bulk out. Its second function of bending sideways leads to a broader neck.

2. The strong brachio-cephalicus muscle, below the spine, has two separate functions which change depending on its fixed point. When the fixed point is on the shoulder, it turns the horse's head to the side in unilateral contraction. When the fixed point is the origin at the head, it lifts

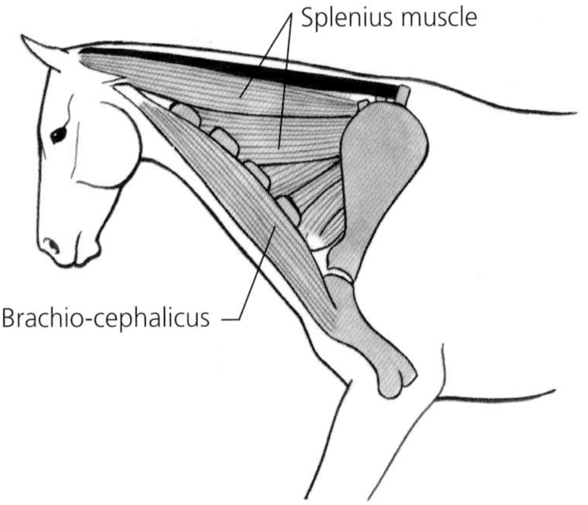

Figure 2.11. The functions of the splenius muscle.

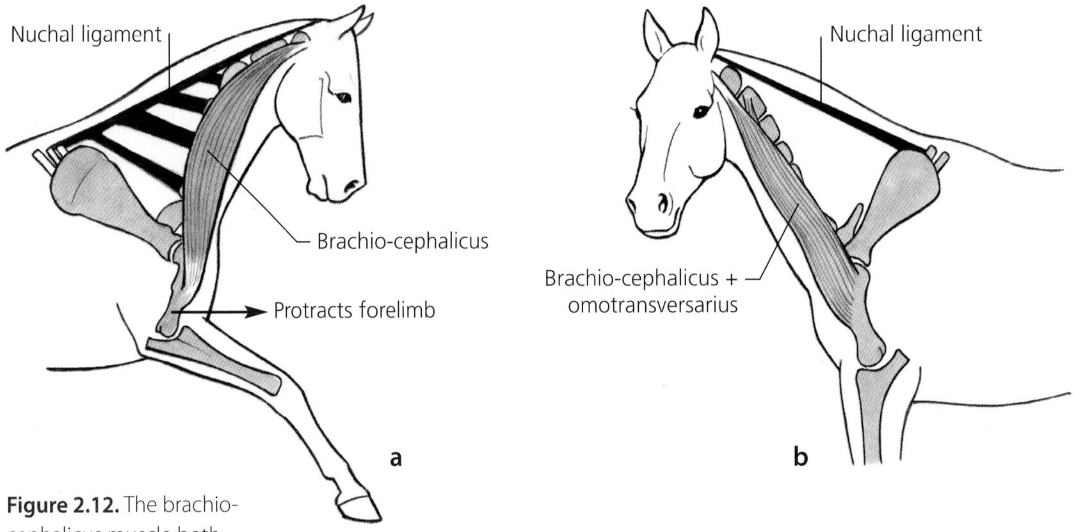

Splenius muscle

Brachio-cephalicus

Nuchal ligament

Brachio-cephalicus

Protracts forelimb

a

Nuchal ligament

Brachio-cephalicus + omotransversarius

b

Figure 2.12. The brachio-cephalicus muscle both protracts the horse's forelimb (a) and turns the horse's head (b).

and swings the forelimb forwards in unilateral contraction. Therefore it is expected to be large and well developed. The brachio-cephalicus muscle is thus active during the swing phase, and passive during the stance phase. When in bilateral contraction, it assists in maintaining the 'on the bit' position. It works together with the omotransversarius muscle.

The multifidus and intercostalis muscles are the deep stabilizers of the spine. They interconnect and work in concert from the top of the neck to the tail. Therefore, when the neck tightens, it affects the entire spine.

The foreleg and shoulder muscles

The forelimb muscles are small compared to those of the hindquarters – the 'engine'. They are used for lifting and placing, for shock absorption, steering and support. The trapezius and rhomboid muscles move the top of the shoulder blade forwards and upwards to retract the forelegs. They are assisted by the latissimus dorsi muscles, which also retract the forelimb. The large latissimus dorsi muscle is also a back muscle because it draws the horse's body over the forelimbs. These muscles work in synergy with the brachio-cephalicus muscles to move the horse's forelegs forwards and backwards. The triceps muscle extends the elbow joint and therefore has to be very supple to prevent restriction of free forward movement. The pectoral muscles adduct the forelimbs and stabilize them onto the ribcage. These muscles therefore have to be very supple for lateral movements in dressage, but also strong to stabilize the forelimb onto the body. The deltoid, teres minor, supraspinatus and infraspinatus muscles are the abductors of the forelimbs and are responsible for all the lateral movements and circles.

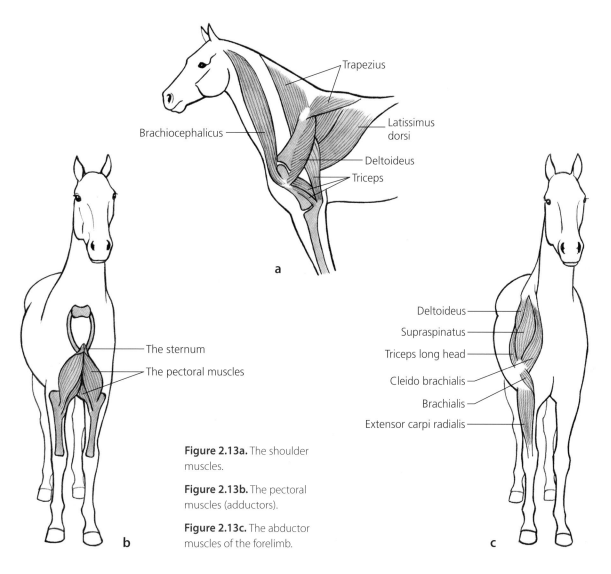

Figure 2.13a. The shoulder muscles.

Figure 2.13b. The pectoral muscles (adductors).

Figure 2.13c. The abductor muscles of the forelimb.

The hind leg muscles

The hip extensors

The middle gluteus and the hamstring muscles extend the hip joint. They are strong and produce horizontal velocity to propel the horse forwards by pushing the body over the legs. They are important for speed in racing, for lifting the horse when jumping and for the extended gaits. The deep, middle and superficial gluteal muscles and the biceps femoris also abduct the hind limbs for lateral movements.

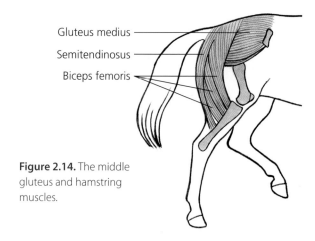

Gluteus medius

Semitendinosus

Biceps femoris

Figure 2.14. The middle gluteus and hamstring muscles.

The hip flexors

The quadriceps femoris muscles flex the hip joint and extend the stifle joint. They flex the hip joint to bring the leg forwards in the swing phase of the movement. This movement is, however, not against a significant amount of resistance. Their strenuous work is the extension of the stifle in the stance phase of the hind leg. They have an important role in stabilizing the stifle joint when the leg is in mid stance and the body is propelled over the hind legs. In addition they are the main locking mechanism of the stay apparatus.

These muscles are very important and have to be extremely strong for collected work – especially the collected canter, piaffe and passage – and for rein-back. They strain easily if their strength is not developed slowly for the very collected work. In the piaffe, they bring the hind legs quite far underneath the body in order to function in the correct position with the least amount of strain.

The quadriceps muscles have to match the hip extensors and stifle flexors in strength to stabilize the stifle in extension during the stance phase when the weight of the body moves over the leg.

The gracilis, adductor and pectineus muscles adduct the hind limb. For

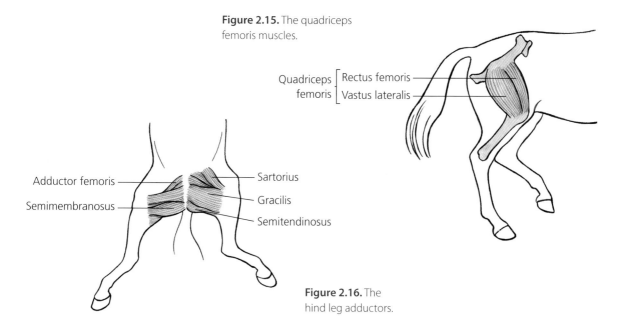

Figure 2.15. The quadriceps femoris muscles.

Quadriceps femoris [Rectus femoris
Vastus lateralis

Adductor femoris

Semimembranosus

Sartorius

Gracilis

Semitendinosus

Figure 2.16. The hind leg adductors.

the purpose of dressage they have to be supple to allow lateral movement, yet strong to stabilize the hip joint and prevent injury.

The back muscles

The trot movement produces natural flexion and extension of the back vertebrae because of the weight of the viscera, which lifts and drops with the movement. The back muscles and the abdominal muscles contract only to control the extent of the hollowing and rounding at each stride to protect the spine.

Contraction of the back muscles hollows the horse's back. Tension and anxiety cause tension in the extensor muscles: the horse hollows his neck, which leads to hollowing and tightening of the back muscles. His steps shorten, his movements become choppy and it becomes uncomfortable for the rider to sit at the trot. This chain reaction can be corrected by eliciting a flexor pattern which brings the neck down and rounds the back, bringing the hindquarters more underneath the body.

The longissimus dorsi muscle runs in sections down the top of the vertebral column from the head to the tail. It connects to the middle gluteus muscle and thus, together with the gluteus muscle, facilitates propulsion at each hind leg stride. These back muscles work as a unit to extend the horse's spine from his head to his tail. When the forehand lifts in the canter, all the back muscles contract against the resistance of gravity and have to support the entire weight of the horse. Therefore, they have to be extremely strong.

The middle gluteus muscles of the hindquarters connect to and pull on the longissimus muscles in the back to lift the whole horse on the hind legs. This rapid process, however, starts at the head and neck and works down the spine to the gluteus muscles.

The longissimus also contracts together with the gluteal muscles when the horse kicks back with both hind legs. This, however, is an easier action because the forehand is designed to carry weight, the neck balances the process and horses only kick out occasionally.

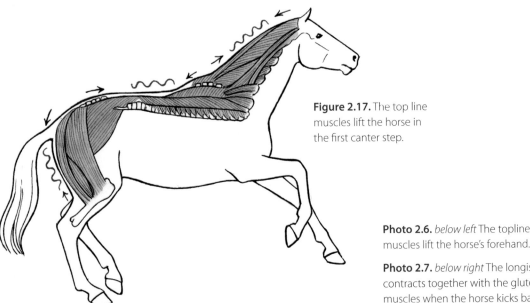

Figure 2.17. The top line muscles lift the horse in the first canter step.

Photo 2.6. *below left* The topline muscles lift the horse's forehand.

Photo 2.7. *below right* The longissimus contracts together with the gluteal muscles when the horse kicks back with both hind legs.

The abdominal muscles and their interaction with hip flexors

The muscles below the vertebral column are all flexors of the spine. The abdominal muscles show very little activity during walk, probably because there is no suspension in the walk, but they contract to support the very heavy viscera.

The iliopsoas muscles flex the spine at the lumbo-sacral joint during the canter and gallop. They also flex the hip joints to bring the hindquarters under in collection, thereby assisting in engagement to bring the haunches more underneath the body. They are not hugely powerful muscles because they do not work against gravity. (This muscle is the tender fillet steak in food animals).

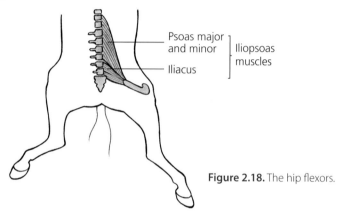

Figure 2.18. The hip flexors.

Equine Anatomical and Physiological Idiosyncrasies

Horses have many anatomical adaptations. Most of these are energy-saving devices.

1. The extremely thick, strong and elastic (rubbery) nuchal ligament and laminae support the horse's heavy head and neck. This ligament runs from the occiput to the summits of the third and fourth (or fifth) thoracic vertebrae. Its diameter ranges between 3 cm (approx 1¼ in) at the top and 8 cm (approx 3¼ in) at the base of the neck. It is connected to the spinous processes of the neck vertebrae with the nuchal laminae. The horse's head and neck 'dangle' on this ligament like a suspension bridge. It is an energy-saving device which ensures that the horse uses little muscular effort against the force of gravity to maintain his head and neck in the neutral position – the upside-down V position. This places his eyes in the optimal position for observation of the landscape.

EXERCISE

Palpate the nuchal ligament with your fingers about 10 cm (4 in) down from the horse's poll. You will find a 3 cm (approx 1¼ in) hard, round band against the muscles. The muscles will feel spongy while the ligament feels dense. Once you have felt this, slide your hand down to about 10 cm (4 in) in front of the horse's withers. Here the band is so broad – about 8 cm (3¼ in) that you will have to open your hands quite wide to grip it below the thick layer of fat on his neck. Above this hard band is quite a substantial layer of fat. Lower down you can palpate the vertebrae. Feel the difference between the textures of the bone, muscle, ligament and fat.

It takes strong muscle action to flex the head and neck down against the enormous tensile strength of the nuchal ligament. As soon as the flexor muscles below the vertebrae relax, the nuchal ligament springs back to its resting position – the upside-down V position of the neck. This strong ligament is the reason why we have to remind the horse contin-

Photo 2.8. The thick nuchal ligament, showing the fat layer above it.

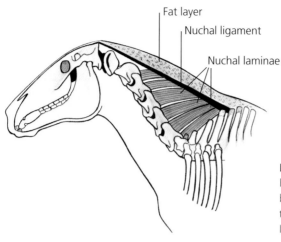

Fat layer

Nuchal ligament

Nuchal laminae

Figure 2.19. The nuchal ligament and laminae. The bigger the crest, the bigger the layer of fat above the ligament.

uously to maintain his round frame. We request him to contract his neck flexors through pressure and release on the reins.

2. The strong and fairly rigid supraspinous ligament binds and stabilizes the spinal column. This ligament is continuous with the nuchal ligament and attaches to the spinous processes of the horse's vertebrae, binding them together. It serves to strengthen the back and maintain its 'rigidity'. It is supported in its function by the deep muscles of the back (spinalis, multifidi and iliocostalis). This ligament also facilitates the task of the hindquarters which push the horse's heavy body over the forelimbs: it braces the vertebrae together to form a solid rod which the hindquarters can push forwards.

When the horse's neck is in the resting position, these ligaments are in their neutral state of tension. When the horse stretches his head and neck down with his flexor muscles, the nuchal ligament is pulled down and this places tension on the supraspinous ligament which then 'pulls' the horse's back up, rounding it in flexion. Simultaneously, the neck flexor muscles activate the flexor muscle chain to contract underneath his abdomen and hips. When the horse lifts his head and neck, the tension on the supraspinous ligament becomes less. When the horse hollows his neck by contracting his extensor muscles, the supraspinous ligament loses some of its tension. This action of the neck activates the extensor muscle chain to hollow the back. This hollow position weakens the stabilizing effect of the supraspinous ligament on the back, thus placing strain on the intervertebral ligaments. Therefore, it is important for the horse's health to ride him in a round frame, especially for a heavy rider.

3. The stay apparatus in the forelimb is an energy-saving device which allows the horse to rest while remaining standing. It is a complicated

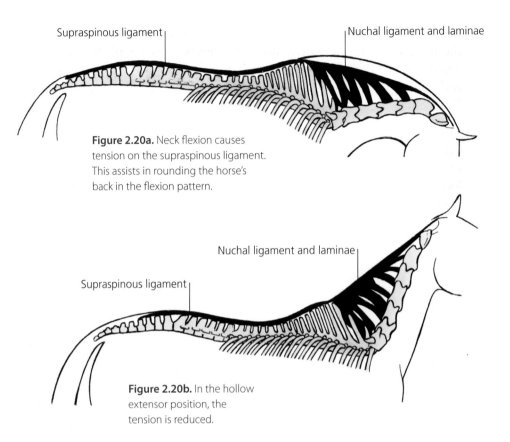

Supraspinous ligament

Nuchal ligament and laminae

Figure 2.20a. Neck flexion causes tension on the supraspinous ligament. This assists in rounding the horse's back in the flexion pattern.

Nuchal ligament and laminae

Supraspinous ligament

Figure 2.20b. In the hollow extensor position, the tension is reduced.

arrangement of tendon and ligament connections which criss-cross the joints to prevent flexion of the shoulder, elbow and knee (carpal) joints and extension of the pastern and fetlock joints. This arrangement stabilizes the joints in a position of support and prevents the collapse of the legs to allow the horse to remain standing with minimal muscular effort. While muscles tire, ligaments and tendons do not. This arrangement assists the strut effect when braking, or landing after a jump.

4. The stay apparatus in the stifle is an energy-saving device which enables the horse to doze while remaining standing. An oval knoblike protrusion (the medial condyle) on the inside ridge of the femur, in the stifle, fits between the medial and middle ligaments. These ligaments are attached to the kneecap (patella). During normal movement of flexion and extension the kneecap glides up and down in the patellar groove of the stifle. The tensor fascia lata muscle tilts the ligamentous hook away from the knob at every stride. When the horse wants to sleep or rest while standing, the medial patellar ligament loops over this knoblike protrusion. The horse does this by contracting his quadriceps muscle and the tensor fascia lata, lifting the patella. When the stifle is fully extended, the medial ligament slips over the medial condyle of the

femur. The stifle is then locked in place. When the horse wants to release the lock, he pulls the patella up and sideways again with the same muscles as he takes the first forward step with his foreleg. The next step is the unlocked hind leg. It is therefore difficult for the horse to take the first step of the walk with a hind leg (see Chapter 10).

5. The reciprocal apparatus is a safety mechanism to guarantee correct coordination, stability and power in the hind legs. A group of ligaments, tendons and muscles at the front and back of the main bones of the hind limb are attached in a specific pattern to ensure that the stifle and hock open and close to the same degree simultaneously.

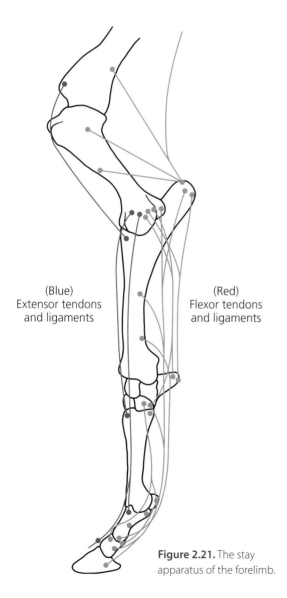

(Blue)
Extensor tendons
and ligaments

(Red)
Flexor tendons
and ligaments

Figure 2.21. The stay apparatus of the forelimb.

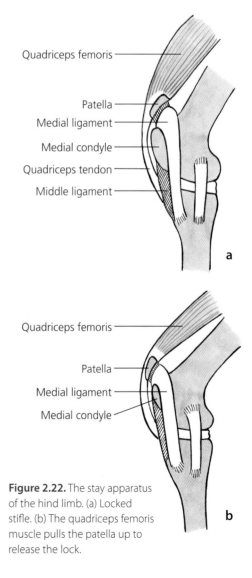

Quadriceps femoris

Patella
Medial ligament

Medial condyle

Quadriceps tendon

Middle ligament

a

Quadriceps femoris

Patella

Medial ligament

Medial condyle

b

Figure 2.22. The stay apparatus of the hind limb. (a) Locked stifle. (b) The quadriceps femoris muscle pulls the patella up to release the lock.

6. The long spines of the second to the ninth thoracic vertebrae (the withers) are for muscle and ligament attachments to secure the horse's heavy head and neck while simultaneously ensuring mobility and balance. (This area also happens to keep the saddle from sliding over the horse's shoulders.)

7. The absence of collarbones assists the horse in speed of movement. The shoulder blades of the quadruped are the main determinant of the length of stride of the forelimbs.[9] The absence of collarbones sets the shoulder blades free to produce a longer stride. The attachment of a collarbone between the shoulder and chest would restrict this movement. The absence of collarbones also greatly assists the horse in balance because it allows the ribcage to swing in between the legs, thus allowing lateral movement. The almost rigid spine complicates the turning method of the horse: bony attachments between the horse's forelegs and skeleton would be an even greater deterrent to turning this rigid structure. (Another very important reason for the absence of collarbones is connected to the horse's weight. A large weight is carried with more ease on upright pillars – the legs. Collarbones would push the legs out to the sides, as in reptiles and amphibians: this produces an amphibian-like gait, which leads to pressure on the lungs and thus impedes flight.)

   In humans, the arms can move through 360° by way of the ball and socket shoulder joints. In horses, with their short and strong pectoral muscles, which stabilize the forelimbs onto the body, the movement of the shoulder joints is restricted. The absence of collarbones allows the forelegs to yield on impact, which improves shock absorption through the joints.

8. The horse's shoulder blade is attached to his ribcage by muscles alone. The absence of a collarbone ensures that the ribcage can swing and tilt from side to side and can lift and descend to lift or drop the centre of gravity. Thus, the rider can tilt the horse's ribcage by pushing it with a leg. This gives the impression of an inside bend during turns, circles, leg-yield, shoulder-in and half-pass (see photo 2.9). The horse lifts or lowers his ribcage with his serratus ventralis thoracis and pectoral muscles (the muscle sling). This gives a trampoline action which protects the viscera and ensures superior shock absorption. It gives the rider a comfortable ride – the proverbial 'soft back'. When these muscles become stronger, the muscle tone increases and the horse grows a little at the withers.

---

9 M. Holmström, 'The effects of conformation', in W. Back and H.M. Clayton, *Equine Locomotion (London*, Harcourt Publishers Ltd., 2001).

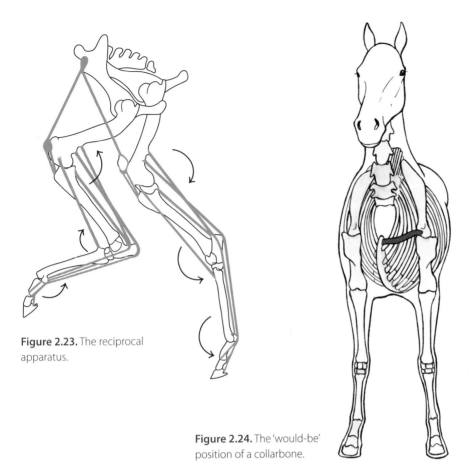

Figure 2.23. The reciprocal apparatus.

Figure 2.24. The 'would-be' position of a collarbone.

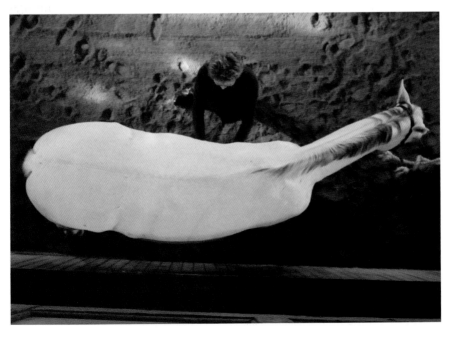

Photo 2.9. The tilting ribcage gives an impression of an inside bend. It also produces a balance reaction which turns the horse's head and neck in the direction of the bend.

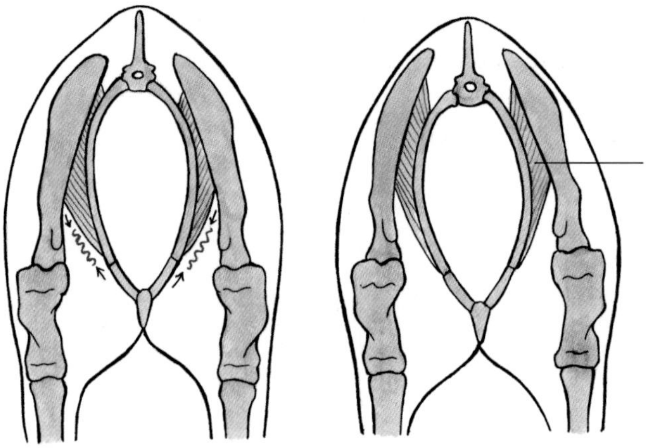

Serratus ventralis
thoracis

Figure 2.25. The serratus ventralis thoracis muscles contract to lift the ribcage which lifts the withers and makes the horse 'grow' in stature.

9. The horse has an extremely long and mobile neck, which he uses to move his head in all directions, giving the ability to see in a wider range. He uses it for balance and for repelling flies. (The horse has mobile appendages, a neck and a tail, at each end for this purpose.) Since the horse has no 'arms' to use for maintaining balance, he uses his neck as we would use our arms.

10. The horse's limb muscles are positioned high and close to his body, thus close to the centre of mass. This ensures that the lower limbs are lighter in order to move faster in flight.

11. The muscles with their long tendons and ligaments in the horse's legs are the source of elastic recoil. They produce a spring action which is an energy-saving device. It stores elastic energy during the extreme stretch of the fetlock joint in the stance phase of the limb. At break-over, the elastic tissues recoil to facilitate flexion of the joints to raise the limb.[10] This ensures that the protraction muscles of both fore and hind limbs use very little power and energy to protract the limbs. Elastic recoil also serves as an important shock absorber.

12. Equine bones are less dense than human bones. This bone lightness facilitates swift flight.

13. In perfect conformation, the horse's pastern and shoulder angles are supposed to be parallel. In practice this is often not the case, but the pastern angle does give the rider, at a glance, an indication of the shoulder angle. A long, sloping shoulder blade (scapula) is most beneficial for good movement.

---

10 W. Back, 'Intra-limb coordination: the forelimb and the hind limb', in W. Back and H.M. Clayton, *Equine Locomotion* (London, Harcourt Publishers Ltd., 2001).

14. The hind hooves are pointed while the front hooves have rounded toes. The pointed hind hoof digging into the ground assists in pushing against the ground, in a way similar to a track athlete using starting blocks. Rapid flexion of the coffin joint at the end of the stance phase pushes against the ground to propel the horse forwards. Thus there is a burst of power as the hoof pushes against the ground.

15. The horse has extraordinarily small feet in relation to body size. This is another energy-saving device which assists elastic recoil of the muscles and tendons. It is important for instant and fast flight. The horse can function with small feet because he has a large base of support with a stable quadruped stance. A small base of support needs large feet for balance. (Compare this to the kangaroo's feet and tail.)

16. The horse's breathing during canter is synchronized with the movement of the stride. When the horse's weight is on his leading forelimb, the 'downhill' position pushes his viscera against his lungs. This assists in forcing the air out of his lungs and he breathes out. When his weight is backward on his trailing hind leg, the viscera move backwards, allowing the lungs to expand. The horse thus breathes in. When young horses initially canter in the arena under a rider they tire rapidly. Young horses often do not have a set rhythm in their first mounted canter sessions and this would lead to a disturbance in their breathing rhythm. Slight tension during these initial canter sessions could also disturb their rhythmical breathing in conjunction with each and every stride.

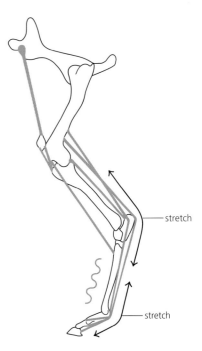

Figure 2.26. Elastic recoil.

3

The Control Centre

The Central Nervous System

The central nervous system consists of the brain and the spinal cord. Every conscious thought and movement starts with the brain, the great initiator. It is the nerve centre, the seat of motivation and it spreads the 'word'. Voluntary movement as well as automatic reactions and responses are dependent on the head and initiated in the brain. Some primitive reflexes however, are spinal cord controlled, but no active thought process is involved. For example, the fast retraction of a limb from heat is a primitive reflex. The tickle on the horse's skin from a fly causes the reflex of the skin to wrinkle and the tail to swat.

The peripheral nervous system

All the nerves between the spinal cord and the rest of the body form the peripheral nervous system. This arrangement can be compared to a telephone network. If the brain and spinal cord (the central nervous system) are the exchange, the nerves to the limbs and organs (the peripheral nervous system), are the telephone lines to each house.

Cephalo-caudal development and movement

All life starts at the head. Even before birth, development starts at the brain and travels down the spine to the periphery. This is called cephalo-caudal development. Nerve development and controlled movement thus start at the head. Postural control in the newborn baby starts with the head; first the baby learns a little head control, then neck control followed

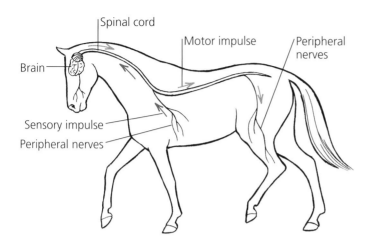

Figure 3.1. A schematic illustration of the horse's central and peripheral nervous system.

by back control and, as the development spreads down the spine, the arms and hands become more coordinated and finally the legs start to take weight and balance. By approximately one year of age, the human baby can walk. In horses, however, all this development proceeds before birth to ensure that the foal is born in readiness to flee. The overall format, however, is still the same.

Just as all voluntary movement for postural control is initiated by the brain and starts at the head and neck, so too does the learning of all new skilled movement. The horse, for example, hears an unfamiliar sound, lifts his head, followed by his neck, then hollows his back, extends his legs, and finally runs away. All this happens in split-second timing.

Photo 3.1. Hollowing starts at the head.

The brain is so powerful that even the *thought* of a movement produces chemical reactions in the nerves and muscles to prepare them for the movement. Studies have now shown that, during times of inactivity, simply going through the thought processes of the activity can make a significant contribution to retaining fitness for it. The chemicals discharged in the nerves and muscles when simply 'practising' in the brain, can help maintain their fitness. This is a powerful learning aid.

As bones cannot move without muscles, so muscles cannot move without nerve input and nerves do not have an input without the brain giving the instructions. These instructions are passed on, from the brain to the muscles, via the spinal cord. Thoughts and actions develop in the head and become chemical stimuli. They jump from one nerve to the next via the dendrites. (A nerve cell consists of a head, a tail and hair-like dendrites at each end.)

In general terms, the nerves from the brain descend down the spinal column to the periphery. The sensory nerve pathways (afferent nerves) run in an upward direction from the sensory organs (skin, eyes, ears, nose, tongue) to the brain. The horse perceives all our aids through his sensory organs. All the sensations are sent to the brain for integration, interpretation and decision-making. The motor nerves carry these 'decisions' from the brain to the muscles to produce action in the head to tail direction (efferent pathways). For example:

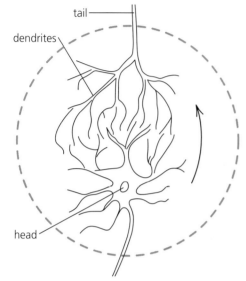

Figure 3.2. Nerve impulses 'jump' from one cell to the next in a head-to-tail direction in the synapse.

1. The sensory organs perceive elements of both the inner and outer environment. The rider's leg pressure on the horse's skin, and hand pressure through the reins on the horse's mouth are sensory stimuli, which move up the spinal cord to the brain in the efferent pathways.

2. The rider's aids are interpreted by the horse's brain according to his memories and his associations. Once the brain has interpreted the message and decided how to react appropriately, it sends the appropriate signals, via the afferent pathways, to the muscles. The muscles do not explain to the brain how to react. They only give the brain the information about their condition and environment such as pain, stretch and position. It is not the muscle doing the job, but the brain telling the muscle what to do.

The eyes, ears and nose

These are the great motivators of the horse, the primary sensory organs on which animals depend for safety. 'The head and mouth region of an animal always makes first contact with its environment and here are developed the special senses, smell and taste, sight and hearing.'[1] The nose, eyes and ears initiate the fright/ flight response of prey animals. They smell, see and hear danger then look in that direction and decide to stay or flee. The movement of the eyes occurs in unison with those of the head and neck. The horse's ears often move in the same direction as his eyes to investigate the situation.

Sixteen muscles control the horse's ear movements. This is an indication of the importance of ear movements in communication with both herd and rider. As soon as the rider's legs are used for communication, the horse will move his ears in the direction of the legs. When the rider talks, the horse moves his ears in the direction of the voice. When he is rewarded with a tickle, he moves his ears in the direction of the tickle. He communicates all his emotions through his ears.

Horses have a large peripheral visual field and react instantly to unusual movements on the periphery. The horse sees movement about 90 per cent faster than humans and lifts his head instantly to perceive it. The rider should pre-empt this through constant awareness of the possibility of movement in the landscape.

The horse does not need to turn his head in the direction in which he is moving because the position of his eyes on the sides of his head allows him excellent lateral vision. He shies or spooks at a 'scary' object while looking at it because he has the ability to assess the lateral space where he has to make his jump without turning his head. When he is on a rough track he will look ahead, assess the going and step over the stone with his forelegs – his integrative sense will ensure that his hind legs also miss the stone.

When we ride in the 'on the bit' position, we remove the horse's ability to survey his surroundings for safety, because the vertical position of his head narrows his field of vision in all directions so that he sees more of the ground close to him and less of the landscape around him. He thus has to rely on the rider for his protection. This position is thus a position of trust and submission, which the rider should appreciate and respect. Is it a wonder that many horses do not enjoy being ridden in this position? The 'deep and round' method of riding (hyperflexion) removes the horse's entire ability to assess his safety. This positioning of the head places the horse's eyes where he can see little except his own body and the ground beneath him.

Figure 3.3. The restricted visual field in the 'on the bit' position.

---

1 R.D. Lockhart, G.F. Hamilton and F.W. Fyfe, *Anatomy of the Human Body* (London, Faber and Faber, 1959).

Part-whole perception

Humans have the ability to form a picture of the whole object when only part of the object is visible. This is called closure or part-whole perception. The horse, however, does not seem to be able to close a picture if he sees only half of it. For example, when he sees only a section of a cow, he cannot recognize it as a whole cow. When he perceives movement it takes some time for him to assess the meaning. Therefore, when he sees part of a well-known, but half-hidden object, he will not recognize it and may spook or shy at it. When he sees a person lying down, he cannot recognize the person as a human being until the person speaks. He then recognizes the 'object' as human because humans are the only creatures possessing a clear verbal language. Another aspect of the horse's powers of perception is that a new, yet familiar, object in the paddock disturbs the whole picture of 'the paddock' and thus the horse spooks at it.

The Head and Neck

Leading function of the head

The head follows the eyes, the ears, the nose and the thoughts. Where they lead, the body will surely follow, but not always in the normal manner (see Circles and Turns in Chapter 11). The head and neck, however, initiate all ambulatory and balance movements such as the flexor pattern and the extensor pattern. The hind legs are the horse's engine, therefore they do not dictate the direction of the head, but the head dictates the direction of the hind legs.

Together with the neck, the head is the horse's main balance mechanism. The object of training, however, is to teach the horse to use his hindquarters and abdominal muscles for balance as well as to strengthen them. *It does not make sense why the equine world is so obsessed by doing everything 'from back to front' since it is so completely against the biomechanics of postural movement.*

EXERCISES

1. Sit back on a chair and try to stand up without moving your head and neck forwards first. It is virtually impossible to do this unless your feet are tucked well under your body. It illustrates how the head leads all movement.

2. Stand upright and walk forwards without leaning forwards from your head, your upper body, or even leaning forward on your ankles. We are able to take small, graceless steps in this way, but to give longer steps we have to lean slightly forwards to move our gravity line beyond the perimeter of our base of support.

3. Stand upright and walk backwards without taking your upper body backwards first. It is possible to take small, stiff steps backwards, but to move back gracefully, as we expect from the horse, we have to incline back slightly.

These exercises illustrate how we move our centre of gravity beyond the perimeter of our base of support in order to move. It is even more difficult for the horse to move backwards because his centre of gravity is so far forward. These exercises also illustrate how difficult it is to initiate movement without the use of the head and neck. Try each one again by inclining slightly in the direction of the movement and note the difference in ease. Now imagine how difficult it is for the horse to move when we are restricting his head and neck as we do when we ride him in the 'on the bit' position.

The neck, the source of balance control

The horse's neck is his great balancing tool and he uses it to maintain and regain balance in each movement or change of movement, in all balance reactions. The relatively rigid main part of his spine does not assist him in maintaining balance and prevents him from regaining balance speedily. Since his adductors have a significant role in stabilizing the limbs onto the body, they do not have enough lateral mobility to contribute sufficiently to the maintenance of balance and they have far less freedom than the arms of primates. The horse's tail is too small and too short to be of much value in the maintenance of balance. The only effective appendage for this purpose is his long, strong, flexible and considerably mobile neck. Its part in maintaining balance is especially important because of his great speed. His long neck is designed to function as a bob weight to move his centre of gravity. He maintains his balance by moving his neck as a tightrope walker would use the pole and as we use our arms to maintain balance.

All our human appendages help us to maintain and regain balance. We use our arms regularly in all balance reactions. When they are not available to us we use our necks and upper body by bending at the waist. If all this fails, we use our legs by moving them faster forwards or sideways. The latter is what the horse has to resort to when we inhibit his neck movements.

EXERCISES

1. Fold your arms and plant your feet. Now ask someone to give you a shove from behind, not too big that you would fall though. Notice how your neck pokes out to help you to maintain your balance. If you are shoved harder, you have to run forwards to maintain balance.

The horse does the same with his neck because his forelegs cannot duplicate the movements of our arms. This is why a horse runs instead of lengthening his stride when pushed forward too much while he is on his forehand.

2. Walk on a ground pole or curb stone and notice how you use your arms to balance.

3. Walk backwards on the curb and notice how much more you need your arms for balance.

4. Fold your arms and do part 2 of the exercise again and note how you move either from the waist or the neck to maintain balance. You may even stabilize yourself by tightening the muscles around you waist (centring).

5. Ask someone to push you sideways while your arms are folded and notice how your neck moves laterally to assist your balance.

EXPERIMENTS

1. Place your horse in a lunge ring. He should be without tack. Ask him to take a few forward walk steps and watch his neck as he takes the first step. Do a few walk-halt-walk transitions and watch his head and neck move slightly forwards with the first step and lift when he halts.

2. Ask your horse to take a backward step. Notice how he lifts his neck slightly and hollows his back in order to change his balance for this movement. This is especially noticeable when the horse has committed to the halt and has his weight firmly planted on his forelimbs as is natural. (If the horse is proficient at backing in the 'on the bit' position he may back without lifting his neck).

A horse's body is not as agile in his ability to regain balance as the cat and dog family with their flexible spines, or humans with the ability to abduct arms and legs. Compared to these creatures, the horse's neck muscle mass is astounding. He therefore has other superior methods of maintaining balance, but he has to be able to move his neck in all directions to do so. He moves his neck sideways when his balance is disturbed laterally, such as in leg-yield. Tension or tightness in the neck thus affects the horse's ability to use it efficiently for balance. When the horse's neck is in the 'on the bit' position, it is of limited value for balancing purposes. He thus becomes vulnerable to disturbances of his equilibrium. His only method of moving his centre of gravity is then his hind legs, which he can move more underneath his body to move the centre of gravity back, or out behind him to push it forward. His hind leg joint-stabilizing muscles become more toned in order to prevent balance disturbance.

The influence of the neck on movement

The great horseman, François Baucher, said, 'The head and the neck are at once the rudder and compass of the rider.' He admits that he has recognized the tremendous influence the neck has on the entire mechanism of the horse.[2]

The flexor and extensor patterns of movement, the tonic neck reactions and co-contraction of the neck, all affect the actions of the horse's hindquarters. Therefore, through correct communication via the reins, the rider can control the movement of the hindquarters to a large extent. The flexor pattern brings the hindquarters more underneath the horse and produces longer hind leg steps. It also encourages freer forelimb action. The flexor muscles of the neck (brachio-cephalicus and omotransversarius) contract and pull the forelimb forwards while the opposing triceps muscle relaxes to allow this forward stretch. The extensor pattern straightens the horse's hips and leads to trailing hind legs and shortened forelimb steps. Co-contraction or tightness in the horse's neck leads to a rigid spine with the consequent swinging hindquarters. Soft lateral bending of the neck maintains the hind feet in line with the forefeet and enhances lateral movement of the legs. When the horse moves his head and neck forwards, his centre of gravity moves forwards and consequently more weight moves onto his forehand. To counteract this change of balance, he brings his hindquarters more underneath his body.

Photo 3.2. The contraction of the neck muscles show how the horse uses his head and neck to initiate all movement and to balance.

2 H. Nelson, François Baucher, *The Man and his Method*, (London, J.A. Allen, 1992).

The tonic neck reactions

These primitive reactions affect human biomechanics and, although they have not been studied in the horse, since the basic neurological functions of all mammals are similar, their effect on the horse's movement should be similar to that seen in humans.

Neck flexion initiates a *tonic neck reaction* that facilitates contraction of the muscles that cause pulling actions of the arms in man. This action will fold up the horse's forelegs as when jumping and should produce more knee action when moving. This is the 'pull' pattern of movement.

The tonic *neck extension* reaction, on the other hand, facilitates contraction of the muscles that cause pushing actions of the forelegs. Therefore, when a horse lifts his head and neck, he will push with his forelegs against the ground. When he 'puts on the brakes', he will want to lift his neck to assist this action. This is the 'push' pattern of movement

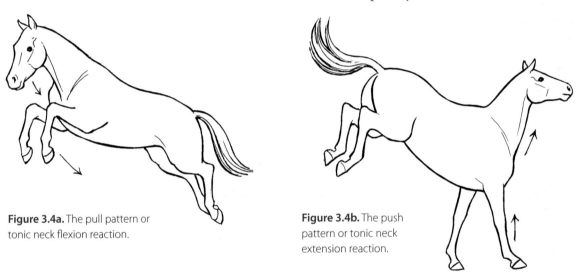

Figure 3.4a. The pull pattern or tonic neck flexion reaction.

Figure 3.4b. The push pattern or tonic neck extension reaction.

The equine neck reaction

This is an automatic reaction specific to the rigid-backed group of animals. It is not found in cats, dogs or humans. When the horse resists the rider pulling his head to the side, his neck becomes rigid. This rigidity of the neck forms a rigid unit with the rest of the horse's spine. His neck will thus influence the movement of his hindquarters through his rigid spine: he will move his hindquarters to the opposite side of the pull on the neck. This reaction is often used to encourage the horse to turn on the forehand. The rider is usually taught to hold onto the rein on the same side as the push from the leg. It is, however, not the logical method of teaching the movement (see Chapter 11). It is important for riders to learn how to inhibit this automatic reaction in movements such as the walk pirouette, shoulder-in, half-pass and flying changes.

This reaction is even more prominent when the horse is in the extensor pattern. It has been shown that the extensor pattern blocks mobility of the back.[3] This is important to consider when riding lateral movements. When the horse lifts his neck, his hindquarters will swing out because of the restriction of movement in his back.

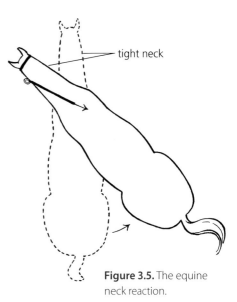

Figure 3.5. The equine neck reaction.

▶ RIDING AND TEACHING APPLICATIONS

The position of the horse's head and neck is paramount to what will happen in the rest of his body. The biomechanical influence of the head and neck on the musculature of the rest of the body has been well researched in humans. Recent studies of equine biomechanics have also shown that the position of the head and neck influences the rest of the horse's body.

1. The horse moves forward more freely and with better balance in the round frame.

2. A tight neck will inhibit the horse's ability to do circles, lateral work, counter-canter and flying changes.

3. Neck flexion encourages engagement of the hindquarters.

4. Neck extension hollows the horse's back and works against engagement of the hindquarters. A tight rein contact indicates neck extension.

5. Neck flexion, as in a bascule, helps the horse to fold his forelegs out of the way when jumping obstacles.

6. Neck extension, or jumping in a hollow frame, works against the folding of the legs in the 'pull' pattern and often leads to trailing legs.

7. Lateral flexion of the horse's head and neck has to be maintained through 'take and give' on the reins to prevent the hindquarters swinging out in the equine neck reaction.

8. Pre-empt the horse's fright reaction of lifting head and neck by conscious awareness of the surroundings. If you notice movement of any nature, prevent him from lifting his head (to see), with 'take and give' on the reins.

---

3 C. Gomez, M. Rhodin, L. Roepstorff, M. Weishaupt and R. van Weeren (research paper presented at the International Conference on Equine Exercise Physiology [ICEEP], 2006).

9. Encourage the horse to round his neck and frame with 'take and give', sponging, squeezing or vibrating the reins, then push him forwards to activate the engine, not the other way around unless he does not move forward freely. This will prevent loss of balance.

▶ JUDGING SIGNIFICANCE

1. A hollow neck carriage means that the horse's back muscles are contracting to produce a hollow back. This inhibits engagement of the hindquarters and should therefore be considered a basic fault.

2. Swinging hindquarters in lateral work and in flying changes are the result of the equine neck reaction because the horse is not yielding sufficiently to the rider's inside hand.

3. An unsolicited flying change during the counter-canter is often a sign that the horse's neck is in co-contraction and not yielding to the rider's hands.

4. A horse who is 'pulled in' will be in an extensor pattern although it may appear to be a flexor pattern. His gait may become choppy with a daisy-cutting action and loss of suspension.

5. Be aware of the false bend which mimics a bend, when the rider is pulling on the inside rein (see The false bend in Chapter 4.)

The neck action in lameness

In forelimb lameness, the horse lifts his head during the stance phase of the affected forelimb in an attempt to lift the weight off it. He then drops his head on the sound limb in stance to keep the weight on the sound side. The swing phase of the sound limb is shorter and the stance phase longer in an attempt to keep the weight off the painful limb.

In hind limb lameness, the horse drops his head and neck during the stance phase of the lame hind limb in trot. This means that he moves his centre of gravity forwards to take weight off the painful hind limb. The problem here is that the hind limb lameness mimics forelimb lameness on the same side. Observing the croup can confirm hind limb lameness – the croup usually lowers during the stance phase of the painful hind limb.

Comprehension, Learning and Memory

Although horses have extremely limited planning ability – if any at all – they have a remarkable associative memory and an excellent ability to understand and to learn. The horse learns to associate every movement on his back and he learns very quickly which movements are meaningful and which he can ignore. For example, the horse knows to ignore the movements such as the rider's initial adjustments of seat or zipping up a jacket. Every time a different rider sits on his back, the horse has to relearn to distinguish the new rider's 'meaningless' movements and meaningful applications. Good riders can feel exactly when another rider has ridden their horse and what that rider has inadvertently 'taught' the horse. For example, if a new rider takes a stronger contact, the horse's contact will feel different to the regular rider. Unfortunately the horse learns incorrect work as fast as he learns the correct work. Although the horse tries his utmost to understand the rider at every step of the way, his ability to understand is often not considered in his training when riders expect him simply 'to know'. Strangely, riders often expect horses to have the ability to understand, know and perform a movement, while they themselves are not in sufficient control of their own body to get the message across to the horse. The proof of this again shows in the excessive use of gadgets and ever stronger bits or tighter nosebands, to control the horse. These are seldom necessary when horses understand what riders are asking of them and when riders are in total control of their own bodies.

Most riders give the horse double messages. There is usually a message to move forwards and a simultaneous message to stop. The 'hold-the-reins-and-push-the-horse with the legs' method of riding is a prime example of the simultaneous stop and go instructions. It seems to work with talented riders who have the instinctive timing and technique to retain the balance between 'push' and 'hold' and also seems to be effective with male riders who can push more strongly than they hold. In most riders, however, it leads to a block in forward movement and confusion in the horse. Riders have a responsibility to ensure that the horse understands their requests. A sure sign that the horse has not understood the instruction is when he responds incorrectly. This is a regular occurrence.

One of the greatest modern developments in horse training is in the knowledge we have gained of learning theory. It is only since Pavlov and his dog, followed by the experiments of Skinner, that conditioned learning has developed into a successful training method. This method of teaching animals is extraordinarily simple yet remarkably successful in helping the horse to understand the rider. There is, however, a method which speeds up this understanding process by leaps and bounds and should be used concurrently with conditioned training. This is the biomechanical method of *facilitation and inhibition of movement* – the use of the horse's automatic balance reactions and patterns of movement to help him understand the rider. By understanding equine biomechanics and how to use them, each rider can ensure that the horse will not only understand their requests, but learn correctly in a fraction of the time of the traditional method. I should point out that there are still no 'short cuts' in training horses; there is only the fast method when the horse understands the rider's use of equine biomechanics and the unnecessarily slow and confusing methods, in which the horse does not understand the rider. The term 'brought on slowly' is often used to describe the latter.

Conditioned learning

Horses also learn through conditioning. In conditioned learning the horse learns to react consistently to signals through positive or negative reinforcement. The rider gives a signal, the horse responds, the rider rewards. For example, with conditioned learning, the rider uses pressure to persuade the horse to move. As soon as the horse moves, the rider releases the pressure. The horse thus learns to react consistently to this pressure. If we add a reward to this system, it becomes positive conditioning and the horse learns twice as fast. We can also add punishment to this system, but it is a well-known fact that learning is far faster with reward than it is with punishment.

Clicker training

Clicker training is pure positive conditioning. The clicker is paired with a food reward. The clicker bridges the gap between the correct behaviour and the reward. For example, if you want your horse to push a toy car you can place a small piece of food in the car. When the horse nudges the car, press the clicker and immediately reward him with a titbit. The horse associates the clicker with the food reward just as Pavlov's dog associated the bell with food. He then starts to associate the action with the food reward and thus learns to do the action alone. After a few repetitions, the horse will react correctly and push the car without the food reward.

Voice 'clicker' training

This method of teaching a horse is extremely satisfactory for both horse and rider. It turns training into a completely positive experience for the horse and, furthermore, he learns faster than with any other method. Food is arguably the most motivating factor in a horse's life, so it works especially well for horses who don't move off light pressure. I have had great success using this method to assist in rehabilitating horses who have become 'dead' to the leg and hand: it lightens them to the aids within a few minutes.

It is, however, a little impractical to do clicker training when mounted, but the voice is a good substitute for the clicker. Instead of a food reward, a tickle on the withers will be as effective once the horse has associated the tickle with the reward. Pair the voice and the tickle with a food reward before starting this exercise. For example, say 'Good boy' and give a titbit. Once the horse understands this, say 'Good boy', then tickle and then give the titbit. Then teach the horse to move forwards. Use leg pressure on his sides and as soon as the horse responds by taking a step, release the pressure, say 'Good boy' and immediately reward him with a tickle. After a few repetitions the horse will react to the leg pressure alone. This method of teaching is especially useful when backing young horses. The voice, together with the lunge whip, is used to teach the horse to 'Walk on' or 'Trot on'. Once the horse is backed, the voice is used together with leg pressure, and the 'Good boy' and tickle are the reward. It works even better if you continue rewarding with food.

Pressure release

This form of conditioning is used once the horse understands leg pressure. Ask the horse to move forwards with the lightest pressure you would like to use. Follow up immediately with strong pressure if he does not react immediately to the light pressure. This can take the form of a tap with the whip or pressure with the spurs. Maintain the strong pressure until the horse responds appropriately. Release the pressure instantly and reinforce the behaviour with a tickle on the withers and a 'Good boy'. It is important that the pressure is maintained until the horse reacts correctly or he will not be able to make the association. The release has to be instant when the horse reacts correctly or he will be rewarded for the wrong step. The horse will respond to light pressure alone after three to four repetitions of 'light pressure, strong pressure, release, reward'. Although the release of pressure is the reward, an extra tickle and a food reward will sweeten the process and the horse will learn faster. This principle of pressure release lies behind the half-halt leg aid and the 'take and give' rein aid. This pressure-release system of learning is so effective that the source of incorrect behaviour can be diagnosed by simply figuring out what action the horse was rewarded for by ill-timed use of pressure.

EXAMPLE

A family had bought a young pony who had been taught to load with ease. Her loading became steadily worse until she would rather rear than walk into the horse box. Why did she start rearing? The person leading the pony had put too much pressure on the lead rein. The pony objected by rearing so the pressure on the lead rein was immediately released. The pony thus learned that by rearing, the pressure is released. Everything up to the point of rearing was also done with releasing the pressure at the incorrect moment. If the pressure had been released the second the horse took a forward step, the rearing would not even have occurred.

Facilitation and inhibition of movement

This is the term used to describe the biomechanical manoeuvring of the horse's body through his automatic reactions. When the rider places the horse in the correct position through the manipulation of his balance and other automatic reactions, the instructions become perfectly clear and understandable. Facilitation and inhibition of movement is the fastest and clearest method of teaching a horse. If we combine conditioned learning plus an extra reward with facilitation and inhibition of movement, he will learn each new movement or instruction immediately and will experience no pressure or confusion.

EXAMPLES

1. When the horse is positioned correctly before the canter depart, he will take the correct lead. If this is rewarded by the release of pressure and a tickle he will make an immediate correct association.

2. We initially teach the horse the concept of a flying change with an exaggerated 'aid', which disturbs his balance. Provided the horse is set up correctly for the changes, this method will not lead to swinging hindquarters and will lead to a correct reaction. The instant reward reinforces this and there is no room for confusion. Once the horse reacts consistently to this disturbance of balance, we refine it to an invisible aid which he understands perfectly as well.

Motivation and intent

The source of motivation is in the brain. The horse is mainly motivated by food, safety and companionship with other horses. With all the training and the best movement in the world, the horse may not perform well if he is not motivated or cannot concentrate on the job. The ability to concentrate, the fright/flight reflex (which includes shying, napping and bucking), obedience/submission, contentment/enjoyment in work and physical comfort all have an effect on motivation to comply with the rider. When a horse is in pain or experiencing discomfort arising from an injury, he loses his basic motivation to move forwards during training – although the discomfort of applied whip and spurs (while unwarranted in this context) will give him an alternative motivation to do so.

The enjoyment of jumping and the motivation to jump have a strong hereditary link. This genetic predisposition to enjoy jumping includes good technique, physical ability and enjoyment of the feeling. Horses, just like people, differ in their motivation and abilities to concentrate and this has to be taken into account when training a horse. Many Olympic riders simply discard horses who do not possess appropriate mental attributes.

Motivation affects inertia and direction of movement. Motivation starts in the head: the head moves in the direction of motivation and the body follows. When a horse is not entirely submissive or in harmony with the rider, he has the ability to oppose whatever the rider asks of him. When a fly is too bothersome, he will shake or lift his head to chase it despite being in the 'on the bit' position. If it is supper time, he may tilt his nose or move his shoulders towards the stable, the latter being the so-called 'falling out' of the shoulders. The horse moves faster and also does better half-passes in the direction of the meal. His canter depart is more likely to be correct when he is positioned towards the other horses and he will be less likely to refuse a fence when another horse is standing on the other side.

▶ RIDING AND TEACHING APPLICATIONS

1. The horse's head and neck are responsible for the initiation and main-tenance of all ambulatory movement. This includes voluntary move-ment and automatic reactions such as the balance reactions, the tonic neck responses, the automatic patterns of movement and locomotion. The horse's brain motivates him to do the movements requested. Good performance is dependent on exceptional and delicate communication between the rider's hands and the horse's head as well as between the rider's body and legs and the horse's body. A superior body language which the horse must understand is therefore hugely important for success in riding.

2. The equine neck reaction has to be inhibited to prevent the horse from swinging his hindquarters out in the shoulder-in, the walk pirouette, and in flying changes. This is done with squeeze and release of the inside rein together with pressure from the inside leg.

3. The entrance to the arena, other horses and the direction of the stable can all be used to teach young horses difficult movements.
   a. Teach the turn on the forehand starting with the horse's head facing away from the entrance of the arena. He will be more motivated to move his hindquarters in order to face the entrance.
   b. Teach leg-yield down the long side of the arena, head to the wall, towards the entrance.

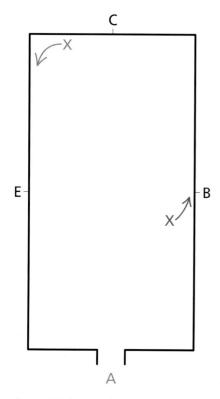

Figure 3.6. Starting the canter where the horse is most likely to take the correct lead. Start the canter at the red cross when the horse is positioned towards the arena entrance. Start the canter at the blue cross if the stables or other horses are in the opposite direction.

c. Choose a place in the arena where the horse is most likely to take the correct canter lead. This will be towards other horses, the entrance of the arena or towards the stable. Ask for the canter depart either between C and the corner or at the part of the circle opposite the stable or other horses.

d. Ask for the rein-back with the horse's hindquarters facing the direction of the stable, the entrance or other horses.

e. When teaching the medium trot, slow horses may need to do it in the direction of the stables. Forward-thinking horses, however, need to do it away from the stable to prevent pushing their weight onto the forehand and losing balance, thus running or breaking into canter.

4. The young and 'green' horse often 'leans' out of the circle when passing the arena entrance or he 'leans' into the circle in an attempt to cut the corner towards the arena entrance. The rider can prevent this leaning with earlier preparation as well as manoeuvring of the horse's shoulders to the other side (see Circles and Turns in Chapter 11).

5. When a horse becomes bored or irritated with continuous schooling, his motivation can be improved with 'voice clicker training' paired with food. The horse's attitude changes immediately to become willing and eager to please. Head turning towards the food in the rider's hand does not become a problematic habit.

▶ JUDGING SIGNIFICANCE

When the horse lifts his head during dressage movements the cause may be loss of balance, a display of negative emotions (resistance), lack of motivation, insufficient preparation for the movement or a sign of discomfort. Only careful analysis will determine the cause. Since the cause is not immediately clear, only the fact of the head position should be noted by the judge. It is the teacher's and rider's job to find the cause.

Emotions and personality

Horses have different personality types which affect their approach to work. Some are submissive by nature and these are so easy to train they almost do not have to be taught. Others are less submissive and more motivated to follow their own desires as set out above. These horses have to be convinced to react correctly, or to concentrate. Some are bold, while others are timid. Most horses, however, will cooperate and react correctly provided they are not in discomfort and the rider explains in a way that the horse can understand.

Horses experience the same basic 'primitive' emotions as do humans. Affection, happiness, sadness and anger are a few examples. This is evident by a horse's depressed-like behaviour when he loses a friend or moves to a new yard. He may stand alone, or with his head in the corner of the stable. Young horses often show short bursts of anger during the first stage of training when they are expected to follow human rules for the first time. This phase soon passes and the outbursts of anger seem to disappear.

The horse uses his head as well as his eyes and ears, to communicate his emotions. In fact, the position of his ears indicates most of his emotions. He will 'throw' his head up or shake it when he is uncomfortable or to display a negative emotion. Stallions' and geldings' eyes become 'soft' when in company of a mare whom they may fancy and then hard when another gelding interferes.

▶ RIDING AND TEACHING APPLICATIONS

1. The rider's approach to each horse should be open-minded and accepting of his specific personality type. The training programme should be flexible to accommodate each type of horse and his speed and ability to learn.

2. Observe the horse's ears and eyes to note their degree of submission and acceptance of the work.

The fright/flight response

Figure 3.7. The fright/flight stance.

The fright/flight response is the horse's instinct to flee from danger and is his only line of adequate defence. It is manifested in many forms of behaviour patterns that are unacceptable as far as the rider is concerned. These range from the lifting of his head and neck, snorting, planting his feet, spooking and shying to bucking, rearing, bolting, etc. The fright/flight response is triggered by the horse's five senses and incorporates his whole body: his visual sense, olfactory sense and hearing are all geared to react speedily to sense danger. They are all situated in his head and to use them efficiently he lifts his head in the direction of the danger. This lifting of the head leads to contraction of all his top line muscles, so all the behaviour patterns listed start with tension in the neck. His neck hollows and this is followed by the hollowing of his back, the lifting of his tail and the extension of his hindquarters. His whole top line, together with his fore and hind legs, goes into the extensor pattern in readiness to take flight. He literally grows taller by contracting his serratus ventralis and pectoral muscles, which push up his ribcage. This makes it extremely difficult for the rider to engage the horse's lower neck muscles, his abdominal muscles and hind leg flexors, which are all so necessary for engagement. In this position the horse is ready to flee unless the rider can inhibit the response.

▶ RIDING AND TEACHING APPLICATIONS

1. 'The flight response has a high coefficient of reinforcement or reward; it takes very few repetitions to consolidate it as a habit.'[4] The significance for the rider is that it is difficult to eradicate and has a tendency to increase. Therefore these behaviour patterns should be avoided at all costs and prevented at the first and tiniest pre-reaction.

2. The first and mildest sign of this reaction is the lifting of the horse's head, which is followed by the tightening of his top line muscles. A rider who learns how to prevent this first sign can inhibit the fright/flight response. There are a few methods of doing this:

    a. A tired horse is less likely to show this response to mild distractions, therefore should the horse be fresh or simply inclined to flight behaviour, lunge him before riding.

    b. This response can be inhibited by maintaining the horse in a low and round frame. Riding him in this frame inhibits the action of the top line extensor muscles and activates the bottom line flexor pattern. (This is the principle behind the use of the deplorable deep and round method of riding.) Once the horse looks down, (or in the opposite direction as when riding in shoulder-in), the 'frightening' objects cannot be detected since all three of his senses needed for this defence are facing in the wrong direction. He will therefore relax. If he cannot lift his head, he cannot go into the fright reflex. Maintaining this low and round frame when the horse is in the fright/flight mode is sometimes difficult, since the rider's arm and body muscles are not as strong as the horse's extensor neck muscles. In this instance, 'take and give' simply has no effect. The rider then has to resort to the centuries-old method of riding *correctly* in running reins to prevent this response, spooking and shying. *Running reins used incorrectly are very harsh on a horse's neck muscles and may lead to delayed onset muscle pain (DOMS).*

    When the running reins are used correctly, they will hang loose when the horse is in a round frame. Should the rider continue to hold them tight after the horse has yielded to the pressure, he will start to

---

4 A. McLean, *The Truth About Horses: A Guide to Understanding and Training Your Horse* (USA, Barron's, 2003).

pull on the running reins. This is because he has not been rewarded with release of pressure. A tight rein means that the horse's neck and back extensor muscles are in contraction. This is completely opposite to what the rider has set out to achieve. It is easy to see when running reins have been used incorrectly; the horse will immediately lift his head and neck when the running reins are removed. A safe alternative to the running reins is balancing reins of correct dimension. The horse may need them for a few weeks only, after which his fright/flight behaviour should improve.

c. Distract the horse's attention by pushing him forwards in a shortened, but round frame. He will then concentrate on the rider.

d. Distract the horse and gain his attention by giving him variety in his work on which to concentrate. Circle after circle, although it does have a mesmerizing effect, will not force him to concentrate. On the other hand, movements such as tight serpentines or small circles at regular intervals will not only relax the horse, but the regular changes of directions will also make him concentrate. Shoulder-in exercises not only help him to concentrate, but also to look away from the perceived 'danger'.

e. Rearing should be prevented at all costs and this is relatively easy. It is usually caused either by the horse's reluctance to move forwards, or him being pressurized to move, yet held in simultaneously, and thus having nowhere to go but up. The first line of defence is to ride with light contact so that the horse does not feel restricted. A horse can only rear when both his hind feet carry weight simultaneously. Upsetting this balance will prevent a rear. Backward steps, piaffe-like steps, lifting of the head and forehand or moving like a rocking-horse usually precede the rear. As soon as the horse presents one of these behaviour patterns, turn him with one rein to unbalance him and take the weight off one hind leg. This should be followed immediately by riding actively forwards on a yielding contact or alternatively, dismounting and lungeing the horse forwards vigorously.

▶ JUDGING SIGNIFICANCE

Tension is either caused by confusion or by the fright/flight reaction of the new and exciting surroundings. The exact reason cannot be determined in a dressage competition and can therefore not be ascribed to incorrect riding. The trainer, however, should ensure that the rider does not confuse the horse and only has the fright/flight behaviour with which to contend.

4

Communication and Self-carriage

The Biomechanics of Contact

Contact serves two purposes. The first and most important is the gentle line of communication between the horse's delicate mouth and the rider's hands, through feel. For this purpose, a round frame is not necessary. The second purpose is to explain to the horse that he is to use his head and neck muscles against the pull of the nuchal ligament to produce a balanced and round frame. This cannot be achieved by riding on loose reins. (It can, however, be taught to horses without rein contact by way of clicker training). The correct contact enables the rider to ask the horse to yield to rein pressure and to move into a round and balanced flexion pattern.

The horse's natural frame

The horse naturally carries his head and neck in an upside-down V frame. His head and neck 'dangle' on his nuchal ligament. The 'on the bit' frame he reserves for special occasions of showing off and excitement or when he 'bounces' from canter to walk or halt. However, he holds it for short periods only. Horses who have only been exercised in this natural position have narrow necks from side to side and the brachio-cephalicus muscle appears to be overdeveloped. The neck muscles are symmetrical on each side of the horse's neck. They strengthen and become bulkier from side to side through regular lateral bending exercises (see Chapter 7 – Misconceptions).

The natural position ensures that the horse's head and neck are free, ready to control balance and to initiate movement. The horse cannot, however, develop the correct muscles sufficiently for sports uses in this natural frame. It does not encourage the flexor pattern or lead to engagement of the hindquarters. Engaging a horse's hindquarters while riding in this natural frame is, however *possible*. We see many jumping and Western horses well engaged yet in this natural frame. This demonstrates clearly that the horse does not round his head and neck from the back to the front. Jean Saint-Fort Paillard had the following to say about this misconception: 'A rider does not push his horse forward or make it seek support from the

Photo 4.1. The natural head and neck carriage.

Photo 4.2. Clear engagement in the natural head and neck frame.

bit; he does not push the horse on the hand. These expressions, as traditional as they may be, have sufficiently proved their harmfulness, and they should be forever deleted from equestrian language. Why? Simply because they do not correspond to anything true, or even to anything possible.'[1] This is an example of thinking in terms of mechanics and not in terms of biomechanics. Expressions such as these and 'curling the horse up like a spring' or 'bending him like a bow from back to front' are examples of thinking in terms of mechanics and not biomechanics.

The horse develops submission: he yields to the hand.

The horse develops impulsion: he moves forward from behind.

These two separate qualities equal 'throughness' when put together. Engaging the horse's hindquarters does, however, encourage the flexor pattern which enables him to yield to the rider's rein with more ease.

Contact and the round frame

The round 'on the bit' frame is evidenced by the nodding position of the head on the first cervical vertebra in the flexor pattern. The muscles below the cervical vertebrae are responsible for maintaining this position against the pull of the nuchal ligament. Contact in this round 'on the bit' position *encourages* engagement of the horse's hindquarters, improves his weight-bearing capacity, places him in a position of submission and makes him more manoeuvrable and more comfortable for the rider. However, it hinders his automatic balance reactions.

At Novice level the lower-longer neck carriage is not dependent on the engagement of the horse's hindquarters. In horses with naturally high-set necks, however, this carriage may automatically be higher.

The rounded head and neck carriage is relatively easy for the young horse to manage, but only for short periods. This is evident when training young horses and novice horses. There are five reasons for this phenomenon.

1. The muscles involved with rounding the neck tire rapidly.

2. The horse needs his head and neck to maintain balance.

3. The horse needs to move his head for normal locomotion.

4. This round position reduces the horse's visual field, which prevents him from recognizing moving objects. The rider will find that the horse consistently lifts his head and neck at the same place in the circle or the arena at every circuit. It is usually because there is something he 'needs' to look at, at that particular spot. Therefore, every time he reaches the

---

1 J. S-F. Paillard, *Understanding Equitation*, (New York, Doubleday, 1974).

Photo 4.3a. The lower novice outline.

Photo 4.3b. The higher neck carriage of the advanced 'on the bit' frame produced by engagement of the hindquarters.

same place, he lifts his head to check the view because horses are programmed to be alert for their own protection.

5. Submission. A horse has to trust his rider completely because one of his main preceptors of danger, vision, is incapacitated.

The novice horse thus lifts his head every two or three strides either by tightening his top line muscles or by simply relaxing his bottom line (rounding) muscles, which allows the nuchal ligament to spring back into its natural position. He therefore has to be reminded every two or three strides to maintain his round position and to encourage and convince him to maintain a steady contact. This is ideally achieved with light, invisible finger movements.

The high head and neck carriage of the advanced 'on the bit' frame is entirely dependent on the engagement of the hindquarters. It cannot be produced correctly by premature lifting of the horse's head or pulling on the reins. As soon as the horse becomes more engaged, his hindquarters move more underneath his body and closer to his centre of gravity. This engagement lifts the forehand so that the neck becomes more arched with a higher carriage.

Trained horses will take a relatively steady contact with little reminding necessary to maintain it because they have developed the necessary muscle power, balance and submission. The horse's head should never be pulled in. A pulling feeling means that the horse's head is moving away from the rider's hands. The horse should voluntarily move his head closer to the pressure: he must make the decision himself.

Balance in the round frame

Perfect contact is all about balance. The horse cannot maintain a steady head position in the round frame and a consistent soft contact when his balance is compromised. In this situation he will lift and hollow his head and neck, stretch it forwards, turn it to the opposite side or 'lean on the rider's hands'. The horse is usually in good balance when he is moving slowly, but if the young horse is pushed forwards too much, his balance could be compromised. The experienced horse, however, can move forward in the 'on the bit' position without losing balance, but needs 'early warning signals' before changing direction or performing transitions. When losing balance the horse may be able to maintain this round frame, but will use his neck muscles in isometric contraction without visible movement: the elastic contact is then lost. To maintain balance in this round frame the horse has to transfer a significant part of his balance function to his hindquarters. He has to engage, specifically, the deeper joint-stabilizing muscles and the hip and stifle flexors.

There seems to be a misconception, especially in the jumping world, that the rider can help the horse to balance by 'holding the contact'. We often hear trainers saying, 'Hold the horse into the jump'. It is actually quite preposterous of us to imagine that we can balance a huge object while it is in fact carrying us.

We have two tools to improve the horse's balance. The half-halt, which may be used with or without forward leg aids depending on the need at the time, and an 'early warning system' to explain to the horse what we are about to ask of him. Light rein contact is essential for both of these tools.

The low and round position

This position lowers the centre of gravity and increases protraction of the hind limbs through the flexor pattern. It thus improves balance and initiates engagement and is therefore important in the training of young horses. However, because young horses often maintain this lower head and neck position for quite some time, this has led to a mistaken belief that the horse will form a habit of maintaining this low position indefinitely. This is not the case. As soon as the horse has the pushing power in his hindquarters, he will start to lift his neck and head naturally. In the low position, the horse's top line is stretched. The nuchal ligament is pulled forward and this pulls on the supraspinous ligament. This rounding contributes to the lifting of the horse's back in the flexor pattern: when the horse's head moves down, the supraspinous ligament pulls his back up. When the horse's head and neck are curled in the 'deep and round' method of riding, the supraspinous ligament takes too much strain. This position can also cause damage to the intervertebral joints and discs.

Light contact

In nature the horse does not have to 'take contact' or have support from the reins. He is responsible for maintaining his own balance. Therefore contact between horse and rider should resemble the natural balance of the horse in which he does not lean on anything and maintains his own balance. It has to be elastic, continuously moving with the horse. The quest for lightness has been an ongoing mission since the days of François Robichon de la Guérinière, being pursued by great masters such as François Baucher, Alexis-François L'Hotte, James Fillis, Nuno Oliveira and Alois Podhajsky. De la Guérinière taught us that 'the horse can be put *sur parole* [on his honour] by means of yielding of the hand, that is, he can be allowed to function on his own.'[2] When the horse is in perfect balance, the contact will be soft. The correct contact is therefore the light ±57 gm (2 oz) of rein weight between the horse's mouth and the rider's hands. (It is the approximate weight of a Mars bar). A recent study found that riders take an average of between 1.5 kg (3¼ lb) and 2.5 k (5½ lb) of rein contact in each hand. This is a sad state of affairs. Imagine the pressure on the bars of the horse's mouth. The bone here is covered by only a thin layer of skin and constant pressure will soon lead to loss of sensation and a 'hard' mouth because the nerve endings become damaged. A contact of this magnitude makes a mockery of the term, self-carriage.

---

2 H. Nelson, Alexis-Francois L'Hotte, *The Quest for Lightness in Equitation* (London, J.A. Allen, 1997).

Dangle a 2 litre (3½ pt) bottle of milk from each hand to experience the approximate amount of this weight. Your hands soon tire. Now imagine how the horse's mouth feels.

With light contact we can explain to the horse, through the principle of 'take and give', that we want him to turn his head to each side. We can also explain to him that we want him to lower his head and/or neck or to lift it up. We eventually do this through delicate and gentle sponging of the reins. Only through light contact can the rider develop correct, invisible aids.

Some horses take a lighter than 57 gm (2 oz) contact. These are usually horses with a high-set neck carriage, long thin necks, low muscle tone, sensitive mouths and with excessive forwardness. They often have hyper-mobile necks and are difficult to ride because the rider has very little feeling on the reins and thus cannot pre-empt actions by the horse. It is, however, important to first establish trust between the rider's hands and the horse's mouth. Only when the horse is comfortable with the bit and its movement and when rhythm, balance and suppleness have been established, should the rider attempt to establish the 57 gm (2 oz) contact.

When the horse moves his head closer to the rider's hands, he moves into the flexor pattern; the contact softens and the reins become looser. This is light contact and is an essential component of correct riding.

Strong contact

When the horse moves his head away from the rider's hands by tightening his top line muscles, the contact becomes stronger. He hollows in the extensor pattern, but this hollowing is not always observable.

There is no biomechanical reason to have a consistently firm contact. If the contact becomes more than 60 gm (just over 2 oz), one of two biomechanical states has arisen, both of which work against engagement.

1. The horse has tilted too much weight onto his forehand and thus pulls on the rider's hands in a balance reaction. *Compare this with a seesaw. When the contact is strong the front end of the seesaw is down. The horse is on the forehand. When the contact is light, the front end of the seesaw is up and the horse's hindquarters are engaged with the consequent light contact.*

2. The horse's top line muscles are bracing in isometric contraction (no change in length) as a defence against the rider's pulling hands.

Strong contact puts uncomfortable, even painful, bit pressure on the horse's mouth. Strong contact has little to do with the horse's jaw, but all to do with the extensor muscles of the poll and the neck, which move the head and neck up and away from the rider's pulling hands. Horses will not yield if the contact is continuously strong. The obsession in the riding world about 'taking up the contact', leads to hanging, pulling and an unyielding contact.

Riders complain that the horse is not 'taking contact', but how much do they want him to take and what biomechanical reason is there to take a strong contact? If the horse is in balance, forward and communication is correct, why insist on a stronger contact? Some of my dance partners complain that I am too light, while others like the lightness. The reason for it is that I follow their movements in unison, which means that their body language is good. The same applies to good communication between horse and rider. Good communication does not need strong contact. Light contact is, however, a little more difficult for riders to feel – but the responsibility is theirs.

▶ RIDING AND TEACHING APPLICATIONS

1. The horse's mouth should be sacred ground to the rider. Once 'spoilt', the horse will never fully trust the rider's hands again and perfect contact will be difficult to attain.

2. Young horses find it difficult to maintain the 'on the bit' position. They not only need regular rest periods, but also need to be reminded to maintain the position.

3. All horses need rest periods every five to ten minutes to stretch their neck muscles from the unconditioned 'on the bit' position.

4. The round frame encourages engagement of the hindquarters and is thus the first step in strengthening the horse's hindquarters for collection.

5. Horses with mouth problems often lift their heads in defence and thus have to be reminded to maintain a consistent yielding contact with gentle sponging or vibration. Horses who have become resistant through incorrect training methods will need stronger pressure initially to convince them to yield to pressure. This is done through 'take and give'. Once the horse responds, the 'take and give' should become gentle. Simply holding on and hoping will not convince the horse. It will only make him resist the continuous pull because there is no reward for yielding.

6. The method of holding the reins and simultaneously pushing the horse forward is against the horse's natural method of moving. It gives two opposing messages and is confusing to the horse. The message with the legs is to 'go', while the message with the hands is to 'stop'. Horses

ridden in this manner often lack forwardness and become stiff in the neck, with an unyielding rein contact. This method of riding leads to hard hands. François Baucher[3] was almost hanged and quartered for suggesting flexions, yet this is the kindest method of making the horse understand that he should yield to the hand. Baucher also advocated the 'pushing and simultaneous holding' method of riding until his accident rendered him without strength. He then developed his 'new method' of hands without legs and legs without hands. This latter method is important when training young horses and novice riders. Both methods are, however, also used on trained horses once they understand the concepts and the rider has developed sufficient technique and timing. Once the horse has learnt to yield to the rider's hands, it is easy to simply push him forwards and use half-halts to improve balance and/or engagement. The alternative seems to be ever-stronger bits, running reins, side reins and ever-tightening nosebands. It has led to the use of the extreme and unnecessary crank noseband, the hyperflexion method of riding and many gag bits (even the names conjure up visions of torture).

7. When a horse continually evades the contact by curling his neck and becoming too light, the rider can encourage a better contact first at the halt, then the walk and finally at the trot. Take up the usual light contact and then, very gradually, lean back on it so that the horse does not yield to it. You will find that he will slowly start to lean back on this contact. It will not be '57 gm' (2 oz) initially, but if you maintain this positive feel and do not pull back, the horse will slowly 'take a stronger contact'. This resembles the contact in ballroom dancing. These dancers are in balance with one another, neither pulling, nor pushing: their dancing is just a harmonious act. Should the rider attempt to take up the contact abruptly, this type of horse will simply curl his head and neck and remain too light.

8. Since the horse's natural balance mechanism is removed by riding in the 'on the bit' position, it is the rider's responsibility to assist the horse in maintaining balance. This is achieved with judicious half-halts, tactful aids and suitable preparation every step of the way. When the rider has a continuous 'conversation' with the horse, it allows him to prepare himself for every new movement or transition.

9. Steady contact is easier on a slow or 'lazy' horse, but almost impossible on a horse who is pulling forward out of balance, or one who is pushed forwards out of his state of equilibrium – especially a young horse. These horses have to be slowed down and balanced with many half-

3 H. Nelson, François Baucher *The Man and his Method* (London, J.A. Allen, 1992).

halts to establish a light and steady contact and rhythm. Riding forwards into a balanced and light contact can only be achieved once the
horse is in balance, contact is consistent and the contact muscles (flexors
below the vertebrae) are sufficiently developed.

▶ JUDGING SIGNIFICANCE

1. The angle of the head and neck in the total flexion range of the 'on the
   bit' position (which I term 'the full nod') is consistent whether the horse
   has a high or a low neck carriage. This means that when the horse
   lowers the base of his neck in a lower frame while in this full nod, his
   head position will be behind the vertical. A clear distinction should be
   drawn between the behind-the-vertical head carriage of a horse who is
   in the correct position and a horse who is evading the bit because of an
   inconsistent or too strong contact. In the latter case, the horse will bend
   his neck from the third cervical joint.

2. The 'on the bit' position seems to be easier for the horse to maintain
   with the full 90° angle, than a slightly larger angle which would place
   his head in front of the vertical. In the latter position the horse is using
   his top line muscles in an extensor pattern. Maintaining it in this position could lead to tightness in his neck and too firm a contact.

3. Resistance, non-acceptance of the bit and strong contact are training
   related problems. The poor horse is unfortunately often blamed.

4. Consistently strong contact is always wrong, yet often seen at even the
   highest levels of dressage.

5. The judging sheet should have separate sections for 'the position and
   seat of the rider' and 'the correct use of aids'. The two are often not
   connected. A rider can sit perfectly, but be extremely ineffective and incorrect in communicating with the horse.

Contact Concepts

Riding from the inside leg to the outside rein

The concept of riding 'from the inside leg to the outside hand' or 'riding
on the outside rein' is a very difficult and esoteric concept for novice riders
and children to understand. The phrase is a metaphor developed for purposes of verbal explanation, but is understood by few. Since the school
movements except leg-yield, renvers and counter-canter are ridden with an
inclination towards the inside of the manège, the horse should have a slight

preparatory bend in the same direction to prevent his balance reactions from interfering with these movements. 'The position' or the bent-straight position is the European term for this slight inside bend.

Biomechanically speaking, the rider's inside leg pushes and tilts the horse's ribcage and the weight to the outside, initiating a balance reaction. The 'take and give' on the inside rein encourages the horse to bend his own head and neck to the inside. This automatically softens the contact on the inside and gives a slightly stronger contact on the outside rein. In other words, the pushing inside leg together with the 'take and give' on the inside rein equals an outside contact. Taking up an outside rein contact is therefore a misconception and unnecessary. This firmer contact on the outside enables the rider to control the horse's shoulder with the outside rein.

Photo 4.4. The correct bend. Riding 'from the inside leg to the outside rein'. Note the contraction of the pony's inside neck muscles with the consequent soft inside rein and straight outside rein.

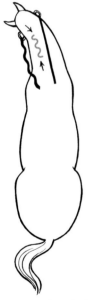

Figure 4.1. When the horse bends to the inside, the inside rein contact automatically becomes softer and the outside contact a little stronger.

The false bend

The horse uses his inside neck muscles to obtain a correct inside bend. Movement starting from a full inside lateral bend through the midline and all the way to a full outside lateral flexion is produced by the outside neck muscles. When a horse appears to have an inside bend, but the contact on the inside rein is stronger than the outside, the horse is tightening his outside neck muscles and is pulling against the rider's inside hand. Therefore the inside bend is false and the incorrect outside muscles are contracting. This type of false bend is often seen in children's riding because they seem to be taught to turn the horse by pulling on the inside rein.

The misconception of taking a strong contact on the outside rein reinforces the development of the false bend. *The rider takes a strong contact on the outside rein which turns the horse's head out, and then has to turn his head back to the inside again to encourage an inside bend. With a strong outside contact this will only be possible if the rider pulls the horse's head to the inside.* He thus only appears to be bent to the inside but is not using his own muscles because he is being pulled to the inside. This is not a true bend and also leads to the overall contact becoming too strong. The horse should bend as an automatic response to the rider pushing the ribcage over and simultaneous 'take and give' on the inside rein. In fact, the more effective the rider's inside leg, the easier it is to convince the horse to bend to the inside. When the horse is bent correctly the rider will feel the outside contact and the horse will have a softer contact or 'feel' on the inside rein. This softness on the inside rein is important in all the dressage movements and when riding through a bend towards the jump. It indicates that the horse is in balance.

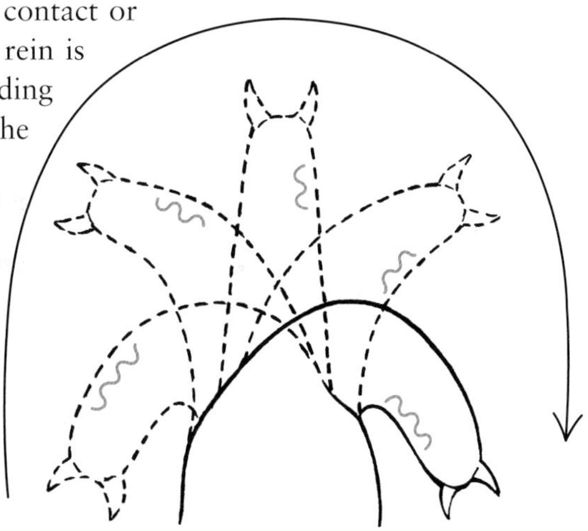

Figure 4.2. The neck muscles on the horse's right side start to contract from the point of full left bend, through to a full right bend as soon as the horse starts to turn his head and neck – and vice versa.

Photo 4.5. The false bend. The horse appears to be bent correctly, but the rider's outside rein has a loop, the contact on the inside rein is tight (notice the pull on the bit) and the horse's inside neck muscles show no definition.

Equal contact

There seems to be some confusion about the concept of equal contact. It is often interpreted as simultaneous and consistent equal contact on both reins. This is a biomechanical impossibility when the horse is ridden 'in position', from the inside leg to the outside rein. According to Gustav Steinbrecht and other notable trainers, when the horse is in a correct inside bend, the rider hardly needs an inside rein.

The only time a horse should have simultaneous equal contact on both sides is when he has to travel on a straight line into the halt, across the diagonal in medium or extended trot, when facing a jump or out hacking. In these situations, he does not need a preparatory bend.

'Equal contact' should rather be interpreted as 'equivalence of contact and suppleness on both sides'. This simply means that the horse should not be

Photo 4.6. The bent-straight position.

tighter or harder when ridden on one rein than when ridden on the other. Although the inside rein's contact, is by definition, softer in the bend, this does not mean that the outside contact should be hard. The horse should yield to the outside contact as swiftly as to the inside contact should the rider request it by squeezing the rein.

▶ RIDING AND TEACHING APPLICATIONS

1. First set up the bend, then ask the horse to change direction or turn. This will ensure that his balance is not disturbed.

2. Practise changes of bend with serpentines to teach the horse to yield instantly to inside rein pressure. Ensure that your inside leg flips the ribcage.

3. When the horse lifts his head during turns, circles and changes of direction, the rider has not prepared him sufficiently with the correct inside bend.

4. Positive contact on the inside, with light contact on the outside (no matter which way the horse is bent), means that the horse is not contracting his inside neck muscles. Ask him to yield with the appropriate form of 'take and give'.

▶ JUDGING SIGNIFICANCE

1. The correct inside bend is evident by the slight loop or soft inside rein and the straight outside rein. The inside neck muscles are defined when the horse has a correct inside bend. In the false bend, the inside rein is tight and the inside neck has a smooth appearance.

2. The horse lifting his neck on turns and circles is an indication that he was not correctly bent before the movement and thus his balance is disturbed.

Contact Problems

The biomechanics of resistance

When the horse resists the rider's hands, he does so with his poll and neck extensor muscles. He lifts his head and neck 'away from the rider's hands'. This causes stronger tension in the reins. When the pull is not accompanied by a visible lifting of his head and neck, it is still caused by his top line muscle tone which is increased through isometric contraction. This top line muscle contraction is an extensor pattern which 'disengages' the horse's hindquarters, thus working in opposition to engagement, cadence, freedom of movement, sequence and 'throughness' of his hind legs. Head resistance is the root of most of the problems which riders encounter in their efforts to control the horse. This is the reason why many riders resort to harsher bits, running reins and other complicated gadgets.

Resistance is caused by one object alone, the rider's hands. When the rider pulls or sets the hands, the horse will either yield or resist. Horses will do almost anything to alleviate pressure. They will first try to yield by moving their heads down and closer to the riders' hands but, if the pressure is not relieved, they will resist and lift their heads away from the pressure of the riders' hands. Every yielding action of the horse should lead to a yielding action from the rider – 'take and give'. Any tightness in the rider's hands, arms or shoulders will lead to resistance.

Photo 4.7. On the other side of resistance are always pulling hands.

Resistance and the 'set jaw'

When the horse resists the contact, the firm response may feel as though he is 'tightening his jaw'. Firm contact has nothing to do with tight jaw muscles, which do not extend the horse's head. The horse's jaw may sometimes appear to be clenched, but if you observe carefully, you will notice a very tight noseband, which restricts the tell-tale opening of his mouth.

Tight jaw muscles (masseters) clench the mouth shut. Notice this when attempting to inspect a horse's teeth. This tight closing of the jaw is a flexor pattern which tightens his neck flexors. His neck will be rigid in flexion and will appear to be in the 'on the bit' round frame. Because of this flexor pattern his contact will be soft when he is ridden on a straight line, but the tight bilateral flexors will prevent him from yielding or bending his head and neck from side to side. The rider usually only notices this 'resistance' when attempting to turn, circle or change the rein. This tight clenching is usually connected to tooth or jaw discomfort.

▶ RIDING AND TEACHING APPLICATIONS

1. Consider the horse's balance in the transitions since he cannot use his head and neck effectively in the round frame. Prepare him for each transition and change of direction with an inside bend and well timed half-halts, with or without simultaneous forward leg aids, depending on the need at the time. Remind him to maintain the round frame with gentle squeezes on the reins ('take and give') and well timed 'early warning' signals.

2. Contact should always stay elastic. Any tightness in the rider blocks this elasticity and forward movement.

3. Ask the horse for a soft contact and then ease him forwards. If you push him forwards before asking him to stay round, he may lose balance and lift his head or he may 'fall' on the forehand. If you push him forwards suddenly without warning, he will attempt to maintain balance by 'leaning on the hand' or running faster.

4. Always yield the reins after the horse has responded to the taking action on the reins, otherwise the horse will resist and the contact will become too firm/strong.

5. When the contact is strong, the horse will be pulling with his forelimbs, but when the contact is light, the horse will push with his hind limbs. This is the same biomechanics as pulling a cart. The horse 'pulls' a cart with his shoulders.

▶ JUDGING SIGNIFICANCE

1. The slight dip in front of the withers, which sometimes goes together with the 'on the bit' position, is usually a sign that the rider's contact is faulty. This should be penalized in the sections on 'acceptance of the bridle', as well as the 'correct use of aids', because it is the rider's responsibility.

2. When contact improves after canter, it is usually a sign that the rider has been maintaining a constant hang, or pull, on the reins. Enhanced impulsion after the canter makes this stronger contact uncomfortable for the horse; he therefore flexes his neck in an effort to relieve this pressure from the bit. The horse yields, the contact softens and the rider then automatically yields a little. If the rider does not yield and if the horse is not a submissive type he will resist this pressure by lifting his head even more.

3. When the horse hollows in any transition, he has usually lost his balance because the rider has not prepared him correctly or horse and rider's timing was not synchronized.

4. The horse resists the downward transition when he is not obedient to the rider's stopping leg aids. The rider is thus 'forced' to use the hands. This excessive pressure on the horse's mouth will make him lift his head, open his mouth and hollow his neck. There should be a clear preparation into the transition.

5. Hollowing of the horse's frame is usually caused by inconsistent or too strong contact. The contact should be yielding and elastic.

6. The rider should be rewarded for establishing a kind, soft contact with the horse's mouth and for having a relatively loose noseband, because this is kinder to the horse. A tight noseband is usually an indication that the rein contact is not established correctly.

7. Head-tossing is usually associated with discomfort such as flies, trickling sweat or back and hind leg discomfort.

8. 'Acceptance of the bridle' is a rider and training responsibility. Inadequacies are not the fault of the horse. Resistance to the hands should be penalized in the *rider* section of the test.

9. Horses at the Preliminary and Novice levels should be rewarded for being in a round frame, even if it is not consistently maintained. This is a progression from the natural frame and consistency could take a while to establish. When the horse is consistently in the natural frame, the rider has not even attempted to ask the horse for the correct flexor pattern.

'Resistances' of the mouth

The open mouth 'resistance'

There is a common misconception that when the horse opens his mouth during resistance, he is 'resisting the bit with his lower jaw'. This is far from the truth and this kind of thinking has done endless harm to many horses. The horse cannot resist with his lower jaw because the lower jaw can only move closer to his chest – towards the rider's hands, when he opens it, not away from them. Only the lower jaw of an animal is mobile. The upper jaw is one with the head and for it to move, the whole head has to lift or flex on the neck. The horse lifts his head or neck to pull the bit from the rider's hands. He flexes his head to yield to bit pressure. When a horse resists he often simultaneously opens his mouth, but he opens his mouth 'against' the bit pressure for one reason alone. His lower jaw yields towards the pulling reins in an attempt to relieve the *painful/uncomfortable bit pressure on his mouth from these pulling reins.*

If the horse were resisting in the jaw, the jaw would move in an opposite direction from the rider's hands and thus close. From this it is clear that he resists with his head and neck extensor muscles, not with his jaw.

The young horse reacts to the first introduction of the bit by chewing it, pulling it up in his mouth and pushing it away with his tongue. He also mouths it, mimicking the submissive response of the foal. If there is no pressure on the bit from the rider's hands, he soon accepts the bit in his closed mouth.

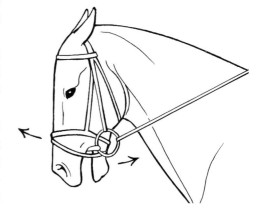

Figure 4.3. The open mouth resistance. He moves his lower jaw towards the pressure to relieve discomfort.

The next phase is the most crucial in the education of the horse's mouth. It is the horse's first introduction to the rider's hands. Should these hands have a taking action instead of a giving action (elastic contact), then the horse will resist the bit and may have mouth problems for the rest of his life. This usually leads to tight shutting of his mouth with nosebands and ever-stronger bits – or he may be pulled in with running reins. All this is an attempt to solve the fault of the first hands to touch his mouth. To summarize these points:

1. The horse will resist the bit by pulling in the opposite direction from the rider's hands. This means that he will lift his head and/or neck. The effect of this is that the rider usually starts to pull back. The lifting of the head and neck increases the pressure of the bit on the lower jaw.

2. This resistance causes pain in the horse's mouth. He therefore opens his mouth in an attempt to relieve the pressure and yield to the pain. Therefore, closing the horse's mouth with a tight noseband simply removes

the symptom. To cure the problem, the horse has to learn to yield to the bit and the rider has to learn to yield the hands the instant the horse yields. The tight noseband may improve the acceptance of the bit in only a few very intelligent, but submissive horses who, when they realize they cannot open their mouth to relieve the pressure, will move their head closer to the pressure. Should the rider then yield, the horse will accept this position. Unfortunately, most riders do not yield sufficiently and the problems persist even with a tight noseband.

▶ RIDING AND TEACHING APPLICATIONS

1. A tight noseband does not remove the cause of the open mouth resistance. First diagnose the problem and remove the cause, then a tight noseband should be unnecessary.

2. Tightening the noseband has no effect on the lateral bending of the head and neck.

3. It is very important to realize that a horse will first yield to uncomfortable pressure, but if it persists, he will attempt to pull in the opposite direction of the pressure (resist).

4. If the horse opens his mouth despite a correct yielding contact on the reins, his mouth and teeth should be checked for abnormalities. A thinner bit may be necessary if his mouth is small.

▶ JUDGING SIGNIFICANCE

1. An open mouth is often a sign of incorrect rein contact. However, it can also be a sign of lack of submission, tension, mouth and teeth abnormalities, or that the bit is too large.

2. A tight noseband can be a sign that the correct rein contact has not been established.

3. Resistances such as pulling, hanging, hard contact and the open mouth resistance are training and rider related and should therefore be penalized in the 'correct use of aids' section of the test.

The protruding tongue and the tongue-thrust reflex

There are many reasons why horses protrude their tongues, but most of them are connected to one or other form of discomfort. The horse protrudes his tongue through the *tongue-thrust reflex* because of uncomfortable pressure on it. The tongue-thrust reflex is a primitive reflex which protects animals from ingesting poisonous foods. The tongue pushes the unacceptable or foul-tasting food/object up and forwards until it is out of the mouth. This primitive reflex occurs in some cerebral palsied or brain-injured people as well. Their tongue's reaction to metal eating utensils is to push them out of the mouth. The horse has the same reaction to metal in his mouth and some horses continue, throughout their training, to attempt to push the bit away with the tongue. This leads to the 'tongue-over-the-bit' problem and the 'busy mouth' problem.

A veterinary check should be the first response to this action. Anatomical abnormalities such as an overshot or undershot jaw, a low and enlarged soft palate, peculiarities in the epiglottis, tooth problems, restricted airways, too large a tongue or inflammation of the tongue caused by bit pressure and injury to the horse's mouth could all lead to the protruding tongue-thrust reflex. If any of these conditions persist, the horse will develop a habit of continually protruding his tongue.

Bitting problems should be checked next. Heavy double-jointed snaffle bits with large centrepieces are often associated with 'softness', but the elliptical centrepiece lies heavily on a young horse's tongue and often leads to the tongue-thrust reflex, of which lip-licking or flicking the tongue out like a snake is the first sign. A good bit should have enough space for the tongue, but not cause discomfort on the soft palate. Thick bits are said to be 'soft', but most horses do not have the space in their mouths for a thick bit. Metal is not a horse-friendly material for bits.

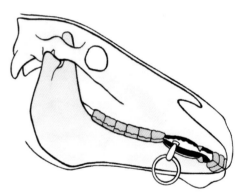

Figure 4.4. The centre piece of the double-jointed snaffle may place excessive weight on the horse's tongue, causing the tongue-thrust reflex.

Photo 4.8. The tongue-thrust reflex.

The next common problem is connected to the rider's hands. Nagging hands, hanging hands or pulling hands cause pressure on the horse's tongue. This pressure can lead to inflammation of the tongue which, as mentioned above, will trigger the tongue-thrust reflex. The horse will protrude his tongue in an attempt to relieve the painful pressure.

Tension and anxiety can lead to a protruding tongue, but this reaction is not that common. Alternatively, sometimes the very relaxed 'dopey' horse protrudes his tongue for very long periods.

▶ RIDING AND TEACHING APPLICATIONS

When your horse starts to flick his tongue out or lick his lips, the next step will be a protruding tongue. Immediate research into the cause of the problem is essential. It could be calamitous simply to tighten the noseband.

▶ JUDGING SIGNIFICANCE

A protruding tongue is a sign that the horse has a problem in acceptance of the bit, but it has many causes. Tension is one of the least common possibilities. The judge should therefore not assume that the protruding tongue is caused by tension but simply point out the presence of the protruding tongue.

The tongue over the bit

This problem usually has the same cause as the protruding tongue – the tongue-thrust reflex caused by pressure and discomfort. The horse attempts to push the bit away with his tongue, but he pulls the tongue up too high and it slips over the bit. Once there, he can only move it back if the tension on the bit slackens.

▶ RIDING AND TEACHING APPLICATIONS

1. It is important to find the cause of the problem. Simply tightening the noseband does not remove the cause, but will leave the horse with a permanent contact problem. While the cause is being investigated, the only acceptable reasons for tightening the noseband to a moderate degree can be as an expedient at a dressage competition (to avoid losing marks for a protruding tongue) or as a temporary controlling measure to avoid the painful 'tongue-over-the-bit problem while jumping. Tightening the noseband severely only leads to more tension and tongue movement. Added to this, the horse will now attempt to open his mouth against the noseband.

COMMUNICATION AND SELF-CARRIAGE

2. When the horse's tongue flips over the bit, the reins have to be released to slacken the pressure on the bit. This is the only way the horse can get his tongue back in position.

3. All tongue, bit and mouth problems disappear when a horse is ridden in a bitless bridle, but the biomechanical principles of yielding to pressure remain the same for both types of bridle: the pressure is simply in a different area.

▶ JUDGING SIGNIFICANCE

1. Tight nosebands are often a sign that the horse has a problem with contact. Although judges may not comment on subjective assumptions, they can watch for signs of contact problems.

2. A horse's tongue slipping over the bit is often a sign of the tongue-thrust reflex and a contact problem.

Lifting the Withers

The concept of lifting the withers seems to be another metaphor used in teaching, but the meaning is not quite clear. Trainers seem to use this concept to teach the rider how to round the horse's frame. Yet, he does not lift his withers to round his frame. The horse literally lifts his withers when he goes into the fright/flight mode: he lifts them in an extensor pattern. This is evident as the horse seems to 'grow' when he becomes excited. As mentioned in Chapter 2, the muscles responsible pull his shoulder blades down and his ribcage up to lift his withers.

5

The Engine and the Brakes

Although horses are quadrupeds and we refer to their four extremities as legs, their fore and hind limbs have distinctly different functions. We can see this clearly by making a broad comparison to the limbs of a biped. In a biped, the 'forelimbs' constitute arms and hands, which are used for balance, to break a fall and for dexterity. The horse's forelimbs are also used for balance and for rudimentary dexterity (pawing). The biped's legs are used for ambulation (the 'engine'); the horse's hind legs are also his engine. Discomfort to the horse's fore or hind legs, or disturbance of their function, will thus have an effect on his ambulation or braking ability.

The Shoulders and Forelegs

The long, straight piers of the forelimbs are designed for weight-bearing during grazing, for braking, to transfer energy upwards, as struts over which the hindquarters can push the body, and for turning.

The horse is designed to carry about 5–10 per cent more of his weight on his forehand than on his hindquarters, especially during stance. The positioning of his neck, however, easily changes this relative distribution by lifting or dropping. During movement, this weight distribution changes continually, (although the horse in nature maintains slightly more weight over his shoulders than the trained horse). However, it is the forehand which has to absorb the majority of the impact. This leaves the horse's hind legs free to propel him forwards. The absence of collarbones ensures that the forelimbs yield sufficiently to concussion in order to prevent injury. The muscle sling, which attaches the shoulder blades to the ribcage, allows the ribcage to swing from side to side and to bob up and down like a trampoline. It assists in balance as well as in shock absorption. The angles of his fetlock, elbow and shoulder joints further damp the concussion by allowing a yielding movement.

The forelimbs have a pulling action whereas the hind limbs push. The more the hind limbs push, the less the forelimbs have to pull. As mentioned in the previous chapter, when the horse 'pulls' a cart, he pulls with his shoulders via the harness while his hind legs push from behind the vertical. Compare this pulling action with swimming and rock climbing. When we swim, our arms pull against the water while our legs propel us forwards. Rock climbers push with their legs and pull with their arms. When the horse is on the forehand, he 'pulls' his body forwards with his forelegs. In racing and in nature, where speed is required, the horse carries about 10 per cent more of his weight on his forehand, but in dressage and in jumping the rider insists that he moves a considerable amount of his weight to his hindquarters. The forelimbs then have less weight pressure, although their job is still to catch the weight and to transfer it upwards, especially when jumping. When the ridden horse carries too much weight on his forelimbs, he will start to 'fall' and move faster.

The horse uses his forelegs as active struts to brake. He does this by pressing them against the ground and transferring the energy in an upward direction (vertical acceleration): 'The front hoof bounces at impact.'[1] That is why a horse jolts the rider in an upward direction when the canter-walk transition is too abrupt. The horse's hind limbs have too many angles to have an effective braking action.

Photo 5.1. The braking action of the horse's forelimbs.

---

1 W. Back, 'Intra-limb coordination: the forelimb and the hind limb', in W. Back and H. M. Clayton, *Equine Locomotion* (London, Harcourt Publishers Ltd., 2001).

109

The planes of movement in the forelimbs

The horse's forelimbs move in four directions. They are designed to move mainly forwards in protraction and backwards in retraction in the sagittal plane. Deviations in this plane are the result of slight asymmetries in the articular surface. The forelimbs are able to move in the lateral plane away from the body in abduction and towards the body in adduction, but the extensive abduction and adduction of the human arms are not possible in the horse. This is because, although the horse's shoulder has a ball and socket joint, the movement is restricted by the pectoral muscles, which have to stabilize the shoulder onto the body. Since the horse's forelimbs have no bony or ligamentous attachments onto his skeleton, this stabilization has to be strong to maintain his leg position underneath his body. The pectoral muscles have to simulate the function of collarbones to secure the forelimbs to the skeleton. The movement range in abduction, adduction, rotation, flexion and extension is thus restricted and the shoulder blades (scapulae) and humerus bones have limited ability to move away from the ribcage. In contrast, the human arm movements are almost limitless.

▶ RIDING AND TEACHING APPLICATIONS

1. Lateral movement should be taught progressively and at a slow gait to protect the stability of the horse's shoulders.

2. It is important to buy a horse with sufficiently sloping pasterns and shoulder blades to ensure good concussion/shock absorption, soundness and comfort.

3. Correct training distributes the horse's weight more to his hindquarters. This is because:
   a. Forward riding interspersed with half-halts promotes more engagement.
   b. The weight of the rider on the horse's forehand triggers an automatic balance adjustment – a change in body schema. The horse has to move an equivalent of the rider's weight backwards to bring his centre of gravity to the centre of his base of support. He thus takes more weight on his hindquarters. Van Weeren[2] found that pastured horses show increased maximal extension of the fetlock and knee (carpal) joints of the forelimbs while trained horses showed an increase of maximal

---

2 P.R. van Weeren, A.J. van den Bogert, A.J. and A. Barneveld (1993), 'Kinematics of the Standardbred trotter measured at 6, 7, 8 and 9 months on a treadmill, before and after 5 months of prerace training', Act Anat. 146: 154–161, quoted in W. Back and H.M. Clayton, *Equine Locomotion*, Harcourt Publishers Ltd. (London) 2001.

extension of the fetlock and hock (tarsal) joints of the hind limbs. This indicates that pastured horses carry more weight on their forelimbs while correctly trained horses move some weight to their hind limbs. Pastured horses carry more weight on their forehand for grazing, natural balance and simply because of anatomical structure.

The Hind Legs

The horse's hind legs are designed to push and propel the horse forwards. His hind legs are the engine; the seat of power. Compare the horse's hind legs to those of the human: their function is ambulation. The hind legs are responsible for the production of energy, impulsion and engagement.

In dressage, while we teach the horse to use his hind legs (engine) for propulsion and engagement, we also ask him to use them for brakes and weight-bearing, even though they are not designed for this purpose. This, in fact, is against his natural inclination because 'the rear hoof slides at impact'.[3] The hind legs have many angles and are designed to bend and to push, not to brake. The angles are necessary to yield to concussion, but they militate against the hind legs being used as struts or brakes. Note how a gymnast lands after vaulting, flexing all of the leg joints to yield to the shock of the ground reaction force, in order to maintain equilibrium and to prevent injury. Simultaneous flexion of the hock and stifle joints increases the shock absorption ability of the hind limb (a straight stifle is associated with less shock absorption ability). The simultaneous use of the hind legs for propulsion as well as for braking is like putting a jet aeroplane's engines into reverse to stop on the runway. It is very difficult and strenuous for the horse. Many riders have not learnt how to ride the horse in such a way as to convince him to use his hind legs for braking. Training the horse to become more engaged does, however, save his forelegs from strain when ridden, although his hind legs often show signs of strain on the tendons in the form of windgalls.

The planes of movement of the hind legs

As with the forelegs, the horse's hind legs move in four directions: forward in protraction and backward in retraction in the sagittal plane, and sideways in abduction and adduction in the lateral plane. Although the hip joint is a ball and socket joint, it does not have a large lateral or rotational range. This is because the powerful adductor muscles stabilize the limbs

---

3 W. Back, 'Intra-limb coordination: the forelimb and the hind limb', in W. Back and H.M. Clayton, *Equine Locomotion* (London, Harcourt Publishers Ltd., 2001).

against the body to keep the horse's legs underneath him and prevent 'splitting'. This arrangement restricts the abduction and adduction possibilities of the joint, but the resultant stability ensures that the horse can produce fast forward propulsion in situations of danger.

From the stifle to the toe, the leg moves almost exclusively in the sagittal plane. In fact, because of the reciprocal apparatus between them, the stifle and hock always flex and extend simultaneously

The horse's hind leg movements differ from human leg movement mainly in respect of the movement range. The human has enormous rotational ability and very supple dancers have over 180° movement in their ball and socket joints. Horses have limited abduction in their hips and their ability to rotate them is small because of the stabilizing function of the adductor muscles.

Some horses swivel in their hind fetlocks at the walk. This is more noticeable on sand than on grass. The cause of this swivel is often attributed to incorrect hock movement, because the hock appears to move laterally at each step. However, the problem lies in the manner in which the horse moves his leg from up in the hip joint. Excessive inward hip rotation as the horse grounds his foot then causes the foot to swivel inwards and the hock to move outwards. It is a common walk pattern probably caused by slack ligaments and low muscle tone.

Figure 5.1. Schematic illustration of the fore- and hind limb joints showing the direction of movement each type of joint allows.

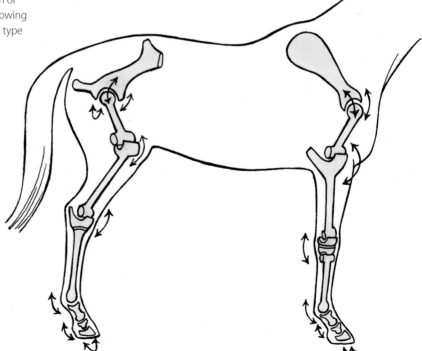

The fetlocks of all four limbs act as springs for shock absorption and to produce elastic recoil for propulsion. 'The spring-like action of the tendons results in a "smooth" gait, but also serves as a shock absorber in the coffin, fetlock, elbow and shoulder joints at the time of ground contact at the beginning of the stance phase.'[4] When the flexible fetlock extends to almost touch the ground, it stretches the superficial and deep digital flexor tendon and the suspensory ligaments. The tension on the superficial and deep digital flexor tendon and suspensory ligament produces elastic energy which it stores during the stance phase to release at push off. 'Energy is released as a result of elastic recoil. [Most of this elastic behaviour is in the fetlock joint, but] the shoulder, elbow and carpal joints show some elastic behavior due to the actions of the soft tissues that cross these joints.'[5] This produces the shock absorption which protects the joints. The elastic recoil is responsible for the cadence in the trot and allows the horse to move forwards at the trot with little energy output. Because of this, horses can trot long distances without becoming fatigued. It is like jumping on a pogo stick.

▶ RIDING AND TEACHING APPLICATIONS

1. Lateral movements do strengthen the horse's pushing ability, but should be taught progressively and at a slow gait.

2. The swivel in the fetlock can be corrected with proprioceptive taping.[6] This is done by pasting sports tape over certain muscle groups to create sensory awareness in the horse. When taped correctly the horse will move in the desired manner to alleviate the pull on his skin.

3. A horse has to be encouraged to use his hindquarters to move forwards. However, if he is pushed out of balance, his forelegs will move into short braking actions which resemble running. Therefore, forward pushing has to be balanced with the appropriate half-halts.

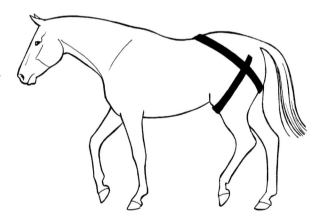

Figure 5.2. Proprioceptive taping to prevent the 'swivel' in the fetlocks as developed by Narelle Stubbs. The tape pulls on the skin as the leg starts to swivel.

---

4 E. Barrey, 'Inter-limb coordination' in W. Back and H.M. Clayton, *Equine Locomotion* (London, Harcourt Publishers Ltd., 2001).

5 E. Barrey, 'Inter-limb coordination', in W. Back and H.M. Clayton, *Equine Locomotion* (London, Harcourt Publishers Ltd., 2001).

6 C.M. McGowan and N. Stubbs, *Animal Physiotherapy*, (Oxford, Blackwell Publishing, 2007).

6

Engagement and Collection

The Biomechanics of Engagement

In biomechanical terms engagement is simply an earlier protraction of the hind legs in respect of the ipsilateral (same side) forelimb. The horse uses this forward position to produce more vertical (upward) propulsion. He does this through more hip and stifle flexion of the hind in the stance phase, lowering his haunches, producing more elastic recoil and a bouncier movement. His hind legs are, however, straighter in the swing phase. Willem Back has found that: 'A shorter stance duration and reduced flexion in the hind limbs [swing phase] cause maximal protraction to occur earlier, so the hind limb reaches the retracting ipsilateral forelimb earlier, which is seen as being engaged in the hindquarters. At the same time, increased fetlock extension illustrates more weight carrying by the hind limbs.'[1] This leads to positive advanced hoof placement in engagement (see Chapter 10). The horse uses his hip flexor muscles (quadriceps femoris and iliopsoas) to step under more and become more engaged, but this protraction uses very little energy because elastic recoil 'springs the legs forward'. The 'heavy-duty' muscle action occurs when the horse pushes against the ground to straighten the stifle in a vertical direction. When the horse's hind legs are more underneath his body, he can use his quadriceps femoris muscles more effectively to produce more vertical propulsion. He thus develops stronger quadriceps muscles. However, this more forward position of the horse's hind legs reduces the size of the base of support and this is more taxing on his equilibrium.

---

1 W. Back, 'Intra-limb coordination: the forelimb and the hind limb' in W. Back and H.M. Clayton, *Equine Locomotion* (London, Harcourt Publishers Ltd., 2001).

Maximal hip flexion has the effect of rounding the horse's back. This is facilitated by the total flexor pattern, which is initiated by the horse rounding his head and neck. Simply rounding the horse's neck however, does not produce the superior engagement required for high-level dressage work or for jumping. This kind of engagement has to be produced by animating the horse's hind legs to produce more pushing power. More power from the horse's hind legs alone, however will only lead to faster forward movement – horizontal propulsion.

The forces of engagement and propulsion push in different directions yet they have to work in concert with one another to produce impulsion and collection. The strong gluteal and hamstring muscles propel the weight in a forward direction. They push from behind the vertical to produce horizontal (forward) propulsion. Engagement, however, is a vertical force and the muscles responsible for this are the quadriceps femoris muscles (in front of the hind limbs). These muscles flex the hip joints and extend the stifle. The iliopsoas muscles flex the spine at the lumbo-sacral joint, dropping the pelvis. The horse flexes more in this joint during the canter and piaffe than at the trot. The quadriceps and iliopsoas muscles bring the hindquarters more underneath the body. The quadriceps femoris muscles then propel the horse in an upward direction.

For the purposes of dressage and jumping the power of engagement has to move in a forward-upward direction. This constitutes impulsion, which is achieved when the forward energy is 'caught' by the rider's hands in half-halts.

Collection is thus a balance between impulsion and engagement in which the hindquarters work in a smaller range of motion. When the hindquarters engage more, they lower. This lowering moves the horse's centre of gravity back, which automatically raises his shoulders and neck and lightens the contact. This elevated forehand is a characteristic of engagement. A collected horse is in perfect self-carriage and balance. A sign of collection and engagement at the canter is that 'the trailing fore-limb leaves the ground just after passing the vertical phase.'[2] Therefore, collection and engagement are not true if the horse is not light in contact. Even a horse with a naturally low neck carriage will raise it when he is correctly engaged.

Engagement does not *necessarily* round the horse's frame from the tail to the head. When the horse stretches his head down and rounds his neck, his back rounds automatically. This interaction, however, does not work as effectively from the back to the front. Although the engagement of the hindquarters pulls the back up and rounds it, the 'pull' on the nuchal ligament in the neck through the supraspinatus ligament will not necessarily bring the head into the 'on the bit' position because the nuchal ligament is too elastic. Therefore the idea that engagement inevitably rounds the neck is a biomechanical misconception and probably the result of thinking in mechanical rather than biomechanical terms. The flexor pattern has to be initiated with some instruction through the reins to encourage the horse to round his head and neck. This principle is demonstrated clearly by the engagement of the cutting and barrel racing horses. They do not necessarily round their necks, but they are clearly engaged. On the other hand, this

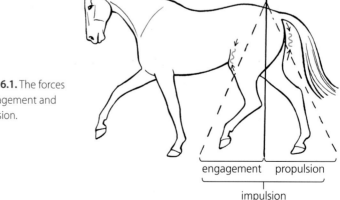

Figure 6.1. The forces of engagement and propulsion.

engagement | propulsion

impulsion

2 Dr H.M. Clayton, 'The canter considered', article in USDF *Veterinary Connection*, October 2002.

flexor pattern initiated by the hip flexion of engagement enables the horse to round his head and neck with greater ease.

EXERCISE

Get down on your hands and knees. Maintain a straight neck as the horse does in the natural frame. Take as large a 'step' as possible with one knee, then take your knee back. Now bend your head and neck down and take as large a 'step' as possible with the same knee again. Your back will round automatically and you will be able to take a longer 'step'. Take a few 'steps' in both the hollow and rounded frame and compare the difference in ease in the two head positions.

Humans do not have a strong nuchal ligament because in the upright stance they do not need to support the neck in the forward position. The head and neck are balanced on the shoulders and the trapezius muscle supports the head. This is why you get a headache or knots in the shoulder muscles when studying and leaning forward.

This exercise illustrates that, although roundness and engagement are interconnected, roundness is initiated by the head, while engagement starts at the hindquarters.

The Energy Circle/Chain

The energy circle is initiated by the rider's leg aids. They encourage forward-propelling energy in the horse's hindquarters. The hindquarters push the energy/movement forwards. They move the body over the forelimbs and propel the horse's forelimbs. The rider's hands, however, 'catch' this energy through half-halts. The half-halts act on the forelimbs via the head and neck through the bit. These half-halts prevent the energy from 'escaping' into faster forward action – 'running'. The energy is thus pushed in an upward/vertical direction by the horse's forelimbs and creates more suspension, which improves cadence and engagement. The rider's legs continue to ask for more energy, which is caught in the rider's hands – this then forms a circle of energy. (Energy is never lost, but is transformed into different matter. Muscular contraction, for instance, is changed into heat.)

▶ RIDING AND TEACHING APPLICATIONS

1. Strong contact and engagement are opposites. Correct engagement of the hindquarters is difficult when the horse takes a firm/strong contact because he is either tipped on his forehand or goes into the extensor pattern with tight top line muscles, both of which are counterproductive

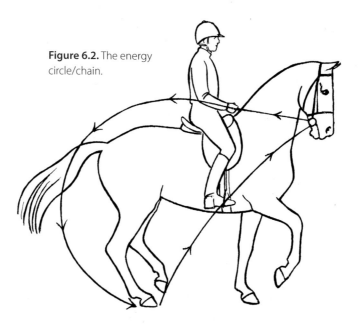

Figure 6.2. The energy circle/chain.

to engagement. Therefore the round frame should be encouraged from the head and neck together with the request for more engagement from the hindquarters.

2. Collection can only develop correctly once the horse's muscles have developed sufficiently and he can move with impulsion, is in balance and can engage his hindquarters.

3. If the horse's hindquarters are simply pushed forwards without the correct rein contact and timely half-halts, the horse will simply run faster and lose balance.

4. The energy circle is produced by forward leg aids followed in split-second timing with checking rein (and knee) aids to 'catch' the energy.

5. The canter is a better exercise for producing engagement and collection than the trot because the lumbo-sacral joint drops the pelvis during canter.

6. At the higher levels of schooling, the piaffe is a superior collecting exercise because of the hip and lumbo-sacral flexion it generates.

7. Even though it is a movement of extension, rein-back exercises and transitions condition the engagement muscles. Rein-back brings the hindquarters into the correct position for engagement, but it does not necessarily *constitute* engagement. Power and impulsion are necessary for engagement and collection. All forward impulsion is lost by doing rein-back exercises. During the rein-back the hip flexors pull the body

over the hind legs while the quadriceps femoris muscles push the hind limbs against the ground when they extend the stifle. The transition between rein-back and the first forward step ensures that the quadriceps femoris muscles push against the ground to produce engagement. Therefore, as a strengthening exercise, the rein-back should be done through trot or canter transitions. The movement can be used to teach the horse to become more responsive to the aids.

▶ JUDGING SIGNIFICANCE

1. Each horse's ability to engage and collect has a unique picture which depends on his conformation and type of movement. The picture of engagement can only be compared to the same horse when not engaged. It is the muscle power and action which leads to more engagement, and this is not visible, although the rider can feel it. A horse with straight leg action can be as engaged as a horse with rounder movement and more flexion in the limbs. Therefore a long-backed horse, for example, should not be penalized for not tracking up as well as a short-backed horse. This would constitute penalization for conformation and not for ability. Horses with straight hind legs can appear more engaged than horses with more hock angle.

2. Engagement is visible as an earlier maximal protraction of the hind limbs. This positive advanced diagonal hoof placement has been shown to be a sign of superior engagement.

3. Hind leg fetlock extension is more pronounced in engagement.

4. An engaged horse shows more hip flexion.

5. The hind legs in engagement are straighter in the swing phase.

6. Engagement and collection should produce more cadence through elastic recoil and vertical propulsion produced by the forward positioning of the hind legs and the braking forces of the forelimbs.

7. The closer the trailing forelimb is to the vertical when it leaves the ground, the more collected the canter. The further it passes the vertical when it leaves the ground, the more the horse is on the forehand.

8. The collected canter has a shorter suspension time than the working, medium and extended canters.

7

Biomechanical Misconceptions

Classical Riding and Biomechanics

To most riders the concept of 'classical riding' seems a little vague. Is it a certain branch of riding, such as Western riding, show riding, natural horsemanship, or is it an art form as compared to competition riding? Or do we follow the dictionary for the definition? If we interpret it as a branch of riding, is it specifically haute école, or is it still open to interpretation because its exact principles have not yet been clearly defined. In the dictionary, the word 'classical' is defined as 'established and widely accepted as traditional; of high quality and lasting value'.

The classical riding methods, which have shown 'lasting value', have done so because they have been based (perhaps without the modern understanding of the subject) on correct biomechanical principles. For example, the phrase 'riding from the inside leg to the outside rein'[1] is meaningless if analysed purely in biomechanical terms, but if performed correctly it tilts the horse's ribcage. It initiates a balance reaction in which the horse will contract his inside side muscles, from his head to his tail. This contraction causes an inside bend, with the consequent stronger outside rein contact.

Misconceptions

We have taken as gospel, through the centuries, many biomechanical misconceptions in horse and rider training and in the movement analysis of

---

1 Since no beginner or novice rider understands this esoteric term, a biomechanical description is: 'ask for an inside bend by pushing the ribcage over with the inside leg'.

the horse. This has led to basing entire systems of training on 'original error'. This was possibly caused by the following:

1. The skill of riding has traditionally been taught through verbal instructions. It is, however, extremely difficult to master a physical skill through a verbal command. Imagine learning to do ballet from a teacher who only shouts verbal instructions. This verbal teaching led to many metaphors, which eventually became literally meaningless rhetoric. For example: 'Ride your horse in front of your legs.'

2. The fault of comparing the large quadruped horse with the bipedal human. Many erroneous assumptions in terms of biomechanics have been made because of this comparison.

3. Viewing the horse in pure mechanical terms, disregarding the effect of biology. Jean Saint-Fort Paillard is one of the few masters who understood the concept when he stated: 'The horse's equilibrium cannot and therefore should not be thought of in mechanical terms, but only in terms of neuro-muscular physiology.'[2] An example of pure mechanical thought is: By holding the reins and pushing with the legs the horse will come on the bit. There is no consideration here whether the horse understands the rider. This method has led to huge discomfort for many horses.

4. Lack of adequate research into equine biomechanics. (These misconceptions may have developed because riding grew as an art form and not as a sport science, and therefore it was not given the biomechanical scrutiny of many other sports.)

While we follow these invalid explanations and misconceptions, we cannot hope to teach the horse (and rider) correctly and this leads to confusion and tension in both horse and rider, with many hours of wasted time.

The following are further examples of assumptions based on inadequate knowledge of equine biomechanics.

Misconceptions about musculature

The 'overdevelopment' of the bracio-cephalic and omotransversarius muscles

The error of thinking behind the so-called 'overdevelopment' of the brachio-cephalicus and omotransversarius muscles (otherwise termed the 'upside down' neck) is that 'these muscles are overdeveloped because the

2 J. S-F. Paillard, *Understanding Equitation*, (New York, Doubleday, 1974).

horse is not ridden in a round outline, but with his head in the air'. The fact, though, is that these muscles have to be well developed because they are the prime protractors of the horse's forelimb: they assist in big movement. The brachio-cephalicus muscle crosses two joints and has to stabilize the head on the neck while 'pulling' the forelimb forwards. The brachio-cephalicus and omotransversarius muscles cover a section of the cervical vertebrae that lies directly underneath them; these vertebrae 'plump out' the muscles and make them appear overdeveloped.

The 'upside down' neck is usually found in young, untrained horses, in horses who only hack out and also in jumping horses who are 'pulled' around the turns – the horses who do not bend sufficiently. The cause of the 'upside down' neck is the *underdeveloped muscles* in the region which act to flex the neck laterally when contracting unilaterally and to extend the neck when contracting bilaterally, not the incorrectly presumed 'overdeveloped' brachio-cephalicus muscle.

In fact, these top line neck muscles only develop sufficiently through lateral bend. They need to be conditioned with correct bending and sup-pling work on circles, serpentines and spirals. Their development is dependent on the horse yielding to the rider's inside hand and using his own muscles to bend laterally to the side. They do not develop when the rider hangs on the reins or pulls the rein to turn or circle.

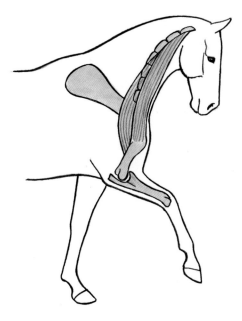

Figure 7.1. The powerful brachio-cephalic and omotransversarius muscles protract the forelimbs.

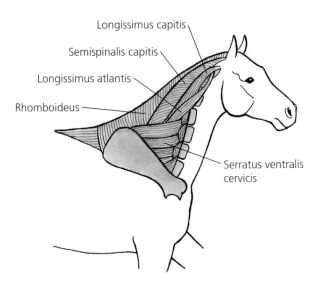

Longissimus capitis

Semispinalis capitis

Longissimus atlantis

Rhomboideus

Serratus ventralis cervicis

Figure 7.2. The muscles above the cervical vertebrae hollow the neck.

'The top line neck muscles hold the horse on the bit'

This faulty belief is connected to the belief that the brachio-cephalicus and omotransversarius muscles are overdeveloped. The top line neck muscles extend the neck and hollow it. The muscles below the vertebrae flex the neck against the pull of the nuchal ligament and place the horse 'on the bit'.

'The hollow in front of the withers is a conformation fault'

There seems to be an assumption that the little hollow area in front of the withers is a conformation fault and that these horses' necks are not set on correctly. This phenomenon is often seen in immature horses or horses lacking condition. The problem disappears immediately when the horse puts on condition and matures.

The hollow area is also apparent when a horse is ridden 'on the bit' incorrectly. In the latter case the rider has too much contact and is pulling the horse in. The horse shortens his neck in defence against the rider's hand pressure. He thus cannot yield correctly to this 'contact'. He attempts to avoid the discomfort by shortening his neck through extension (hollowing) at the base of the neck. The correction is instant when the horse is ridden correctly. This is a pattern which incorporates both the flexion as well as the extension patterns and as such is uncomfortable for the horse. The head is in flexion on the neck, but the base of the neck is hollow in extension. It is easily corrected by teaching the horse to move in a low and round frame in order to develop the correct muscles.

'The horse uses his back muscles to round his back'

This is sometimes presented as 'he must use his back'. It is not quite clear in the literature how the horse has to 'use his back', but he certainly does not use his back muscles to round his back and they do not develop from rounding, they stretch, except during the canter.

EXERCISE

Use your back. What is your reaction to this instruction? You will immediately contract your back muscles. Note that your back hollows when you 'use' it.

The horse rounds his back with his abdominal muscles and his hip flexors (iliopsoas). He 'swings' his back when his top line muscles relax and he is in a round frame. The horse's back becomes rigid when his back muscles are in contraction such as when he is in fright mode. In this position the back cannot 'swing'. The horse's back muscles have the function of stabilizing and protecting the spine and lifting the forehand in the canter.

Photo 7.1a. The dip in front of the withers is an example of a mixed pattern of movement. The horse has her head and top of her neck in flexion while the base of her neck is in extension. This position shortens the neck away from bit pressure. The contact is thus not comfortable for the horse.

Photo 7.1b. The same horse as in (a). The dip disappears as soon as the correct light contact and frame are established and the horse feels comfortable. (The fact that the saddle cloth has slipped mid-test does not detract from this.)

When they contract, they tighten the spine and hollow the back. When they tighten, the sitting trot becomes uncomfortable for the rider.

Certainly, the horse uses his back muscles when he is working, but this is in concert with all of his muscles during movement and is not strong contraction against resistance. The back muscles work especially in concert with the abdominal muscles to protect the spine. There is always movement in the horse's spine, therefore the back muscles contract and relax at every stride, but they can only work smoothly when his back is not in a state of tension. His lumbar longissimus muscle is attached to the gluteus medius muscle which extends the hip. This is to ensure that when the horse lifts his forehand, as in canter, there is a strong connection between the back muscles from tail to head.

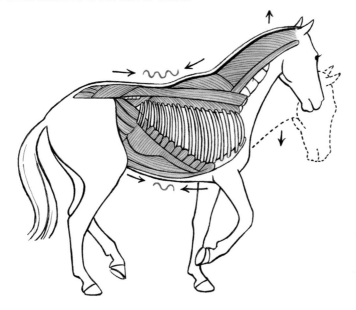

Figure 7.3. The abdominal muscles and hip flexors act to round the horse's back. The back muscles hollow and weaken the horse's back. Note the strong connection between the hindquarter extensors and the back muscles.

Misconceptions about the horse's mouth and the bit

'The horse resists the bit by opening his mouth'

This is sometimes presented as 'he resists with his jaw', but this is a bio-mechanical impossibility. It is not possible for the horse to resist with his lower jaw because it moves *towards* the rider's hands. See 'Resistances' of the mouth in Chapter 4 for a full explanation of the biomechanics of opening the mouth.

The horse is 'holding onto the bit with one side of his mouth'

Horses with tooth problems may resist bending to the painful side. Some horses 'play' with the bit and tend to pull it between their pre-molars, but do not hold it for any length of time. These horses can usually be identified through the chips or hooks on their teeth. The biomechanics of this 'holding' feeling is that the horse actually pulls the reins to the opposite side by using his opposite neck muscles. He turns his head slightly away from the pulling rein or he simply tightens the opposite side muscles against the pull, but appears to maintain the correct bend. He thus resists the bend by tightening his opposite neck muscles, which makes it *feel* as though he is holding on with his mouth. When he relaxes his opposite neck muscles and contracts the turning muscles, he will yield to the stiff side. It is all about use of neck muscles and yielding to pressure. In such cases it is always a good idea to have the horse's teeth checked by an equine dentist.

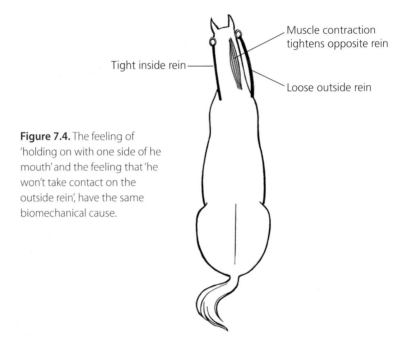

Tight inside rein

Muscle contraction tightens opposite rein

Loose outside rein

Figure 7.4. The feeling of 'holding on with one side of he mouth' and the feeling that 'he won't take contact on the outside rein', have the same biomechanical cause.

The horse 'won't take contact on the outside rein' when on his stiff side

The biomechanical meaning of this is that the horse is not yielding to inside rein pressure. He is thus bent to the outside and not contracting his inside neck muscles to bend to the inside. This position, even when the outside bend is not that conspicuous, will slacken the rein on the outside. No matter how hard the rider pulls on this outside rein, the horse will continue to yield to it slightly unless he is asked to bend his neck to the opposite side (inside). To have a positive contact on the outside rein the horse must bend away from this rein – to the inside and he must place more weight on his outside leg and shoulder. There is no point in taking up a stronger contact on the outside rein because the horse will simply bend more to the outside.

The horse 'puts his tongue out because of tension'

There are many reasons why the horse might push his tongue out, of which tension is the *least* common. Reasons include anatomical abnormalities such as a too large tongue or a malformed epiglottis. As mentioned in Chapter 4, the tongue-thrust reflex is the most common cause, but habit, too large a bit and breathing difficulties are contributing factors. In dressage judging the horse loses marks because of this problem, which is often incorrectly attributed to tension.

The horse stretches down to 'seek the bit'

This phrase probably originated as a metaphor, but eventually took on a literal meaning. Horses, like humans, do not particularly enjoy having foreign metal objects in their mouths – especially since, in many riders' hands, these may prove uncomfortable if not painful. Therefore, they do not 'search' for objects which may in some instances even feel like instruments of torture. The horse will stretch his head and neck down and round *as though* 'seeking the bit', but this stretching is a reaction to being contained in the inner range of movement. The horse's muscles tire and need to stretch from time to time. When permitted, he therefore stretches his head and neck forward and low. This position stretches and relaxes all the muscles he used to maintain the 'on the bit' position. The bit itself has nothing to do with this equation. Horses stretch down and round in *bitless bridles* when the riders request it.

Photo 7.2. Stretching down in a bitless bridle.

Misconceptions about nerve impulses and response to leg aids

'Tapping on the horse's sides triggers reflex actions'

There is a commonly held theory that 'tapping on the horse's sides triggers nerve fibres into simple reflex actions which make the horse lift his spine to round his back and step forwards'. This theory is based on the fact that the intercostal nerve is in this area and stimulates the appropriate muscles to contract. There are many problems with this theory. First, the intercostal nerve's most superficial area is in front of the girth where the rider's leg does not reach. Second, leg pressure is perceived by the sensory nerve which, as seen in Chapter 3, first sends the impulse to the brain which integrates it and then sends the message to the muscles to react. Third, we cannot simplify communication to simple reflex actions, because bodies function in coordinated systems. If simple pressure on nerves caused random reflex responses we would have chaos.

In reality the horse learns a new language from the rider. Through correct repetition of the pressure-reaction-release system of communication (conditioned learning), together with the facilitation of his automatic reactions, the horse learns to contract the appropriate muscles below his spine to round his back. He rounds his back by first dropping his neck followed (as though in one action) with rounding of the back.

EXERCISES

1. Try to initiate a rounded back by tapping or pressing your legs against the horse's ribs, but with long reins and no rein pressure. The horse will not round his back or lift his withers. He will probably simply walk forwards. The horse needs some form of rein restriction to explain to him that he is to yield and initiate the movement with his head. Some 'classical' practitioners ride horses in a round frame with a rope around the neck. These horses are usually also ridden on a loose contact in a double bridle with long shanks. They have already been trained to maintain this position before riding them with a rope alone.

2. Hold the reins to prevent forward movement, then tap or press the horse on his sides and note the reaction of rounding.

Neither the young, recently backed horse, nor the retired racehorse reacts to the tapping of the legs against his sides because it is meaningless to them. These horses remain planted and one can almost feel them thinking: 'What on earth does this uncomfortable pressure on my ribs mean?' In fact, if a rider does this while backing a young horse, he may go into fright/flight mode and buck or rear at this tapping. If tapping on the horse's sides did have this reaction, then all the riding school ponies would be trotting around in a round frame from all the leg flapping.

The horse learns to react appropriately through conditioned learning in the lunge ring; the words 'Trot on' or 'Walk' being followed by signals from the lunge whip. When he reacts by stepping forwards the pressure is released instantly: this is the reward. Young horses usually only understand the leg aids after association with the word 'Walk' together with the whip. This usually takes one or two sessions on the lunge. This reaction can also be learnt without teaching it on the lunge, when the rider's leg pressure produces ever more discomfort and thus the horse may eventually react by taking a forward step in his attempt to relieve the pressure. When this is rewarded instantly by the release of the pressure, the horse learns that he has responded correctly. This latter method, however, may be a little confusing for the young horse because he has to find the correct response by trial and error and this may lead to unnecessary tension.

'Lazy' horses do not react at all to this tapping on the ribs. It takes an association between a light leg aid and a tap from the whip or spur pressure to teach such a horse to react appropriately. The whole point of dressage is to ride in harmony, with invisible aids. A light squeeze of the calf on the horse's sides should therefore elicit an immediate forward step, and light squeezing of the reins should elicit an immediate yielding of the head.

'The horse steps away from leg pressure to nerve fibres on his ribs'

The notion that the horse steps away as a reaction to leg pressure on the 'bundle of nerve fibres' on his ribs is linked to the same principle as the previous misconception. When a horse steps sideways away from the leg pressure he does so as a reaction to the disturbance of his balance or to move away from the discomfort. This is not a spinal cord reflex nor is it from pressure on nerve ganglia. Sensitive horses, such as some Thoroughbreds, may well be ticklish in the area because of the superficial nerves and thus move away from pressure on the ribs in front of the girth. This, however, is of little use to the rider, whose legs do not reach this spot.

As with leg pressure that signals 'forward', young horses have to be taught to move off this leg pressure; they do not do so automatically. It is taught either by strong leg pressure pushing against the horse's ribs or by light pressure reinforced with light tapping of the whip. It can also be taught from the ground by pushing the quarters over with the hands or knuckles behind the centre of gravity. The young horse usually resists this pressure before yielding to it. The pressure from the leg has to be behind the horse's centre of gravity to disturb the balance of his hindquarters and make them step to the side.

'The horse pivots around the rider's inside leg'

This is another teaching metaphor turned into 'fact'. An animal can only pivot around a fixed object. The rider moves with the horse at all times: the rider's leg is not fixed to the ground, therefore the horse cannot pivot around it. The fact is that the rider pushes the horse's ribcage to the side to tilt it and this creates the optical illusion of bend.

'The horse has to lift his back to bring his hind legs under'

There seems to be a misconception that the horse has to lift his back to create a space underneath his body to bring his hind legs underneath him. The horse has enough space underneath his body to engage his hind legs no matter whether his back is lifted or not. Proper engagement of his hindquarters is, however, not possible when the horse is contracting his back extensor muscles and thus hollowing. A round frame, on the other hand, encourages the flexor pattern with abdominal contraction and hip flexion (engagement) and the resultant lifting and rounding of the back (the flexor pattern). The rider then activates the horse's hind legs to become more engaged (usually through transitions and half-halts).

When the head and neck stretch down, the hind legs have to move underneath to move the centre of gravity backwards. This is an automatic balance reaction. The horse does not initiate the movement from his ribcage, but from his head and neck. The horse's back can be rounded by initiating the flexor pattern from the hindquarters, but if there is no restriction on the head and neck, or there are no half-halts, the horse will simply move forwards faster. The abdominal reflex and the hip flexion reflex round his back, but not necessarily his neck – and these reflexes are not possible to elicit from the mounted position. Even tapping the horse under the abdomen is of limited value to the mounted rider: it only serves to confuse the horse.

Misconceptions about engagement

The need to 'engage the inside hind leg'

There is a common belief that the horse must 'engage his inside hind leg', especially at the canter. When the horse 'falls in' on his 'stiff' side, it is said that he is not engaging his inside hind leg. The fact, however, is that the horse is avoiding weight-bearing or engaging sufficiently, on his *outside* hind leg. He thus pushes his weight over to his inside hind leg and this pushes the hindquarters in. When ridden correctly, horses weight the outside legs when they have an inside bend. It is thus the outside hind leg which has to engage sufficiently.

Photo 7.3a. The hip flexion reflex. Note how the rounded or 'lifted' back does not round the horse's head and neck.

Photo 7.3b. The abdominal reflex lifts/rounds the horse's back, but does not round the horse's head and neck.

EXERCISE

Get down on your hands and knees. Bend your waist to the side. Notice how your weight moves to the opposite side.

This same biomechanical principle applies to the horse's lateral bend. When the horse pushes his weight to his inside legs he will lose the inside bend.

Horses, like humans, tend to be stronger on the dominant side of their bodies. They consequently tend to use the stronger side muscles more regularly. If you observe carefully you will notice that the horse loses the inside bend in every upward and downward transition on the non-dominant (stiff) rein. This is because he uses the dominant side muscles to initiate these transitions (see exercises, Chapter 10.)

Misconceptions about bending and circling

'The horse must bend evenly around the circumference of a circle from head to tail'

Research has now shown that the fairly rigid spine of the horse cannot bend to follow the curve of a circle or a turn. Although there is some ability to bend laterally, it is only at the end range that it can take any effect (see Figure 2.5a, page 43). This means that unless the horse 'bites his butt' (end range of movement), lateral movement in the spine will be insignificant. Therefore requesting a slight bend around the curve or the circle will not bend the spine from the thorax to the tail. Instead, the horse tilts his ribcage, which gives an impression of bend.

'The trotting horse takes shorter steps with his inside legs on a circle'

The commonly held theory that the horse trots on a circle by taking shorter steps with his inside legs is an over-simplification which may be based on comparing the quadruped horse with the biped human. The bio-mechanical process is complex in the quadruped because of the automatic diagonal trot pattern of movement combined with the fact that the horse's spine does not bend evenly round the circumference of the circle. It does not seem possible for the horse to take shorter steps with his inside legs because the inside foreleg is coordinated in trot with the outside hind leg, which would thus also have to take a shorter step. This would defeat the object and destroy the purity of the gait: if both inside fore and hind legs took shorter steps, the horse would lose the trot sequence. (See Circles and Turns in Chapter 11 for a full explanation of this concept.)

Misconceptions about balance

'The horse is on the forehand when long and low'

There is still a mistaken belief among some people that the horse is markedly on his forehand when in the long and low or low and round frame. As soon as the horse stretches his head and neck low and round, his centre of gravity moves forwards and more weight moves onto his forelimbs. He thus has to make a balance adjustment to push his weight backwards.

He has one of two options. When he allows his centre of gravity to move forwards he will lose balance, take a firmer contact or hang on the rider's hands and run with shortened steps. Alternatively, he moves his centre of gravity back in an automatic balance reaction, by moving his hindquarters more underneath his body. Thus the contact will become light and he becomes more engaged. Light contact is an indication of balanced weight distribution.

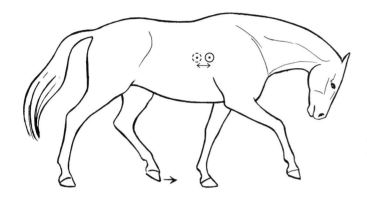

Figure 7.5. The forward and low head and neck position automatically moves the centre of gravity forward. The hindquarters moving more underneath the body, in a balance reaction, moves the centre of gravity back again.

'The rider's movements and position have a major effect on the horse's balance and performance'

Contrary to popular belief, mild changes in the position of our weight and posture do not seem to have a major effect on the horse's ability to perform dressage or jump small fences. The many explanations for this are given in Chapter 9.

'The horse will go on his forehand when the rider's seat is out of the saddle'

There exists a very common and mistaken belief that the horse will go on his forehand when the rider's seat is out of the saddle or when the rider leans forwards. If riding were this simple there would be no horses on their forehands. All riders would simply sit upright and their horses would, miraculously, be engaged. The truth is that it is very difficult to bring a horse *off* the forehand if you do not have your seat in the saddle. Without the seat in the saddle, the rider cannot use body and leg muscles effectively to encourage the horse to engage his hindquarters. Most of the show-jumping and cross-country horses however, are well engaged, yet their riders all ride in a half seat. See also Chapter 9.

General misconceptions

'It's the horse's fault'

The most common of all misconceptions is that riders are convinced that they are riding and communicating correctly and that the fault is with the horse. We often hear the phrases, 'but he knows what to do' or 'the horse is strong' or 'he rushes the fence', etc. The fact is that the horse does not know unless we explain clearly with single messages. The horse is only strong or rushes because the rider has not taught him to be light and responsive.

I explained to an experienced rider that all unbacked horses have soft mouths and her reply to me was that she backed a horse who had a mouth problem from the onset. What she was trying to say was that her hands are perfect and that the fault lay with the young horse who had never had a bit in his mouth!

Every 'problem' horse I have ever encountered either received double messages from the rider or had some sub-clinical lameness or other.

'The horse performs all the dressage movements in nature'

This is another common misconception. The fact is, that although he does many of the dressage movements in nature, he does them in a totally different fashion from under saddle. Chapters 10 and 11 elucidate how the horse does these movements in nature as compared to the dressage and jump trained horse and give detailed analysis of how the horse functions biomechanically.

'The horse was not created to be ridden'

This is often said and yet, of all the animals, this is the one almost perfectly suited for the job, for the following reasons.

1. The horse's spine is fairly rigid and has extra protection through the very strong ligaments surrounding it in all directions. This creates an excellent weight-bearing surface. Compare this to riding a cheetah with its extremely flexible back.

2. The presence of the solid and large ribcage adds strength to carry an average sized rider.

3. The horse's spine is almost horizontal which facilitates the rider's balance. Imagine riding a giraffe, with its sloping back.

4. The shape of the spine is perfectly suited to fit a comfortable saddle secured by only one strap.

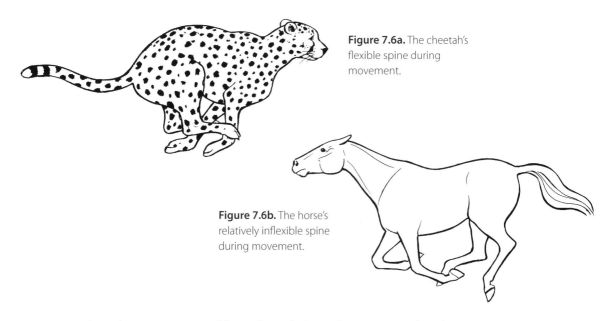

Figure 7.6a. The cheetah's flexible spine during movement.

Figure 7.6b. The horse's relatively inflexible spine during movement.

5. Horses have long, manoeuvrable necks to help with steering and with balance to assist smooth transitions between the gaits.

6. They have superb shock absorption attributes (long pasterns, flexible fetlocks, 'springs' attaching the legs to the ribcage and more, which leads to more comfort for the rider.

7. They have a long and substantial mane for us to grab when in danger of falling!

8. Their teeth are spaced favourably for accepting a bit.

9. Their biomechanical reactions make them very manoeuvrable for the rider.

10. Their tractable temperament makes them submissive enough to be ridden.

11. Horses have developed extreme sensitivity to outside stimuli as a consequence of their limited ability for defence. This sensitivity is the rider's key to invisible aids.

12. They are equipped with an amazing memory which makes them very trainable.

Horses often break down because humans do not condition them appropriately for the expected tasks and uses, not because they are unsuited to the job.

8

Trends, Fads and Gadgets

Many trends, fads and gadgets have appeared and disappeared through the ages, all to enable the less-than-perfect rider to control the less-than-perfect horse. Only the very straightforward and logical methods have shown the 'lasting value' associated with classicism.

New fads and gadgets still appear at regular intervals. Some high-profile rider finds a 'trick' to improve a small, idiosyncratic error in their horse's training: other riders notice the success of the method (no matter that the horse and rider were successful before the 'trick') and many copy it blindly without understanding what biomechanical effect it has on the horse. They often do not copy the method correctly, appropriately (as the originator had intended) or with the all-important feel of the originator. They use it as an attempted panacea for all problems. This often leads to failure and to the mental and physical anguish of horses involved. A recent example of this is the 'deep and round' (hyperflexion) method fashioned by some leading riders. Although, no doubt, the originators were under the impression that they had solid reasons for employing this form of riding, many other have followed blindly, causing great discomfort to their horses. Riders tend to think too much about what to do (mechanics) rather than about what they want the horse to do, i.e. how to communicate in a way the horse can understand (biomechanics).

Bits

A great variety of bits have appeared and disappeared according to the 'fashion' of the time. Some were extremely cruel, others horse-friendly, but most of these bits were designed especially to be more effective in stopping the horse, not for the comfort of the horse. Yet the simple and effective snaffle has been around for millennia. At least twenty-two centuries ago the Chinese were already using a simple snaffle bit (not dissimilar to the modern snaffle) in their horses' mouths.

The linked snaffle bit has withstood the test of time because it remains one of the most comfortable bits for the horse. The link in the centre allows space for the horse's tongue. The width of the jawbone prevents the link of the snaffle from touching the horse's palate, provided it is the correct size for the horse's mouth. However, when a horse has a low palate combined with a narrow jaw, the link presses against the palate. Some of the new fashionable bits rest on the horse's tongue and this can lead to the tongue-thrust reflex. The ideal shape would not put undue pressure on the horse's tongue or on the palate. The centre piece in the double link snaffle should have a small diameter so as not to cause the tongue-thrust reflex.

The modern trend is towards bitless bridles, the soft hackamore and pressure halters. These are certainly kinder to the horse than the unpalatable

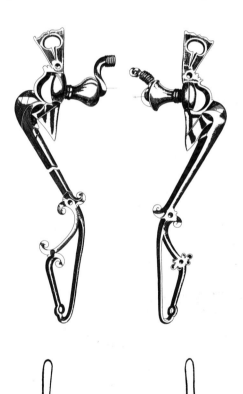

Figure 8.1a. *left* Branches of 'unfriendly' bits used during the sixteenth and seventeenth centuries.

Figure 8.1b. *below left* Drawing based on the type of snaffle bit buried with the terracotta horses in Xiang, China *c.* 210 BC.

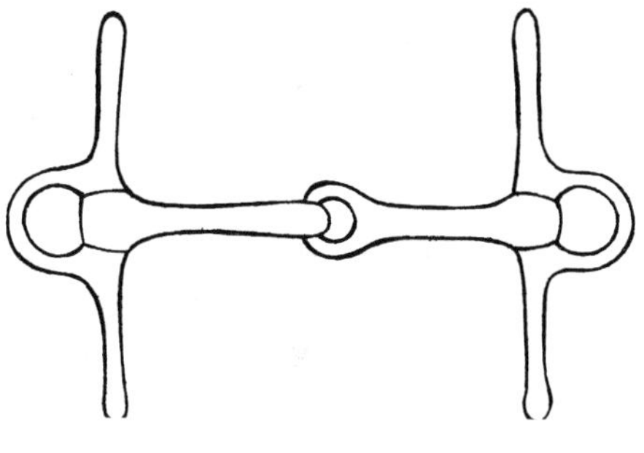

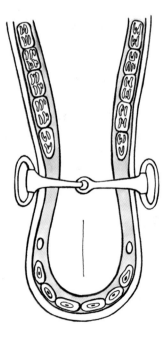

Figure 8.2. Provided the snaffle bit fits snuggly to the jaw, the link should not cause undue pressure on a normal palate.

metal bits we put in the horse's mouth. Ivory, bone or horn are more suitable for a horse's mouth in principle, but unfortunately bits in these materials are not available and might come with other inherent problems such as a tendency to shatter. Unfortunately, the perfect solution has not yet been found. Modern metal alloys seem to be a little more horse-friendly than steel, but further research is necessary to find the ideal solution.

The biomechanical effect of the bit in the horse's mouth

The effect of the bit in the horse's mouth is based on the fact that the horse will do almost anything to alleviate even light pressure. The rider moves the bit by squeezing the rein. The horse then yields to the discomfort of a hard metal object in his mouth by moving his head and neck in the direction of the pressure. If the pressure is not released by the rider's instant yielding to the horse's reaction, the horse will try a different method of relieving the pressure. He will usually pull on the bit in an opposite direction in an attempt to pull it away from the rider's hands. If the rider does not yield and the pressure continues despite the horse's pulling, the horse will simply pull harder. A tug of war ensues between the rider pulling and the horse pulling harder because he is stronger. If the horse is successful in making the rider yield even once only, he has been rewarded for pulling and will then try harder the next time. The stage is now set for the horse to develop a 'hard' mouth. If riders adhere to the principle of pressure – horse yields – release of pressure, then every horse will have a soft and responsive mouth. Unfortunately, most riders do not realize that they are not releasing the pressure in a timely fashion, or completely, or that they reward the horse with ill-timed release of the pressure when he pulls.

Photo 8.1. A twentieth-century bit. The loose rings inside the horse's mouth would encourage even more movement of the tongue. (Compare this with the movement a tongue stud produces in the human mouth; the wearer's tongue never stops fiddling with it.)

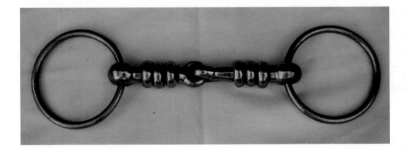

Spurs and Whips

Many varieties of spurs have come and gone; some extremely long, others very sharp. It is the same with whips – cruel whips, long whips, noisy whips and whips with metal tips: each of these has had its day. An extreme example was the *gaule armé* which Federico Grisone used – a long stick with a sharp spur at its end. Fortunately, such extremes are rare nowadays, but it is still important to know how to use spurs and whip in an effective and ethical way.

The biomechanical effect of the spur

As with the bit, the same principle of the horse's inclination to do almost anything to avoid pressure applies to the effect of spurs. The correct way of using spurs is as follows. The rider should give a light aid with the legs. If the horse does not yield instantly to this light aid, it should be followed immediately with effective spur pressure (not tapping, but constant pressure until the horse reacts.) The instant the horse reacts to this pressure, it must be released. Within four repetitions of this light leg pressure-release followed by spur pressure and instant release when the horse reacts, the horse will yield instantly to only the light pressure from the rider's legs. The horse learns the preamble to the spur pressure and learns that the spur pressure will be withheld if he reacts instantly to light leg pressure. Spur pressure alone and constant tapping with the spurs does not teach the horse to react instantly to light aids. Therefore, such methods should only be incorporated to solve idiosyncratic problems in training.

The biomechanical effect of the whip

The same principle of the horse's reaction to other pressure should apply to the use of the whip. The rider uses a light leg aid and if the horse does not react to this light pressure it should be followed immediately with a tap of the whip. After four repetitions, the horse will react to light leg pressure alone. The rider has to decide how light and invisible the leg aids should be. The light pressure, followed by spur pressure or a tap with the whip, will lead to light and invisible aids. Punishing the horse with the whip is unacceptable because horses cannot understand this concept. It leads to fright/flight behaviour.

Nosebands

A variety of nosebands to compel the horse to close his mouth, have seen their day. New and tighter nosebands are still being produced, but the horse only opens his mouth or protrudes his tongue in his attempt to avoid discomfort. If the rider learns to ride effectively with a soft and elastic contact, the need for a noseband will disappear. A noseband is quite unnecessary in riding, as evidenced in Western riding.

The biomechanical effect of the noseband

When the horse opens his mouth he brings his lower jaw closer to the rider's hands in an attempt to relieve the pressure. When we force the horse's mouth shut with a tight noseband, we only remove the symptom of the problem. The horse then has no alternative but to bring his head closer to the rider's hands in an attempt to avoid the discomfort on the bars of his lower jaw. This does not take away the cause of the problem. The cause of the open mouth or protruding tongue should be investigated. The horse may have a tooth, tongue or palate problem. The biggest problem is however, the rider's pulling or hanging hands. If the rider does not release the pulling pressure, the problem will continue.

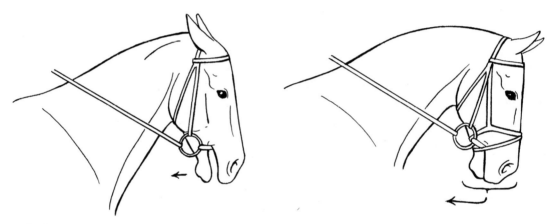

Figure 8.3 The horse opens his mouth to relieve the pressure on the lower jaw (*left*); the closed jaw 'forces' the upper jaw to move closer to the pressure together with the lower jaw (*right*).

Auxiliary Lungeing Equipment

A variety of devices intended to 'encourage' the horse to engage his hindquarters have been in fashion over the years. These include the De Gogue, the Chambon, standard side reins, German side reins and the new Pessoa system of ropes and pulleys, amongst others. Most of these, except for rubber bands, work on the pressure-reward-release system of learning.

A recent study by Biau et al comparing three types of lungeing 'aid' (rubber bands, the Chambon and the 'Back lift') showed that only the Chambon had any effect on the horse's hind limbs at the walk and trot and this was quite modest.[1] All three devices in the study produced 'increased forelimb activity'. This was probably the result of a balance reaction to

---

1 S. Biau, O. Couve, S. Lemaire and E. Barrey, 'The effects of reins on kinetic variables of locomotion' (proceedings of the Sixth International Conference on Equine Exercise Physiology, 2002).

the restriction placed on the horses' necks. They therefore moved their forelimbs faster to maintain balance. When working in the Chambon, however, the horse is able to use his head and neck to move his centre of gravity with little resistance.

Side reins

These work on the pressure-reward-release system of learning. The horse yields to the constant pressure of the side reins, which automatically yield the instant the horse yields. The pressure is thus relieved. Riders' hands do not yield as instantly as do side reins. Horses eventually find their balance in side reins by bringing their hindquarters more underneath them, provided they are not pushed forwards too vigorously.

Running reins

These are the most common gadgets which riders use. They have been in use since the Duke of Newcastle invented them about 350 years ago. Newcastle, however, used them on the cavesson. Unfortunately, they are used incorrectly most of the time today to 'pull in' the horse's head and this is highly detrimental to the horse. *No rein or other auxiliary equipment should be used to pull the horse's head down or to maintain it in this position by force.*

The correct biomechanical action of running reins

Running reins should only be used to explain to the horse that he should use his own muscles to maintain the correct head and neck position, otherwise the exercise will have the opposite effect. Used incorrectly, they will lead to contraction of the neck extensor muscles against the pull of the running reins. When the rider releases the reins in this case, the horse will hollow his neck immediately and thus the exercise will be futile.

When it is used correctly, the reins will *hang* loose most of the time and only become active momentarily if the horse lifts his head too high. The horse should be given regular stretches when riding in this round position.

'Rubber bands'

The 'rubber band' stretches from the girth, through the bit rings and over the poll. It is supposed to help the horse to 'come on the bit'. This is one of the most ineffective gadgets of all. It teaches the horse nothing and does not even encourage a correct frame. It only lulls the ignorant rider into a false belief that the contact is correct.

Photo 8.2a. The incorrect use of running reins. Running reins should only be used to explain to the horse that he should use his own muscles to maintain the correct head and neck position. The incorrect tight use of the running reins will have the opposite effect.

Photo 8.2b. The correct (loose) use of the running reins will teach the horse to yield to pressure because the pressure is released.

The biomechanical action of the 'rubber band'

The horse cannot yield to this elastic pressure because it is always inconsistent. Also, when the horse does attempt to yield to it, the pressure cannot release completely. The horse's top line muscles, the extensors, thus work constantly against the elastic pull, which reinforces the extensor pattern. As soon as the rubber band is removed, the horse will lift his head again.

Rein Effects

'Sawing' hands

The habit of mindless left-right 'sawing' in the horse's mouth at every stride developed during the 1970s. Horses reacted by moving their heads from side to side, instead of yielding because many riders did not understand the concept of yielding to pressure. This left-right swinging of the horse's head is a sure sign that the horse has not yielded to the rider's hands/bit.

The biomechanical action of constant left-right 'sawing'

The rider pulls the horse's head to the right, but the horse does not yield, therefore his head springs back to mid position immediately the rider releases the rein. The rider then pulls the head to the left, but if the horse does not yield to this his head will spring right back to mid position again as soon as the rider releases the rein. The process is repeated with little success even though the horse has not yielded to the pressure. The horse certainly does not understand that he should yield to the pressure and for the rider it is a case of 'do what you always do; get what you always get' – no yielding.

For any action of this sort to be successful, the horse has to understand that he should yield to pressure and this should be followed by instant release of the rein pressure. It is essential that the horse yields to the pressure before the rider releases the rein or his mouth will simply become less sensitive. However, riders who adopt this approach usually yield at the incorrect moment thereby rewarding the horse for non-yielding. They often also hold on after the horse has yielded, which simply encourages the horse to pull more.

Strong outside rein contact

The 1990s brought the 'strong outside rein contact'. This led to the 'false bend' with the resultant rigid contact, which is still prevalent in the riding of today. This false bend is also described by Gustav Steinbrecht in the nineteenth century.[2]

The biomechanics of a strong outside contact

This strong outside contact developed from the concept of riding the horse 'from the inside leg to the outside rein'. Good riders realized that this

---

2 G. Steinbrecht, *The Gymnasium of the Horse*, (Ohio, Xenophon Press (tr. H.K. Buckle) 1995).

inside bend led to a positive contact on the outside rein. Because of the innate crookedness of the horse, he gives a positive contact when ridden in one direction, but not to the opposite direction. This means that the real bend is not sufficient on the 'stiff' side. Instead of suppling the horse and asking him to bend correctly, riders started to 'take a stronger contact' on the loose outside rein to 'force' the horse to pull away and 'take the bit'. The loose feel on the outside rein has nothing to do with the horse's so-called refusal to 'take the bit', but all to do with his difficulty in bending his neck to the opposite side. Bending to the inside automatically gives a positive contact on the outside rein. When the 'take and give' on the inside rein is not effective, the rider is usually not using enough inside leg pressure to tilt the ribcage and the horse does not yield to the 'take and give' on the inside rein. Contact should never be consistently strong.

The concept of equal contact in both reins

This concept seems to be widely misunderstood. This is necessary in showjumping when riding straight towards the fence only, and for hacking when riding on a straight path. It is counterproductive in a dressage arena wherever the horse should be slightly bent in 'position' to prevent loss of balance. The horse is, however, on equal contact when riding down the centre line to halt and across the diagonal in medium and extended trot.

In all movements requiring a bend, the contact on the inside will be softer if the horse is ridden correctly and using his own muscles to turn (see Chapter 4 'Riding from the inside leg to the outside rein').

The *quality* of the contact should, however, be equal *on* both reins. That is to say, the quality of the contact on the outside rein should be the same no matter whether riding to the left or to the right and the soft quality on the inside rein should be the same when riding in both directions. In other words, ideally and as a result of correct suppling work, the horse should not have a stiff side.

Counter-bend

In the exercise of counter-bend or counter-flexion in trot, the horse moves on a straight line or circle with his neck bent to the outside (of the arena/circle). The exercise seems to be used to convince the horse to take contact on the outside rein.

The counter-bend of the horse's neck in canter and counter-canter are, however, good suppling and balancing exercises and are of great value for the preparation for flying changes. Such counter-bending teaches the horse to balance with ease no matter where his head and neck are.

The biomechanics of counter-bend or counter-flexion

By taking a stronger contact on the outside rein the horse can be encouraged to move more weight to his outside shoulder and leg. However, this is the result only if it is done correctly and the horse understands what the rider wants. Unfortunately, the horse will usually bend his head to the outside without moving his weight as well and this defeats the purpose and leads to the false bend. In dressage we want an inside bend. If, instead of taking a stronger contact, the rider rather *opens* the outside rein and taps the horse on his inside shoulder, he will immediately move his weight onto his outside shoulder. If this is done together with 'take and give' on the inside rein, the horse will bend to the inside and automatically place more weight on his outside foreleg. Outside flexion is thus not necessary.

Rein releases in jumping

These have now gone the full circle. During the 1970s, riders moved their arms forwards towards the horse's mouth to give the horse freedom to stretch his head and neck to bascule. The 1980s brought the crest release and the half-crest release. The 1990s brought the non-yielding hands, with riders keeping their hands on the horse's withers. The poor animals could not stretch their necks forwards adequately, but tried as best they could. The latter two methods were only an excuse for the rider to lean on the horse's neck for balance. Today, it seems that there is a movement back to

Photo 8.3. The logical rein release, yielding towards the bit. (The rider however has not maintained her centre of gravity over her base of support. That is why her legs have moved back.)

the arms yielding towards the horse's mouth. Hopefully this logical method will gain momentum. The horse needs his neck for balance, to gain the correct height, to bascule over the fence, to land after the fence and to regain balance for the fast move off towards the next fence. This, he can only do if he has freedom of his neck.

'Deep and round' (hyperflexion)

The 'deep and round' method of riding, which is in extensive use today, has been proved to be detrimental to the horse's physical and mental well-being. All studies have shown significant differences in horses' movement and back mobility between this position and the horse's natural position. Significant changes to nature usually lead to more friction and consequent injury. We can only hope that riders will soon 'see the light' and send this method of riding to the trash bin where it belongs.

The biomechanics of 'deep and round'

The horse is usually asked, with running reins, to flex his neck so that his chin is a few centimetres away from his chest. This position is neither physically nor psychologically advantageous to the horse, and the ethics of using it are highly questionable. It removes all the horse's defence mechanisms. His neck is immobilized and thus useless for balance purposes. He cannot see anything but the ground beneath him, his own legs and the ground at his sides. He is actually looking at the world upside down, as a rider would when standing on their head. No wonder the poor horse becomes totally submissive.

This position can cause muscle and ligament strain, pressure on the nerve roots, constriction in the blood vessels, intervertebral disc pressure, nuchal ligament strain and constriction of the horse's air supply. Although recent research has shown that this position increases back mobility, this does not mean that this abnormal mobility is good for the horse's spine. The horse's rigid spine is important to support his heavy viscera and it is what makes him so rideable. Loosening the spinal ligaments can have a devastating effect on his spinal stability and cause serious problems. More humane methods to improve athleticism are available to all riders.

EXERCISE

Take 10 minutes of your time to get into a kneeling position and crawl around with your chin stuck to your chest. After doing this, it is very doubtful that you will ever ride in the 'deep and round' position.

Photo 8.4. The inhumane and unethical deep and round method of riding.

If the horse is ridden correctly and the rider's requirements are explained to him in a manner that he can understand, he will be light in hand and engaged in his hindquarters. All new trends and gadgets should be tested through logical biomechanical analysis before riders follow them blindly. Ideally, they should not be used at all.

9

The Biomechanical Effects of the Rider's Movement on the Horse

In this chapter we will investigate whether the relatively small adjustments a rider makes have a practical effect on the horse's balance and coordination. These are the associated movements which riders make in order to learn the coordination necessary to manoeuvre the horse. Invisible aids are dependent on superior motor coordination skills as well as superior balance. It can take years for riders to fine-tune their coordination and balancing abilities into these independent coordinated movements.

We know that the rider has a profound effect on the horse's balance and movements – his performance. In order to solve riding problems it is important to investigate whether training difficulties are caused by the rider's basic weight displacement and position or by the rider's actual use of the body and general lack of effectiveness. Only with correct diagnosis can problems be solved.

The Horse's Responses to Initial Backing

There is no doubt that when a young horse is backed, he has to adapt to the object on his back. The rider represents two entities:

1. The sensation and weight of the physical object.

2. The commander on his back, which he has to *understand* and obey.

Horses become accustomed extremely quickly to the weight of the rider. They have exquisite balance and feel and adapt automatically to the rider within the first ride even though their kinematics change. It then becomes 'normal' for a horse to carry a rider. The rider's weight then does not surprise him, upset him, cause him discomfort or interfere with his adjustments of balance unless the rider is too heavy for the horse. (The rider/horse weight ratio affects the horse's back.)

If backed progressively, the horse will adapt his balance automatically to each new gait in a few minutes because he has excellent balancing mechanisms. Newly backed young horses may lose freedom of movement initially, but the movement always returns and improves through schooling, provided it is not the rider blocking the movement. Many horses, however, do not lose much freedom of movement.

There are many variables, apart from the rider's actual weight, involved in this transitory loss of movement. These include the growth spurts when the hindquarters become higher than the withers, the effect of the girth pressure on the sternum, actions of the rider's arms and body which may block forward movement, contradictory messages from the rider and moving in an enclosed or circular area. Horses do not move repeatedly in 20 m circles in nature – see Circles and Turns in Chapter 11. The fact that the movement returns means that the horse has adapted to any of the above factors and has strengthened his previously unconditioned muscles.

The Biomechanics of Adaptation to the Rider's Weight

Once the horse has developed his muscle power and balance and regained his movement, he will automatically adapt to the small weight changes of a rider and not simply lose balance each time the rider's body moves out of alignment with his centre of gravity. Side-saddle riding and riders with disabilities are evidence of this.

Various research studies have shown that kinematics change when horses carry a rider, but does this happen in response to small changes in the rider's position? The rider's weight on the horse's back produces a lower average peak vertical ground reaction force in both fore and hind legs. This means that there is less upward acceleration of the horse's body because of the rider's added weight.[1] Trained horses show more tarsal and fetlock extension of the hind limbs, while horses at pasture show more carpal and fetlock extension in the forelimbs.[2] Other studies have shown that weight moves onto the horse's forehand to adapt to the rider's weight, but moves to his hind limbs when he lifts his neck high.[3] These studies thus

---

1 W. Back, 'Intra-limb coordination: the forelimb and the hind limb', in W. Back and H.M. Clayton, *Equine Locomotion* (London, Harcourt Publishers, 2001).

2 Ibid.

3 M.A. Weishaupt, et al, (research paper presented at the 7th International Conference on Equine Exercise Physiology, Fontainebleau, 2006).

show that both correct training and the horse's balance reaction of lifting his forehand, moves more weight to the horse's hindquarters.

The weight of the rider may put more weight on the horse's shoulders, but if the rein contact is light enough, the horse simply adjusts his neck position to re-establish equilibrium. If the seat of the saddle is perfectly in line with the horse's centre of gravity, the rider's weight will be equallydistributed over the horse's limbs.

Two separate beings, each with their own balance reactions, are involved in the rider/horse partnership and, although they form a unit, it would be useful to look at them individually.

The rider's balance reactions

The Law of Active Balance is simple. The body is arranged in a movable schema around the centre of gravity. As soon as one part moves, another part will automatically rearrange itself around the centre of gravity so that the body always stays in balance. Thus the rider's own balance is maintained around the body's centre of gravity no matter how the rider sits. The rider does not have to think about this consciously (unless, as a consequence of some outside force, balance is lost to the extent that the rider starts to fall). For example, when a rider moves both shoulders forward slightly, this will automatically place the legs and feet further forward and push the hips further back (unless the rider is gripping with the legs or tightening the back muscles as a learned reaction from many years of being told to keep the lower leg back). The pure automatic response will negate the need for the horse to adapt, because there has in effect, been no weight change on his back. When one part of the rider leans to one side, overall body schema will ensure that other body parts move to the opposite side.

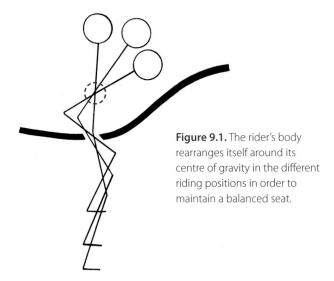

Figure 9.1. The rider's body rearranges itself around its centre of gravity in the different riding positions in order to maintain a balanced seat.

EXERCISES

1. When next mounted, lean over to one side, but do not bend in the waist or push your hips to the opposite side. Notice the discomfort and the tension in the muscles on your other side.

2. Lean over to the side but, this time, push your hips to the opposite side and bend your waist laterally. This second position is more comfortable than the first and is the body's natural balance reaction. The weight distribution on the horse does not change.

3. Turn your head and upper body from the waist, to the side. This position does not affect the horse's centre of gravity because you are turning around your axis. Therefore, looking to the side should not affect the horse's balance whatsoever.

The horse's balance reactions

Jean Saint-Fort Paillard had the following to say about the horse's balance adaptation: 'It is completely untrue to claim that the rider's weight unbalances the horse to any considerable degree. It entails only a very slight modification of its natural equilibrium. A very slight change of posture thus permits the horse to re-establish it completely'.[4] The horse's superior balance mechanisms and great stability allows him to adapt with great ease to the rider's movement.

1. The horse has four legs, one at each 'corner', similar to a table. This is an extremely stable base of support. To disturb a four-legged base one would have to place all of one's weight on the edge, and only when the weight moved beyond the table leg, would the table topple. Thus it would be difficult for a rider to unbalance a horse while sitting inside the perimeter of his base of support. Thus, also, the horse's ability to carry weight cannot be compared to the bipedal support base of a person.

2. The horse's four-legged support stands over a large rectangular base. Since his base is rectangular, leaning forward and back over this base will have little significant effect on the horse's balance mechanism. An erroneous comparison is often made between a horse (a heavy quadruped) carrying a light rider on his back and a bipedal human carrying a person of similar weight on their shoulders.

---

4 J. S-F. Paillard, *Understanding Equitation* (New York, Doubleday, 1974).

3. Horses are very heavy, and this gives them great stability. A very heavy table will not topple even when you stand on the edges beyond the base of support.

The horse's reactions to the rider

Weight-bearing capability

If we assume incorrectly that the position and weight distribution of the rider alone has a major effect on the horse's balance mechanism, we will never be able to correct the real problem. As Sea Biscuit's jockey said after he was questioned about the effect of his weight on the horse, 'The horse weighs 1,800 lb [816 kg], I'm just an afterthought.' In handicaps, the highest-weighted (best) horses still win sometimes and, even when they don't, they still move only fractionally slower than their lighter-weighted rivals. Steffan Peters says, 'I weigh 150 lb [68 kg] and my horse weighs nearly 1,800 lb [816 kg], so I don't think that I gain much by pushing with my seat.[5] The average rider weighs between 55 kg and 80 kg (120–176 lb), the average horse between 500 kg and 600 kg (1,100–1,320 lb). That makes the rider's weight roughly 10% of the horse's. In terms of carrying capacity, this is negligible. A 75 kg (165 lb) mountaineer carries a pack of approximately 25 kg (55 lb) – or 33% of his weight – on only two legs. A good comparison is the ability of a mother to carry a three-month old baby on her back. The modern trend is to ride ever-larger horses so that the rider to horse ratio becomes even smaller.

EXPERIMENT

Kneel on all fours and place a six-month old baby on your back between your shoulder blades. A six-month old baby has some back control, but his mother will have to support him a little. Move in all directions and feel the effect of this weight. The baby will not, however, be able to move with you as a rider does on a horse. Ask the baby's mother to move the baby's upper body and note the effect (or lack of it).

Response to changes in weight distribution

Proof of the horse's ability to maintain rhythm and balance despite weight changes on his back can be seen when the Cossack riders circumnavigate the horse without visible loss of rhythm or balance to the animal. When

---

5 Peters, Steffan, *Dressage Today*, February 2002.

vaulters perform intricate manoeuvres while vaulting on and off the horse, the horse maintains the same rhythm and balance. Showjumping and event riders change from the half seat to the full seat without adversely affecting the horse's rhythm or balance. When small Thoroughbred horses are 'playing' polo with large riders 'throwing' their weight from side to side to reach the ball, the horses continue on a straight track. Note how a horse can stand like a rock while a rider mounts from the side. When a heavy rider mounts a little horse, the horse's back may drop, but it will lift again as he starts to move. (Of course, these days in equestrian sport, we are more likely to see small riders on big horses.)

Photo 9.1. *above* This big man's entire weight is in one stirrup, yet the horse shows no sign of balance disturbance.

Photo 9.2. *right* A small polo pony moving straight despite the very tall rider's weight being mostly to the right.

The horse's automatic balance reactions will lift his forehand to push the rider's weight backwards if the weight goes on his forehand or moves beyond his base of support. The effect of the rider's position is actually opposite to popular belief, but remains extremely small because of the rider/horse weight ratio. Let us apply Newton's Third Theory to this: every action has an equal but opposite reaction. Theoretically, then, if the rider leans forward, the horse feels the weight on his front fetlocks increase. He therefore lifts his neck or moves his hindquarters slightly more underneath his body and the equilibrium is re-established. This slight adaptation of the hindquarters and the insignificant amount of the rider's weight is not sufficient to trigger a reaction that actually engages the hindquarters or produces collection.

(According to this same theory, the horse will maintain perfect balance by moving to the opposite side of the added weight: when the rider leans left, the horse leans right and vice versa. However, even this often does not seem necessary because riders have to make their own redistribution of weight to remain in balance and the effect of any default in this process seems almost insignificant to the horse.)

In summary, when necessary, the horse adapts his body with an automatic balance reaction to the changes of weight and then simply continues in the direction of his intent.

EXPERIMENT

Get down on your hands and knees. Place a 6 kg [13 lb] object on your back between your shoulders. Notice how you push your shoulders up and your buttocks back slightly to rearrange your body schema. Thinking about it, however, inhibits the automatic reaction.

Rider expertise versus positioning

The rider's forward position may appear to affect the horse's balance, but recent research has shown that the regularity of the horse's movement is influenced by the expertise of the rider.[6] Thus effects on balance arise from the rider's technique and timing of the aids – that is to say they are dependent on the rider's *use* of the body and not simply where the body is placed.

For example, when a rider leans in a forward-sideways direction to see whether the horse is taking the correct canter lead, this position prevents correct use of the body. The rider cannot 'push' the horse's ribcage over to get the correct bend. The rider's arms, being forward, are wrongly

---

6 C.Y. Guezennec, et al, 'Analysis of horse-rider interaction by accelerometry' (research paper presented at the International Equine Exercise Physiology Conference, 2006).

Photo 9.3. When the rider falls on the horse's neck, the horse lifts his neck and pushes his centre of gravity back.

positioned to give a half-halt into the canter. The seat, not being in the saddle cannot give the correct weight aids. Thus an incorrect strike-off, or failure to strike-off, is caused by incorrect body use and not by a disturbance of the horse's balance. In this example, it is the rider's *lack of expertise* that seems to impact on the horse's locomotion more than the rider's *weight*. The horse's movement, however, affects the rider and this can have a knock-on effect. For example, a trot which affects the rider's balance will consequently affect the rider's use of body, which may result in signals that affect the horse.

The horse's centre of gravity and the rider's position

1. The horse is constructed to carry a significant amount of weight on his forehand and is comfortable in that position. His centre of gravity is closer to his shoulders than to his hind legs. Good riders move the horse's hindquarters underneath to engage. This moves the horse's centre of gravity backwards. Once the horse has moved his centre of gravity backwards to adjust to the rider's weight and the rider has

engaged the horse's hindquarters, small positional changes and movements of the rider will not disturb the horse's balance. The rider can move from sitting trot to a forward seat or to rising trot without affecting the horse's rhythm and balance.

2. The horse's centre of gravity moves continuously as his body schema changes while he is moving. The horse simply adds the rider and saddle to his body schema no matter where the rider sits. Thus they all form a unit.

3. Stability is good when both horse's and rider's gravity line correspond and dissect the horse's base of support. Since the rider's body maintains its own equilibrium, a deviation to one side is balanced by a deviation to the other side. Thus there will be no significant change in the gravity line. The rider's seat should be as close as possible to the horse's centre of gravity. Unfortunately, the positioning of saddles relative to the horse's centre of gravity varies and saddles do not necessarily place the rider exactly in alignment with the horse's centre of gravity (although the construction of modern saddles seems generally to assist in achieving closer alignment). The better the position of the saddle, the less adaptation the horse will need. The point, however, is that it is easy for the horse to deal with minor discrepancies – if the rider is not completely aligned with the horse's centre of gravity, small positional errors do not make too big a difference, except during half-pass, travers, renvers and pirouettes – see Chapter 11, page 240.

It is interesting that Native American riders, riding bareback, are in such harmony with their horses despite sitting further back than many other riders. When riding bareback, we sit further back simply because it is more comfortable to do so, yet the horse maintains his balance with ease. If the rider simply leaning forwards put the horse on his forehand, one would expect that the trend for saddle-fitting would be to place the saddle further back on the horse to ensure that this added weight would bring his hindquarters more underneath, but we know that this is not the case.

Effects of Intent and Motivation

The horse's intent and motivation play significant roles in the direction in which he moves. He is motivated by three main influences.

1. Food. When it is close to dinner time he starts to lose concentration and moves towards the food (stable).

2. Home (stable). When he moves in the direction of home he will walk

faster and take the straightest possible route.

3. The herd. When there are other horses close by he tends to 'lean' towards them or attempts to look in their direction.

When the horse is intent on moving towards these influences, no amount of weight changes will disturb him. The rider may lean over as far as possible, but unless control is exerted with the rider's hands and legs, the horse will continue to walk towards the stable, food or herd. It is the rider's expertise which prevents this.

When a showjumping horse is really intent on 'running out' at a fence, he will do so, even though all the rider's efforts and weight are employed to guide him towards it. How many riders have fallen off their horse while leaning to one side to encourage him to turn when he does not want to?

There is another key motivation for the horse, and this is avoiding discomfort (harsh 'aids'). Through repetition the horse learns to react and move away in order to avoid the discomfort of strong 'aids' or the whip and spurs.

Photo 9.4. The rider is leaning to the right, yet the horse continues straight.

EXPERIMENT

Do this experiment in a manège with an open entrance. Release your reins completely and ensure that your legs do not guide the horse at all. Lean over to one side, but ensure that your inside leg does not inadvertently place more pressure on the horse's side and that you have no effect on the reins. Note the horse's reaction. Lean over to the other side, being careful not to change your leg or hand positions, and note the horse's reaction. Your horse will either walk towards the gate, the stable or other horses. He will generally continue in the original direction for a few strides until he finds that he is in control. You will probably find that he moves in the same direction whichever side you lean towards.

Photo 9.5a. The rider is purposely leaning to the side, yet the horse continues straight on the centre line. Note that the loose reins have no effect on the horse's direction.

Photo 9.5b. The rider has 'collapsed' his waist on his left side, yet the horse continues moving on a straight line.

Effects of Learned Behaviour

Meaningful weight changes *do* affect the horse. He learns quickly which changes he should ignore (meaningless) and to which he should react (meaningful). He habituates easily to the meaningless changes which he has to ignore. He learns this by association and conditioning and by the rider's intent. Although the horse is good at picking up clues, these have to be meaningful and repeated correctly.

EXAMPLE

Should the rider ask the horse to turn left by the usual method and combine this with leaning to the left or left weight displacement, the horse will soon react to this left weight displacement. He will then turn left every time the rider leans left whether the other aids are given or not. When the rider does not 'teach' the horse by leaning left, the horse will not react to the leaning at all because he has not learnt it.

Meaningful and meaningless weight changes

It is from the first contact with the rider that the horse learns to differentiate between meaningful movements (weight changes) and meaningless movements. The meaningful weight changes become the aids. Meaningless weight changes are all the superfluous movements we do while we ride. We adjust our seat at the halt, we lean over to tighten the girth, shorten the stirrup leathers or check whether the horse has halted square, we blow our noses and do up our zips. We open and close gates. We even remove or add clothing. These weight changes have little effect on the horse's balance. Therefore the rider can lean forwards, backwards or sideways and the horse will not react unless it is meaningful to him. He learns to ignore the meaningless weight changes.

EXAMPLE

When the rider pushes the horse's ribcage or hindquarters over, the horse understand that he is to yield. If the rider leans over in the direction of the inside leg while pushing the horse's ribcage in the shoulder-in, the horse still knows what to do and ignores the 'leaning', but rather listens to the actual instruction. (Even so, this is not ideal from a training perspective.)

A slight weight change will thus not affect the direction of the movement unless it is meaningful to the horse. If horses were so obedient as to react immediately to every weight displacement, meaningless as well as

Photo 9.6. The rider purposely leaning over, but the horse continues with the shoulder-in.

Photo 9.6. The rider purposely leaning over, but the horse continues with the shoulder-in.

meaningful, we would have little control over them. If getting the horse off the forehand were as simple as leaning back, then there would be no horses on their forehands.

All riders have a weak and a strong side. Their aids are thus slightly different on each side of the horse. The horse learns that the aids on one side differ from the other, yet he responds appropriately to these slightly differing aids. The horse too has a weak and a strong side and this difficult side remains difficult whether it corresponds with the rider's weak or strong side.

Figure-ground perception

Figure-ground perception plays an important role in communicating with the horse. It is the ability to distinguish foreground objects, movements or noises from background objects, movement or noise. When we have a discussion with another person, their words are the foreground on which we concentrate. All other objects and sounds, such as barking dogs, become the background, which we learn to ignore. The horse learns to distinguish between the foreground movements/weight changes (the aids) on his back which become meaningful, and the meaningless background movements and weight changes such as adjusting stirrups and girth, sneezes, rein adjustments, etc. The latter he ignores.

▶ RIDING AND TEACHING APPLICATIONS

1. A newly backed horse should be allowed the freedom of his head and neck for a few weeks to help him adapt his natural balance to being ridden.

2. It is not the weight of the rider which affects the horse, but the interference and attempt at control of the horse, which impedes his balance reactions. Riders should search for the blocking effect in their bodies when the horse leans on the forehand or does not move forwards. We tend to stabilize ourselves by blocking movement in our bodies.

3. Certain situations prevent the rider from maintaining the perfect seat. When training young horses, when correcting a difficult problem and when learning a new technique, the rider's seat may be compromised, but this will not have a significant effect on the horse's balance. It is more important for the horse's well-being and understanding that the rider is effective when riding than it is to sit perfectly yet be ineffective. It is, however, important to aim towards sitting correctly for the 'finished' product and during competitions.

4. When weight changes are to be used as aids, the rider should ensure that the horse understands the meaning. These weight aids should then be repeated until the horse responds consistently.

5. The saddle dictates where the rider sits. Therefore it is important that the saddle seat corresponds with the horse's centre of gravity once the horse is engaged.

6. Able-bodied riders do not usually sit crooked. If the rider is crooked, check for scoliosis, a twisted, crooked, lopsided, uneven or sliding saddle or different length stirrup leathers.

7. Rising to the trot produces left/right asymmetry in the ground reaction forces. Therefore muscle development in the horse may become asymmetrical if the rider does not change the diagonal on a regular basis when rising to the trot. However, it makes little difference which diagonal the rider chooses as long as it is changed when changing the rein or at regular intervals when hacking out or during endurance rides.

▶ JUDGING SIGNIFICANCE

1. The rider's seat should be aesthetically correct for dressage, but it is more important that the horse understands the rider's aids and reacts appropriately and in harmony.

2. Leaning forwards is not aesthetically correct, but it does not place the horse significantly on his forehand as long as the rider's seat can be used effectively. (However, with the rear of the seat off the saddle, it is unlikely that the full range of effects will be available.)

3. An asymmetrical seat does not have a substantial affect on the horse. Many riders have some or other degree of scoliosis which gives them an asymmetrical seat, yet their horses learn to adapt. However, an asymmetrical seat is often caused by a crooked saddle and this could make it difficult for the rider to be effective.

4. It is more important to be effective when riding and to develop the horse's muscles correctly than it is to sit in a perfect position, yet be ineffective and give confusing messages to the horse. Misunderstanding causes tension, confusion and slow learning which are more detrimental than an insignificant weight change.

5. The marks for good seat/position should be separated from those for 'the correct use of aids', because a perfect seat does not necessarily correlate with effective riding. Yet, good positions should be rewarded.

10

The Gaits – Nature Versus Training

The analysis of equine movement has, historically, relied heavily on classicism and tradition. It is only since the development of photography that all the gait sequences have been correctly analysed. Recent development and research into equine biomechanics has now enabled us to draw comparisons between the kinematics of equine movement at pasture and the movement of trained horses.

Many studies have shown that training changes the natural movement of pastured horses. The swing duration increases with training while the stance duration decreases.[1] Good training seems to improve movement for riding purposes in the long run. Bad training, on the other hand, can stifle movement to the point of causing 'bridle lameness'. Correct training, through engagement of the hindquarters, shifts the horse's centre of gravity back, lightens the forehand and renders it more mobile. Research has shown that pastured horses carry more weight on their forelimbs while correctly trained horses move some weight to their hind limbs.[2] It is common that some horses lose their free movement at the beginning of their training and then regain it again later. Training also increases the development of 'positive advanced diagonal hoof placement' (see later this chapter).

Arguably, the major difference is that whereas the trained horse is expected to work in the flexor pattern, the horse at liberty moves predominantly in the extensor pattern. For example, the extensor pattern is

---

1 W. Back, 'Intra-limb coordination: the forelimb and the hind limb', in W. Back and H.M. Clayton, *Equine Locomotion* (London, Harcourt Publishers Ltd., 2001).

2 Ibid.

necessary for flight and the natural horse in flight mode needs his hindquarters behind him in order to propel with his gluteal muscles. He will also frequently need his head and neck in the neutral or hollow position for balance, control and visibility.

Many variables are involved when comparing pastured horses to ridden horses, the most important being the rider's type of contact, feel and timing. The majority of riders inadvertently block the horse's shoulders with less-than-perfect contact and thus interfere with the horse's balance. In addition to rein contact, the 'on the bit' position, freedom of the neck, leg effectiveness, balance and the effect of stabling and eating out of a manger all have an effect on the movement of the ridden horse. The stabling affects joint flexibility because the horse does not have to stretch his legs or his neck in order to graze. On the other hand, pastured horses do not, for example, necessarily maintain a constant rhythm while trotting to enable the tester to compare movement adequately. The many variables in these studies prohibit the ability to ascertain the exact cause of certain observed differences in movement.

Principles of Gait Analysis

The gaits of the horse are all automatic patterns of movement controlled by the central nervous system (CNS) in whole, coordinated patterns or systems. Neither man nor beast has to think consciously about moving, except when learning new complicated dance or gymnastic patterns. Movement is controlled by the central nervous system in whole coordinated patterns or systems. For the purpose of analysis however, the movements are dissected into individual parts.

Transitions between gaits are automatic and the one gait follows the other as the horse speeds up or slows down. 'Gait transitions are triggered when musculoskeletal forces reach a critical level.'[3] Dressage training removes this natural trigger when the horse learns a new coordination pattern, discarding the intermediate steps as, for example, trot to halt. In the natural downward transition there is little braking; the movement simply slows down until it 'triggers' the next gait. In dressage, the downward transitions have a larger braking deceleration,[4] therefore the horse's legs push harder against the ground to brake into the next gait. The transition period in the trained horses become longer, to allow smooth

---

3 E. Barrey and S. Biau, 'Locomotion of dressage horses' (paper presented at conference on Equine Sports Medicine and Science, 2002).

4 Ibid.

deceleration.[5] This ensures that the braking is not abrupt. The rider achieves this by giving half-halts until the horse is balanced sufficiently for a smooth downward transition

Knowledge of the sequence of each step of the horse's gaits is only a part of the understanding of the horse's movement. Simply lifting and replacing the feet does not enable an animal to move forwards. If this is all the body has to do, horses would only be able to move on one spot – piaffe.

The knowledge of the exact sequence of steps of all the gaits will:

1. Help the rider to feel the sequence.

2. This will enable the rider to prepare the horse effectively for the transition from gait to gait and from movement to movement, which will prevent the horse from losing balance.

3. It will also enable the rider to synchronize the aids with the horse's next step.

Therefore the transitions will be clean and smooth.

This knowledge will avoid, for example, errors such as when the rider's 'aids' for walk to canter are given at the wrong moment, in which case the horse will take the wrong lead, or take a few shuffled, hurried steps to correct his leg sequence before the first canter stride.

Biomechanical analysis of movements is described, where applicable, from the antigravity stance position – the halt – and from the transition from one gait to the next. Therefore, the following analyses may differ from the sequences described in traditional riding literature. The traditional description starts from the hind leg. This, however, is mostly not the natural method of the horse.

The natural movement is described according to how horses generally move at pasture, but this does not mean that horses always move in this manner. At liberty, horses have the ability to move and initiate movements by moving their heads in any direction, depending on their motivation at the time. Horses have the ability to move in nature exactly as they wish and they may have moments when they move exactly as when mounted. However, in nature, they generally choose the most economic method, which is often *not* as they move when mounted. Also, while the analysis is described in fine detail, horses actually perform automatically as in one fluid and graceful movement.

---

5 Ibid.

The Walk

Biomechanics of the walk

Let us first consider the human walk. Do we initiate the walk by simply lifting one leg followed by the other?

EXERCISE

Stand perfectly upright against a wall and attempt to take a step forward without inclining your head, neck or body forwards at all. It feels unnatural and stilted. Now start to walk normally. Notice how you have to incline your head, neck or body forwards slightly to initiate the movement and then, to a lesser degree, at each step.

The procedure is as follows: We walk forwards by leaning slightly forwards from the head. We then take a step, lean forwards again and then take the next step. Walking is basically a series of falls and then steps to rebalance. This forward lean serves to move our gravity line beyond the perimeter of the lines connecting our base of support. It is not really noticeable until we become conscious of it. *This forward inclination is initiated automatically by the head and neck. It is not initiated by our legs, unless intended. It is the same with the horse. He does not naturally initiate forward steps with his hindquarters.*

How does the horse bring his gravity line beyond his base of support? He can only do this by stretching his head and neck forwards followed

Figure 10.1a. The human body inclines slightly forward from the head, neck, waist or ankles, to take the first step.

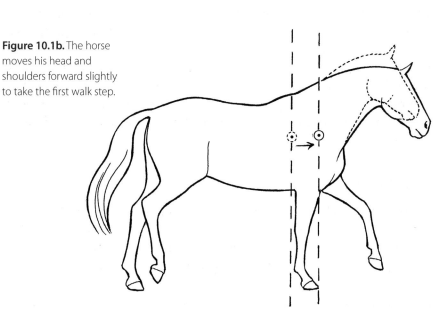

Figure 10.1b. The horse moves his head and shoulders forward slightly to take the first walk step.

166

by leaning his shoulders forwards. He then takes the first step with a fore-leg, followed by the opposite hind leg. The process is then repeated for the next step.

EXERCISE

Do transitions between walk-trot and halt-trot with your horse loose schooling in the lunge ring. He should not be wearing any apparel as this can inhibit his natural balance mechanisms. You will notice that he drops his neck down slightly and forwards for each upward transition and lifts it for each downward transition.

This is the horse's natural method of taking a forward step and of stopping. *He uses his head and neck*. In equitation, however, we ask the horse to move forwards in the 'on the bit' position. This prevents him from using his natural automatic balance reactions to move.

EXERCISE

Get down on your hands and knees with your thighs perpendicular to the floor. You will notice that you take most of your weight on your arms and hands. This is what the horse does as well. Lean forwards until you lose your balance and react. You will notice that you 'take a step' with one arm first (say left). You will then place your weight on this left arm and hand which will free the opposite (right) knee to move. Your weight on the left hand will automatically free your other hand (right) to move next. You will now slowly move your weight over onto the newly placed right hand. This will free the weight off the opposite (left) knee to allow it to take the next 'step'. This sequence works in the same manner for most quadruped animals and is the most economical energy-saving method of moving at the walk.

The walk is a four-beat movement, experienced by most riders as a two-beat feel (the rider's body moves forward and back in a two-beat rhythm. The rider usually feels and sees the horse's foreleg movements. Feeling the hind leg movements is quite difficult but, to do so, try the following exercise.

EXERCISE

As the horse is walking, lift both of your knees forward and up, high off the saddle, until your seat bones (ischial tuberosities) dig into the saddle. You will feel the horse's hips rise and fall very distinctly as the horse takes each step. Slowly move your legs back in position while maintaining this feeling.

In the walk each leg is grounded separately in the sequence as illustrated.

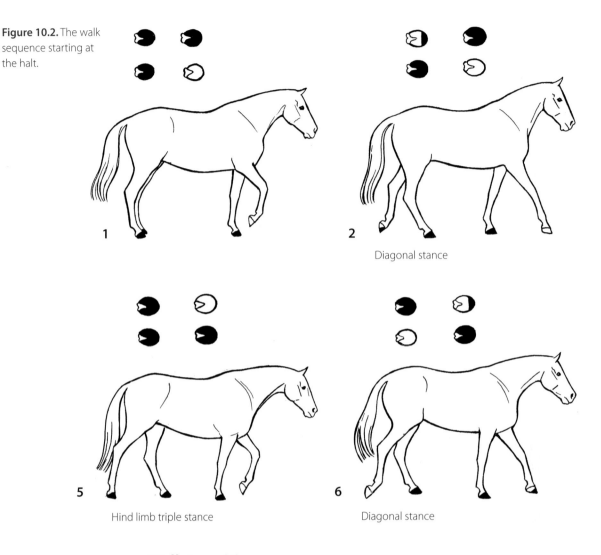

Figure 10.2. The walk sequence starting at the halt.

1

2

Diagonal stance

5

Hind limb triple stance

6

Diagonal stance

Walk transitions

The natural halt to walk sequence

The mounted horse initiates the walk pattern from the square halt in the same manner as described above. When he moves his head and neck forwards his gravity line and his centre of gravity move forwards. When he takes them far enough forwards, his gravity line moves beyond the perimeter of his base of support. He thus takes the first step with a foreleg to 'catch' his balance. His second step is with his opposite hind leg, which pushes his centre of gravity forwards again. This is the step which pushes against the ground to propel his body over his foreleg. Because the hind legs are directly connected to the horse's spine, they push his body over his weight-bearing forelegs, which makes him take the second foreleg

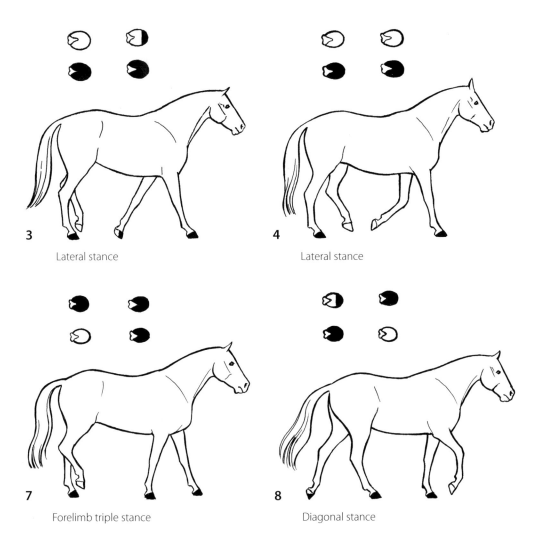

3 Lateral stance

4 Lateral stance

7 Forelimb triple stance

8 Diagonal stance

step. His weight now starts to move over to the new grounded side and the opposite hind leg moves forwards. This moving of the centre of gravity is the reason why the horse stretches his head and neck forwards and back at each stride of the walk and why the rider's arms should follow to allow it.

During the walk the horse always has at least one fore and one hind foot on the ground which means that there is no moment of suspension, the base of support stays large and he has good stability. This large base of support with hind and forefeet grounded means that his back hangs like a sling between the fore and hind legs. This ensures that gravity does not resist the action of his back muscles. Back muscle contractions are thus not powerful in the walk.

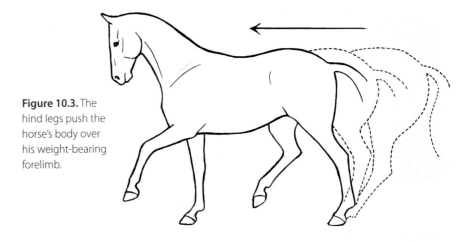

Figure 10.3. The hind legs push the horse's body over his weight-bearing forelimb.

Forward transition to walk 'on the bit'

This is less straightforward for the horse than when he has the freedom of his head and neck, especially when the rider incorrectly pulls/hangs onto the reins. (This pulling/hanging on is one of the major causes of tension in horses and the loss of the correct walk sequence – see Faults in the Walk.)

In the 'on the bit' position, the horse cannot use his neck effectively to move his centre of gravity forward and back. Therefore, his hind legs have to push his shoulders forwards beyond his base of support to take the first step and then move his centre of gravity back again. He thus has to flex his haunches for this step. This is why riding transitions in the 'on the bit' position improves engagement of the hindquarters and contributes to the development of power in the hind legs. This work could therefore be used as a first step in the initial stages of rehabilitation after a lay-off.

▶ RIDING AND TEACHING APPLICATIONS

1. The knowledge of the walk sequence helps the rider to develop feel and to plan and prepare the horse for walk to trot transitions and walk to canter transitions.

2. A rider who can feel the individual hind leg movements has the ability to time the aids to influence the horse's hind leg activity. When the leg aid is given as he grounds a hind leg, he will push harder with that leg. Give the aid on the side of the pushing hind leg. If you use your seat muscles only, the horse will usually push for a longer stride. If you use your legs, the horse will generally speed up the frequency of the walk steps.

    Visual clues: Give the leg aid when the opposite foreleg grounds and the shoulder is at its most forward position, because the opposite hind leg grounds split seconds later.

Photo 10.1. The 'on the bit' walk prevents the horse from using his neck to move his centre of gravity at each step.

Feel sensation on the legs: Give the leg aid when the horse's ribcage bulges against the leg.

Feel sensation on the seat: Use the leg on the same side when the horse has pushed your hip to the most forward position.

3. Knowledge of the walk and trot sequence is particularly important for lateral stretching in lateral movements. For a bigger crossing step of the outside hind leg in leg-yield, push as the horse grounds his inside hind leg. For a larger opening step of the inside hind leg, push as the outside hind leg grounds. This will ensure that the leg in the swing phase takes a larger step. The same principle applies to increasing the lateral steps of the forelegs.

4. A rider who can feel the movement of each hind leg will be able to feel whether the horse has engaged his hind legs. It is extremely difficult for a novice rider to feel when the horse is engaged and to feel the difference between a slow movement and an engaged movement.

5. A rider who hangs onto the reins during walk is giving the horse two opposing messages – the legs say 'walk on', but the hands say 'stop'. This is extremely confusing to a young horse and will lead to tension and other problems in walk.

Faults in the walk

Shortened, hurried steps

A naturally faulty walk is almost unheard of in young, unbacked horses. This only develops during or after training. The biggest culprit is tension, usually caused by holding the horse in with the hands and simultaneous pushing with the legs. This double message is not only confusing to the horse, but also blocks his shoulder movement and interferes with his natural balance mechanisms. 'Chasing' the horse into a hurried walk has the same effect. The obsession with an 'active walk' places pressure on riders who, in trying to obtain it, do so incorrectly, pushing the horse prematurely into a faster walk. The horse lifts his head in a balance reaction. His top line muscles tighten and he speeds up his foreleg action into hurried shorter steps. Tension in the top line muscles cause tension in the extensor muscles of the hindquarters and this is counterproductive in terms of engagement. When the horse is not engaged adequately he will have too much weight on his forehand, which will also lead to hurried steps as he runs to maintain his balance. These problems can all be prevented by maintaining the horse in a round frame with a light (57 gm [2 oz]) contact and slowing the horse down with correct half-halts. The latter help the horse to maintain balance with his hind legs.

The shuffle

The shuffle is often the fault of anticipation before the walk to canter transition or before the walk pirouettes in the higher levels of dressage training. It is very rare in Novice level horses. The horse's tension rises as he anticipates the transition. He then takes faster and shorter steps to prepare for the canter transition, especially if the rider does not prepare him with early warning 'signals'. The rider then holds on with a stronger contact in an attempt to prevent this. This leads to more tightness of the top line muscles and slowing down with shorter, faster and less elevated steps – the shuffle. Slowing down a hurried walk with the reins alone is another cause. The rider's legs are taken off the horse's sides in an attempt to slow down the hurried steps and this creates the shuffle.

'Pacing'/lateral movement

The pace is a lateral paired movement in which the horse lifts and places his lateral pairs of legs simultaneously. This is how a giraffe 'walks' because of the length of its legs. In horses, it is a natural gait in *some* breeds, which may appear spontaneously. Some other individuals may have a hereditary ability to pace. The gait is also seen in long-legged, short-coupled foals, but it usually disappears when they mature.

Research has shown that the walk pattern alters naturally at slower speeds: 'Even in highly trained dressage horses, a regular four-beat rhythm of the footfalls was observed in only one of six horses.'[6] Incorrect schooling is, however, the major culprit of the pace in the dressage-trained horse. It is unfortunately seen quite regularly and unnecessarily in Advanced dressage competitions. The lateral paired sequence can appear in what are supposed to be walk, trot and rein-back. The good news, however, is that incorrect lateral movement can easily be schooled out of the horse in both walk and trot. It is, however, very difficult (although possible) to school out of the rein-back since, in this case, it is not a training error, but the horse's natural inclination.

The horse loses the walk sequence and paces when the forelimbs move too fast or when the hind limbs move too slowly. This happens when the rider pushes him forwards too fast while blocking the forward movement with the hands, pulling or hanging on and attempting to 'hold' the horse into and in the collection. The horse speeds up his foreleg action because of the rider urging for activity. The blocking through the reins slows down the hind leg activity. The foreleg thus leaves the ground prematurely and changes the sequence of the walk steps into pace steps.

▶ RIDING AND TEACHING APPLICATIONS

It is often recommended that the collected walk should not be practiced 'as this could lead to pacing or shuffling'. The problem, however, is not the practice of the collected walk, but its *incorrect* practice. If the collected walk is ridden correctly, the horse will not develop problems.

1. Correct any shortened, hurried steps by first relaxing your seat. Then use half-halts and yield the reins. (Tight reins increase tension.) Once the horse has slowed down, ask him to move forward with your alternating seat muscle contractions alone (subtle aids with the seat; not 'driving' or 'pushing'). Maintain the round frame with a soft, elastic contact.

2. The pace is entirely avoidable if the rider slows the horse down and collects the walk correctly with half-halts followed by yielding of the reins. When the horse is in a collected frame with a soft and elastic contact, he is using his own flexor muscles to maintain the position and thus there is no tension of his top line muscles, which is a major cause of pacing.

---

6 E. Barrey, 'Inter-limb coordination' in W. Back and H.M. Clayton, *Equine Locomotion* (London, Harcourt Publishers Ltd., 2001).

If the activity is insufficient, push the horse forwards with your seat muscles rather than your legs and 'catch' the impulsion with half-halts using alternate rein pressure followed by yielding of the reins. Use your legs if the horse does not respond to your seat, but take care that this does not lead to hastened steps of the forelegs,

3. Correct the shuffle with as many half-halts as necessary by closing your knees and using checking rein aids, followed by instant yielding with the hands and knees to allow the horse to take longer steps. Push the horse forwards with your seat muscles alone (see point 1). The seat aids tend to facilitate a longer hind leg step whereas the leg aids tend to speed up the walk steps.

▶ JUDGING SIGNIFICANCE

1. A good walk has to have a regular four-beat rhythm. It unfortunately often changes to a lateral rhythm at even the higher levels of dressage, but this indicates incorrect training methods and should therefore be penalized quite heavily.

2. The degree of overtracking is often dependent on the horse's conformation and therefore not a good sign of the correct activity or length of stride desirable for the walk variants.

3. Swing in the back allows a longer stride. Tightness in the back is often caused by mental tension.

4. It has been shown that there is a significant correlation in the kinematics of the walk and that of the trot with regard to the intra-limb coordination pattern, stride duration, protraction and retraction range and maximal range of fetlock extension and hock motion. Despite the differences in their respective sequences of movement, the quality of the walk is thus a good predictor of the quality of the trot.[7] If the walk is inadequate, then the rider has probably caused negative interference with incorrect training methods. An inadequate walk is a major training error and easily corrected. It should be penalized significantly in the movement section of the test as well as in the 'effectiveness of aids' section especially at the higher levels of dressage competition. Poor walk movement is seen even at the very highest level of competition, yet some judges make excuses for the horse, claiming that he 'has a bad walk'. As stated earlier, naturally bad walks are very rare in horses.

---

7 W. Back, 'Intra-limb coordination: the forelimb and hind limb', in W. Back and H.M. Clayton, *Equine Locomotion* (London, Harcourt Publishers Ltd., 2001).

Walk to halt sequence

The natural halt

In nature the horse will initiate the halt by lifting his head and neck in the pushing pattern and moving his centre of gravity backwards. The horse will naturally take his weight on his forehand in the halt and thus stop first with his foreleg, followed by a hind leg; the other foreleg follows and he takes the last step with the second hind leg. Horses seldom halt square in nature. This spread of the legs ensures a more economic halt as it increases the size of the base of support. It allows the horse to use his hind legs to move off like an athlete in starting blocks.

The halt in the 'on the bit' position

This position prevents the horse from using his head and neck to move his centre of gravity back. He thus does one of two adaptations to the natural sequence.

1. He will pull on the rider's hands in an attempt to lift his head and neck in the decelerating push/brake pattern with his forelegs. When attempting to lead a horse who won't move, you will notice that he presses his forelegs into the ground and leans back slightly. This is the braking pattern.

2. His other alternative is to bring his hindquarters more underneath his body to move his centre of gravity back. However, he only does the latter if the rider, through 'take and give', does not allow him to take a

Photo 10.2. The natural halt with the hind legs in 'starting blocks' ready to push off.

stronger contact. The hind limbs with their many joint angles are not designed for the braking action.

In dressage we ask the horse to become more engaged and lift the forehand. We then ask him to brake with the hind legs. When the horse's hind legs are engaged sufficiently, he will place more weight on them and conclude the halt with a foreleg. When the horse halts with too much weight on his shoulders, a hind leg will take the last step.

▶ RIDING AND TEACHING APPLICATONS

1. Knowledge of the exact sequence of the halt aid is essential to ensure a square halt. The rider's hands explain to the horse to take a shorter step with each foreleg separately. The right hand, with a 'take and give' action, 'blocks' the right shoulder from moving forward. The left hand then 'blocks' the horse's left shoulder from moving forwards. The rider can thus control the exact length of the foreleg steps and make them smaller with each stride to prepare the horse for a square foreleg halt. As the horse starts to halt with one forelimb the rider should squeeze slowly with both calves, to ensure that the horse takes the last squaring up step with his second foreleg. The rein on this side should be

Photo 10.3. The perfectly square halt.

'blocked' to such a degree that the horse will not step beyond the first planted limb.

2. By feeling the hind legs individually the rider can ensure that the horse's last hind leg step will square out the halt. When the horse moves a hind leg last, the rider will know that the horse is carrying too much weight on the forehand.

3. When the horse pulls into the halt, he loses the engagement of his hind legs. The easiest method of moving the collected horse's weight backwards into the halt, is with 'lifting' and collecting half-halts for three strides into the halt. This is especially important in the transitions from trot and canter into halt. Maintain superior lightness of the forehand and light contact into the halt.

4. With the above method the horse will usually perform a square halt. If the horse is not square behind, novice riders should not tap the trailing hind leg because, although this can be effective when done by advanced riders with good feel and tact, done by less experienced riders it can often lead to fidgeting at the halt. Rather, walk the horse forward and repeat the halt. Reward the horse when the halt is square. The more engaged the hindquarters, the squarer the halt becomes. By the time the horse learns the piaffe, his halt will be square automatically.

▶ JUDGING SIGNIFICANCE

Both the judge and the trainer can assess with ease whether the rider has the horse properly engaged at the walk and the halt. When a hind leg takes the last step, the horse has too much weight on his forelimbs.

The Trot

Biomechanics of the trot

The trot is a two-beat diagonal movement with a moment of suspension in between the diagonal support phases. The horse lifts and places diagonal pairs of legs simultaneously (or almost simultaneously). Recent research has shown that the diagonal pairs of legs do not always touch the ground in perfect symmetry (see 'advanced diagonal hoof placement', later this chapter). After each moment of suspension the horse has to land on diagonal pairs of legs 'simultaneously'. This diagonal rather than lateral stance increases the size of his base of support and thus improves his balance. The longer the suspension phase, the greater the need for good balance.

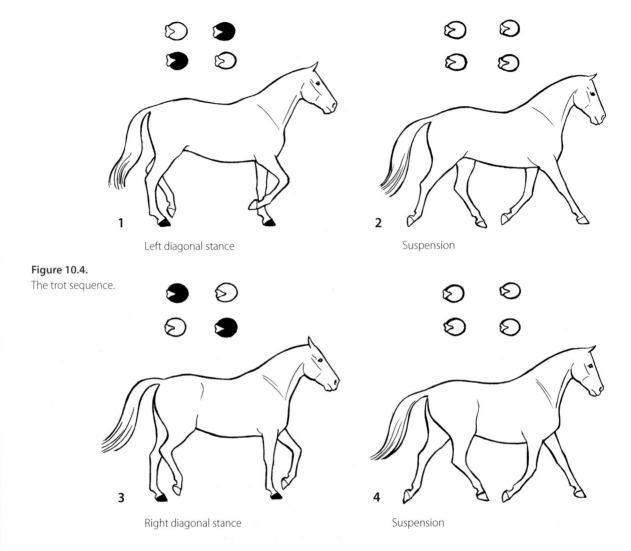

1 Left diagonal stance

2 Suspension

Figure 10.4.
The trot sequence.

3 Right diagonal stance

4 Suspension

Although there is a moment of suspension, the muscles of the back and hindquarters do not have to work against the gravitational force during the trot. This means that the back muscles do not have to contract as strongly in trot as during the canter (see later this chapter). The back muscles, however, coordinate with and assist the hind leg extensor muscles each time the horse extends a hind leg. At trot, the horse's overall height is lower than his standing height. This appears to be another energy-saving mechanism designed to improve gait efficiency. This may be a result of the spring-like action of the serratus ventralis muscles or because of added flexion of the joints to assist propulsion, elastic recoil and shock absorption. (As the forelimb extends in the stance phase, the serratus ventralis muscle relaxes to allow the trunk to spring down and so dampen the concussion.)

EXPERIMENT

Lunge your horse without side reins. Watch carefully as he initiates the trot from the walk. Notice how his head and neck first move forwards when he initiates the movement and then lifts in the trot. Repeat a few times to accustom your eye to the movement.

Elastic recoil in the trot

During the trot the horse has to push with his hind legs, one at a time. He needs a big push to lift his entire weight and propel it forwards. He does this by flexing all his hind leg joints to produce a spring action. This is why a horse with long pasterns and flexible joints with good angles often has a longer than average moment of suspension. The joint moves through a longer arc to increase elastic recoil.

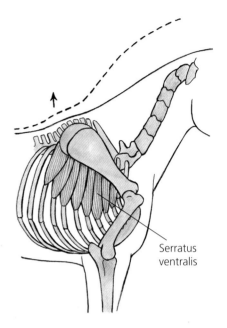

Serratus
ventralis

EXERCISE

Practise a little Irish step dancing with your body completely erect and your arms immobile next to your sides. Jumping up and down is not too difficult. Now attempt to take a forward step. The only way to step forward in this position is to use 'bounce'. You can jump forward with this bounce, but your step will be high and short. It is almost impossible for ordinary folk to leap forward in this erect position.

Figure 10.5. The serratus ventralis muscles relax and stretch to drop the withers for shock absorption. When they contract, the horse grows in the withers.

In the horse's case, his 'bounce' is elastic recoil; it is an energy-saving mechanism to improve gait efficiency. When he is in a round frame and cannot use his neck to move forward, he uses elastic recoil to jump forwards. His steps thus become more rounded with more spring, comfortable and smooth. Because the round frame initiates the flexor pattern, this 'bounce' is enhanced with more engagement of the hindquarters.

Advanced diagonal hoof placement

Recent slow motion analysis has shown that there is usually some dissociation of the diagonal placing of the limbs in the trot.[8] This phenomenon is called advanced diagonal hoof placement. When the hind limb hits the ground about 20–30 milliseconds before the diagonally opposite forelimb[9]

---

8 W. Back, 'Intra-limb coordination: the forelimb and hind limb', in W. Back and H.M. Clayton, *Equine Locomotion* (London, Harcourt Publishers Ltd., 2001).

9 E. Barrey and S. Biau, 'Locomotion of dressage horses' (paper presented at conference on Equine Sports Medicine and Science, 2002).

(positive advanced diagonal hoof placement) it allows the hind limb to push earlier during the stance phase. This is associated with a well-balanced good quality trot. Greater elevation of the forehand and more engagement of the hindquarters, through correct training, seem to increase the dissociation and positive advanced diagonal hoof placement.[10] The negative version of this form of hoof placement occurs when the forelimb is placed before the hind limb; this may be the cause of forging.

▶ RIDING AND TEACHING APPLICATIONS

1. It is important that the rider changes diagonals whenever changing direction. If a rider does not change the diagonal when rising to the trot the horse's muscles will develop asymmetrically and he may develop repetitive strain injury [RSI] from the rider sitting continuously on the same diagonal. It is of no consequence which diagonal the rider chooses, provided it is changed every time the horse changes direction. The particular diagonal the rider chooses, does not seem to make any significant difference to the effect of the aids, the horse's balance or his ability to engage his hindquarters. (The rider should also change diagonals when riding on a long straight track, such as when taking part in endurance rides.)

Photo 10.4. Positive advanced diagonal hoof placement in the engaged medium trot. The left hind will clearly strike the ground a little earlier than the 'diagonal' off fore.

10 H.M. Clayton, 'Performance in equestrian sports', in W. Back and H.M. Clayton, *Equine Locomotion* (London, Harcourt Publishers Ltd., 2001).

2. Choose a horse with conformation that will produce good elastic recoil. Sloping pasterns of a good length, forward-sloping shoulders and correct angles of shoulder and elbow joints are indicators.

▶ JUDGING SIGNIFICANCE

1. With the knowledge of advanced diagonal hoof placement it is now clear that placing a hind leg slightly before the diagonally opposite foreleg is a sign of engagement of the hindquarters and should not be penalized.

2. The opposite, however, where the forefoot is placed before the diagonally opposite hind foot, is a fault and a sign that the horse is not fully engaged, but on the forehand.

Upward transitions to trot

The natural halt to trot

In nature, the horse usually takes a few intermediate walk steps before moving into trot. His head and neck initiate the movement by moving forwards to move his centre of gravity forwards. He then lifts his head and neck and continues to keep them relatively high and steady during the trot. Once trotting, the elastic recoil of the fetlocks, combined with the stronger ground reaction force, propels the horse forwards and this negates the need to use his head and neck to move the centre of gravity continuously. The horse thus springs from one diagonal to the other.

The 'on the bit' halt to trot

When 'on the bit', the horse cannot use his head and neck to move his centre of gravity forwards to take the first step. He has to learn to go directly from halt to trot, from no impulsion to superior impulsion. He therefore has to use elastic recoil to 'spring' into the trot. He simply lifts a diagonal pair of legs, and pushes down on his fetlocks to spring off the other diagonal pair. The automatic use of elastic recoil ensures that his head and neck remain steady in trot, therefore the rider's arms do not move forwards and back at each stride as in the walk.

The natural walk to trot

In nature the horse will choose the moment for the transition to coordinate with the diagonal stance phase of the walk. He then stretches his head and neck forwards and hops onto the opposite diagonal pair of legs. His head and neck are then carried high and quiet as the elastic recoil takes over, together with horizontal propulsion from the hind legs.

The 'on the bit' walk to trot

In the 'on the bit' position the horse places one hind leg to come in sequence with the diagonal foreleg as he feels the instruction. When the horse has diagonal legs in stance, he springs off and jumps to the opposite diagonal for the first trot step. When the aid is not synchronized with the horse's diagonal stance phase, he will speed up his steps until a diagonal pair is in stance phase and then spring into trot. Therefore this transition will not be as smooth.

▶ RIDING AND TEACHING APPLICATIONS

1. The timing of the aids and the reaction time of the horse are crucial to encourage a clean first trot stride. For a smooth transition it is important that the horse takes the first diagonal trot step from the diagonal support/stance phase. Therefore the rider should give the aid as the horse lifts a foreleg. At this point he will have a diagonal pair of legs in a stance phase and he will have time to organize the first trot stride. As feel develops, a rider will learn to give the aid at the correct moment when the horse is about to go into the inside diagonal stance phase. (The top riders have developed their feel to such an extent that the timing of their aids is instinctively correct.) The horse will then jump onto the outside diagonal, which is the 'sitting' diagonal. The rider will then post correctly immediately. (Although, as previously noted, there is no 'correct' diagonal in biomechanical terms, it is traditionally accepted that the rider sits on the outside diagonal. This, assuming that the ridden work involves frequent changes of rein, ensures that the diagonal is changed regularly.)

2. It is unnatural for the horse to initiate the trot without the freedom of his neck. The rider should therefore ask for the trot transitions very tactfully and only ease him into the next gait. This will assist him in maintaining his balance and encourage engagement of the hindquarters and a smooth transition. During the walk to trot transition the horse will naturally want to lift his head and neck to initiate the movement. If the horse is to maintain the round frame in the transition, the rider has to explain to him, by means of 'take and give', *throughout* the transition, that he should keep his head down. He has to be eased into the transition or he will lift his head and neck. Sharp or sudden leg taps will lead to interference with balance and the consequent lifting of the head and neck.

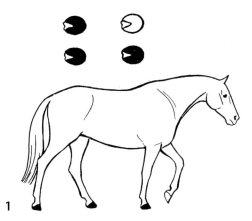

1

Walk hind limb triple stance: give aid
as forelimb lifts

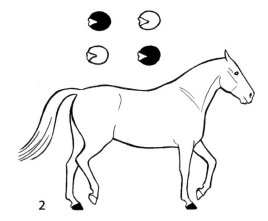

2

Walk diagonal stance – first trot step

Figure 10.6a. *above left and above right*
Walk to trot transition, correct timing.
When the aid is given in the hind leg
triple stance phase, the horse will lift
one hind leg and spring from this
diagonal stance into the first trot step.

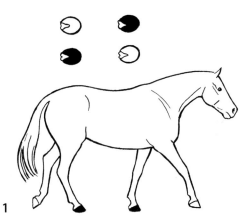

1

Walk diagonal stance: giving the aid
here will be too late

Figure 10.6b. *left and below* Walk to
trot transition, incorrect timing. When
the aid is given in the diagonal stance
phase it will be too late for the horse to
spring into diagonal action and he will
speed up the steps until the opposite
diagonal is in stance.

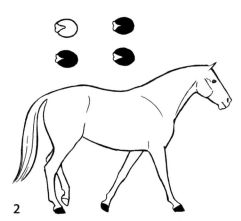

2

Walk forelimb triple stance: the horse
speeds up the walk steps

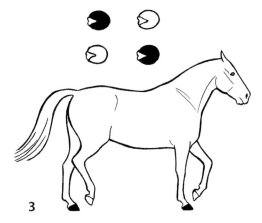

3

Diagonal stance – first trot step

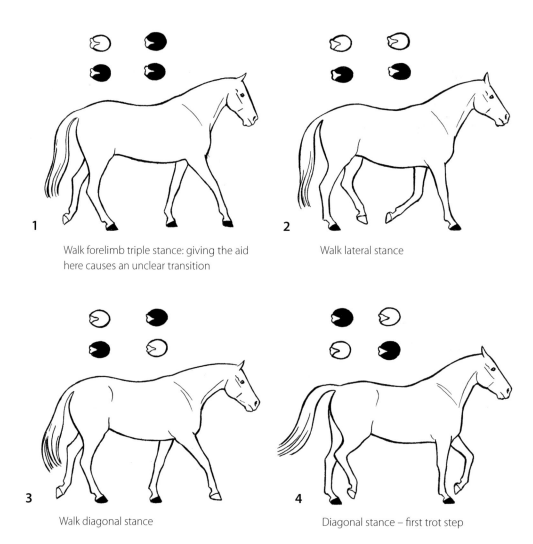

1 Walk forelimb triple stance: giving the aid here causes an unclear transition

2 Walk lateral stance

3 Walk diagonal stance

4 Diagonal stance – first trot step

Figure 10.6c. Walk to trot transition, incorrect timing. When the aid is given when the horse is in foreleg triple stance the next stance phase is lateral and the diagonal stance phase only follows after this. The horse has to speed up his step sequence into trot and this leads to an unclear transition.

3. Easing the horse into the trot transition with squeezing leg aids gives him the opportunity and time to organize and coordinate his leg sequence for a clear spring from the diagonal stance phase, into the trot. He will then not speed up and the transition will be clear.

▶ JUDGING SIGNIFICANCE

1. Bear in mind that when a green horse lifts his head in the walk to trot transition it is usually not a resistance, but a natural balance reaction to take a forward step.

2. Unclear walk to trot transitions usually mean that the rider's timing is faulty or that the horse did not respond instantly to the aids. This should be noted in the collective marks for the correct use of aids.

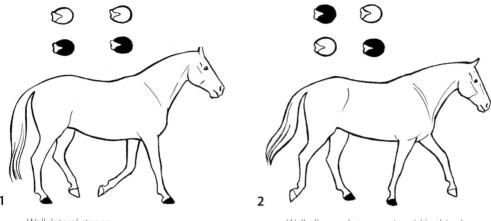

1 Walk lateral stance

2 Walk diagonal stance: give aid in this phase

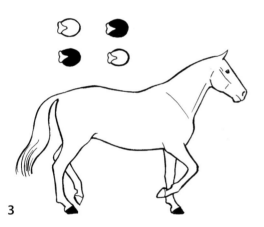

3

The horse into the first trot step on the opposite diagonal

Figure 10.6d. Walk to trot transition – correct timing. When the aid is given during the diagonal stance phase, the transition will be smooth because his next step is the opposite diagonal in trot.

Downward transitions from trot

The natural trot to walk

In nature the horse simply trots slower with shorter strides until the lack of impulsion leads to the walk. He grounds one diagonal. The other diagonal dissociates (breaks up) to place the forelimb first, followed by the opposite diagonal hind limb. The walk sequence then continues. It is thus the forelimb which takes the first step of the walk sequence.

The 'on the bit' trot to walk

The ridden horse has to brake with his forelegs instead of simply slowing down because he is asked to go straight from an active trot to a walk.

When the horse is in the 'on the bit' position, he cannot use his neck in the push pattern to brake, nor to move his centre of gravity back unless he has ample preparation from the rider. When he is not prepared and balanced into the transition, he will lift his neck to balance, brace on his foreleg and 'fall' into the walk. This is the reason why green horses and horses with novice riders lift their heads and necks into the walk transition. The horse appears to hollow in the downward transitions, but is in fact using his neck for balance.

▶ RIDING AND TEACHING APPLICATIONS

1. The horse should be prepared for the transition a few strides ahead. This is done with half-halts, asking the horse to maintain a round frame and slowing down into smaller trot steps. The horse will then know that a transition is imminent and will prepare himself for a balanced, clean transition.

2. The rider can encourage a smooth transition by coordinating the aid with the suspension phase. The horse will brake as his diagonal pair of legs hit the ground. He then proceeds with the walk sequence with the opposite forelimb taking the first step.

3. Since we remove the horse's main balancing tool, it is the rider's responsibility to assist the horse to balance, especially during the transitions. This is done with as many half-halts as is necessary, together with 'take and give' on the reins to explain to the horse that he should not lift his head and neck.

4. To ensure that the horse maintains the yielding round frame, the rider has to ask him to yield, with squeezing of the reins, throughout the transition.

▶ JUDGING SIGNIFICANCE

1. Unclear transitions mean that the rider's timing of the aids and preparation of the horse are not adequate. They should therefore be penalized in the collective marks for correct use of the aids.

2. Lifting of the head and neck in the downward transition is often a sign of loss of balance as well as a sign that the rider has not prepared the horse adequately by explaining that he should not lift his head to balance. It is a sign of resistance only when the horse is ignoring the rider's preparation and aids for a downward transition. Therefore the fault is usually rider related. 'Resistance' implies that the horse is at fault.

Lengthened forms of trot

The natural lengthened trot

The natural lengthened trot is usually the horse's natural way of moving in the paddock. The shoulder movement is free and loose and the head and neck are stretched forward. The hindquarters show normal long strides and usually do not move wide behind. As soon as the horse loses balance and starts to move wide, he generally breaks into canter. Horses do not do correct medium or extended trots in nature because 'engagement of the hindquarters' is not their natural method of moving.

Lengthened, medium and extended trot in the 'on the bit' position

The trot is lengthened by prolonging the suspension phase through stronger pushing from the hindquarters. 'Suspension in the medium and extended trots is twice as long as that of the collected and working trots.'[11] The stride frequency, however, stays the same. Therefore, while the actual speed of the movement (miles per hour) increases, it appears to be slower. The fetlock extension increases, which magnifies the elastic recoil and this assists in prolonging the suspension phase. *The development of power, engagement and elevation of the forehand are therefore necessary in order to prolong the suspension.* Power is developed from engagement and collection exercises. When the horse is in the 'on the bit' position, he has to have a long and round frame to lengthen his trot. When he is in a shorter 'on the bit' frame, he can only lengthen or extend the trot correctly once he has developed strong and engaged hindquarters because:

a. Propulsion has to be in a forward as well as upward direction. Therefore he needs both well-developed stifle extensor muscles (quadriceps femoris) for vertical propulsion and hip extensor muscles (gluteal and hamstring muscles) for forward impulsion.
b. He has to move with superior balance with more weight on his hindquarters so that he does not need his neck for balance. He should be able to depend entirely on his hindquarters for balance before medium or extended trot is requested.

If his hindquarters have not developed enough he will tip his weight on his forehand, lose balance, run, move wide behind or break into canter. Many novice horses have not developed sufficient strength in the hindquarters to increase the suspension as required in a medium trot. The medium and

---

11 H.M. Clayton, 'Performance in equestrian sports' in W. Back and H.M. Clayton, *Equine Locomotion* (London, Harcourt Publishers Ltd., 2001).

extended trots develop in concert with engagement and collection and are thus not appropriate movements in the lower-level dressage tests.

▶ RIDING AND TEACHING APPLICATONS

1. The development of extension and collection clearly go hand in hand and both need well developed hindquarters. Therefore novice horses should only lengthen the stride by lengthening and lowering the frame. This will bring the hindquarters more underneath and thereby strengthen them. Only once the horse can engage and collect sufficiently, should he be taught the medium and extended trots.

2. As soon as the horse's weight tips on the forehand during a lengthened trot, he will take a stronger contact because his top line muscles will tighten. His hips will lose their protracting capacity and he will move into hoof placement whereby his forefeet will tend to impact before the diagonally corresponding hinds. He will immediately take faster running steps, forge, go wide behind or 'fall' into canter. It is important, especially in training, to maintain a light contact with 'take and give' of the reins *throughout* the movement, together with appropriate half-halts. Only when the horse has developed the correct muscles sufficiently, should the contact become 'holding' for that extra power and balance.

3. When the lengthened or medium trot is requested too early in training before the horse has developed pushing power, he will 'tip' on his forehand and will attempt to maintain balance by running or moving wide behind. A horse who does not have the natural extension may need to work on quite advanced collecting exercises such as canter to walk exercises and piaffe, before being ready to do a medium trot. The horse should only be pushed into a medium trot when he has developed enough power in his hindquarters to push for more suspension. This will lead to positive advanced diagonal hoof placement and will ensure that the horse takes his forelimb out of the way of his protracting hind leg.

4. Good stride length is dependent on increased scapula movement, therefore the scapula muscles need to be very flexible. This flexibility can be enhanced by doing stretch exercises. The most effective method of suppling these muscles is with the correct use of trotting poles.

5. Endurance horses should not be ridden in extended trot for too long distances as this may cause repetitive strain injury to joints, ligaments and tendons from hyperextension of the fetlock joints.

▶ JUDGING SIGNIFICANCE

The lengthened trot in the Novice tests is a double-edged sword. It is included in the test to encourage the rider to allow the horse to free his movement. Unfortunately, it leads to premature pressure on the horse to perform at medium gaits. The lack of engagement when pushing the green horse forwards to lengthen his stride can lead to many faults in the trot. When dressage tests require a 'lengthened trot', riders tend to ask for a medium trot because this is rewarded by the judges. However, few horses have a natural medium trot and most of the horses at the lower levels have not developed enough power to hold the prolonged suspension. This movement thus degenerates into running, tipping on the forehand and breaking into canter and this is not good for their training. A clear distinction should be drawn between a lengthened trot and a medium trot. It would be more judicious to replace the lengthened trot in the Novice tests with a movement in which the frame is lengthened by stretching the head and neck in the low and round frame with a light contact. This would prevent the horse from 'falling on his forehand'. It would naturally lead to a longer and freer stride, which facilitates engagement of the hindquarters. This is the precursor to teaching the medium trot and will facilitate the development of the movement.

Faults in the trot

Forging

This is a sign that the forefeet impact before the diagonally corresponding hind feet. Horses carrying too much weight on the forehand often forge, especially those with big movement. Although forging is a problem of long-striding and short-coupled horses, it disappears as soon as the horse becomes more engaged in his hindquarters. The horse's forehand lifts, diagonal placement improves and his fore hooves thus lift out of the reach of his hind hooves. Forging also appears when the hooves are too long.

Pacing

The trot can transmute into pacing when a horse has some muscle imbalance, or in a horse who has a natural inclination to pace. In the pace the horse's lateral pairs of legs are grounded and lift in unison. Both swing and stance phases of the pace are usually shorter than in the trot and the stride frequency is faster. The base of support during pacing is small, therefore the horse's balance is influenced and the suspension phase in this movement is thus smaller and shorter. During the pace the horse has to carry his head and neck high and in extension to assist his balance. This means that his top line muscles are tight. The horse moves his weight from side to side to coordinate and balance on the small base in the lateral stance phases, whereas, in the diagonal trot, his weight is distributed evenly over both sides of his body at every stride.

Wide hind limb stance

This has three causes.

1. Conformation. Horses with short backs and long legs often widen the stance to prevent the hind limbs from touching the forelegs.

2. Loss of balance.
   a. Horses trot wide behind when they are pushed forwards too fast while on the forehand. They broaden the base of support to maintain balance.
   b. Pushing the young horse forwards too early in training, before he has developed sufficient power and engagement, means that he cannot balance on his hindquarters and 'falls' on the forehand.

3. Any tightness in the contact or top line will mean that the horse is in the extension pattern, even when this 'hollowing' is not visible to the naked eye. This pattern leads to widening when the horse is pushed forwards too much.

▶ RIDING AND TEACHING APPLICATION

1. Pacing is corrected with ease by asking the horse to lower and round his head and neck and to slow down. This stretches and relaxes his top line muscles and prevents hollowing. It is important that the contact remains light. As soon as the contact tightens the horse will be using the incorrect top line muscles. Improve the trot sequence and balance with many half-halts and working in large circles. Trot very slowly and with little impulsion. Once the horse has accepted the diagonal gait, the impulsion should be improved.

2. Short, hurried strides are often a sign that the horse's feet are sensitive. He therefore shortens the stance phase by lifting them prematurely. (Slippery footing will have the same effect.) The horse's forelimb stride may be shortened as a result of discomfort in his shoulder muscles. Short, hurried strides also appear when the horse is pushed forward onto his forehand and he balances himself by 'running faster'.

3. Lack of suspension is often another sign of discomfort in the feet: the horse appears to be skating. The stride and suspension improve as soon as the feet improve.

4. The widened stance of the hindquarters is fairly easy to correct. The most important aspect of the correction is to maintain a soft contact in a long and round frame. Throughout the lengthening movement the rider should continuously squeeze the reins to convince the horse not to tighten his top line muscles. The slightest firmness in the rein will mean that the horse is tightening them. *Ease* the horse into a longer stride by simply rising higher and sitting deeper to ensure that he does not lose balance. Then slowly ask for more lengthening while explaining every step of the way that he should not tighten his top line. As soon as the contact hardens, do a half-halt to balance the horse, then ease him for-wards again.

The Canter

Biomechanics of the canter

The canter is a three-beat movement followed by a moment of suspension. However, the rider may experience the *feel* of the movement as a two-beat rhythm in that the seat moves forward and back in each stride, in which case the three footfalls are felt as one beat and the period of suspension as the second beat. This two-beat rhythm is usually in the same tempo as the two-beat forelimb movement of the walk. Therefore the music for canter in a musical kür can have either a 6/8 rhythm or a slower two-beat rhythm at the same tempo as the walk.

Although the leading (inside) hind limb is more protracted than the trailing (outside) hind limb, 'the trailing limbs produce most of the forward propulsion.'[12] This means that the trailing outside hind limb has a large horizontal propulsive force. It carries the weight of the entire horse and is the seat of power and engagement. The diagonal pair supports the horse's weight while propelling it forwards. The inside leading foreleg takes the most strain in the canter. The vertical ground reaction force is largest in the leading forelimb.[13] This means that it has to 'catch' and balance the weight of the entire body and then transfer this weight in an upward direction.

The horse at liberty does not generally canter straight (that is, his hind limbs do not move in line with his forelimbs). He often canters disunited for a few strides after a flying change. He may stay in counter-canter around shallow curves until his balance is significantly disturbed; he then

---

12 H.M. Clayton, 'Performance in equestrian sports' in W. Back and H.M. Clayton, *Equine Locomotion* (London, Harcourt Publishers Ltd., 2001).

13 Ibid.

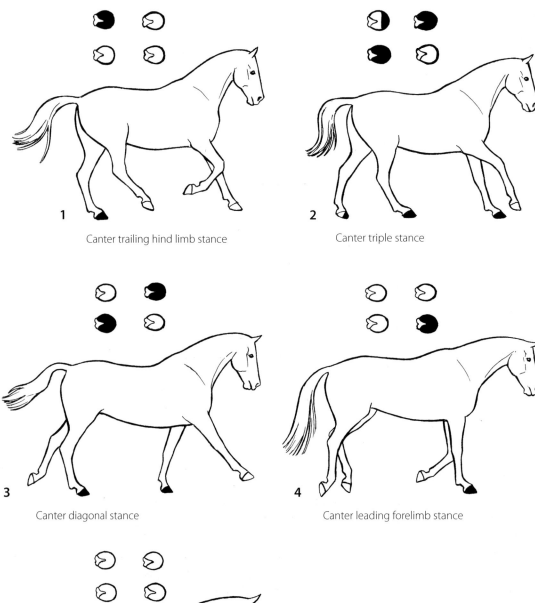

1 Canter trailing hind limb stance

2 Canter triple stance

3 Canter diagonal stance

4 Canter leading forelimb stance

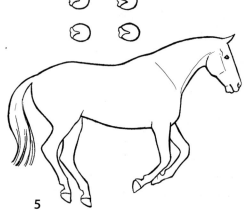

5 Canter suspension

Figure 10.7. The canter sequence.

does a flying change. Under saddle, the horse is straightened by the rider riding in a slight shoulder-fore position to bring his shoulders in line with his hindquarters. This is quite difficult for novice riders and novice horses, yet is expected in Novice dressage competitions.

▶ JUDGING SIGNIFICANCE

1. The outside hind leg (the trailing hind limb) is the one to watch for power and engagement – how far underneath the body it moves. The inside hind leg is often incorrectly presupposed to be the more important leg for engagement.

2. There should be some leniency towards the hindquarters falling in during the canter in the lower grades. Horses only become straight when they are supple and can do shoulder-in.

Upward transitions to canter

Horses in nature usually do transitions gradually with intermediate steps from one gait to another when they are relaxed. They do not usually skip a gait, but go from halt to walk, to trot and to canter. Skipping a gait is not physically economical for the horse. However, when in a state of heightened anxiety or awareness, they will move with ease from walk or halt straight into canter.

The natural halt to canter sequence

The horse in nature initiates the movement by lifting his head and the base of his neck and tightening his entire top line muscles from his head down his neck and back, in extension, to lift his forehand off the ground. This is similar to a swimmer swimming butterfly stroke. His strong back and hip extensor muscles, including the hamstrings, the gluteals, the longissimus and multifidus muscles, take most of the strain. Both hind legs push off the ground to lift his entire forehand. This is followed by the placing of the outside (trailing) foreleg and lifting of the (outside) trailing hind leg, which then leaves the inside hind leg and the outside foreleg for the diagonal stance phase. His inside (leading) foreleg is the last in stance, after which his whole body bounds into suspension. The coordination of powerful muscle function and superior elastic recoil of all four fetlocks produces the suspension. During the canter and gallop the fetlocks of the trailing hind and forelegs almost touch the ground. The huge mass of the body being pulled down by gravity onto the ground via the fetlocks creates enormous ground reaction force.

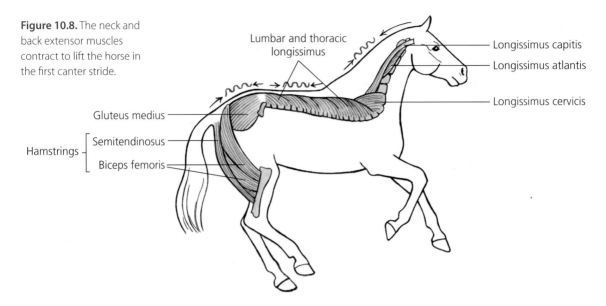

Figure 10.8. The neck and back extensor muscles contract to lift the horse in the first canter stride.

Lumbar and thoracic longissimus

Longissimus capitis

Longissimus atlantis

Longissimus cervicis

Gluteus medius

Hamstrings — Semitendinosus

Biceps femoris

Photo 10.5. During the canter the fetlocks of the trailing limbs almost touch the ground.

The 'on the bit' halt to canter

Horses appear to have two methods of initiating halt to canter. The more economical method is to push with the trailing (outside) hind leg and lift and step with the diagonal pair of legs. This is followed by the leading forelimb and the moment of suspension. The second method is as described by the natural method wherein the horse pushes with both hind legs. Maintaining the 'on the bit' position is extremely difficult during this manoeuvre. Without the assistance of the head and neck extensor muscles, the horse's back and hind leg muscles (hamstring and gluteal muscles connecting to the longissimus muscles) have to exert enormous power. The neck extensors at the base of the neck have to contract isometrically (without shortening) when the neck is in this position. This type of contraction is strenuous, therefore the muscles have to be extremely strong. This is not a movement for young or inexperienced horses.

The natural walk to canter

When he is in a relaxed state the horse usually goes from walk to trot to canter. When in fright/flight mode he may go into canter from the halt or from two or three walk steps. In the latter case his head and neck are carried high. He uses the extensor muscles at the base of his neck, together with his back extensor muscles, to lift his shoulders

The 'on the bit' walk to canter

It is against the horse's natural inclination, and quite difficult to move from walk directly to canter, while maintaining the 'on the bit' position. The horse is prevented from using his head and neck extension muscles to lift his forehand. This leads to more strain on the back muscles from the withers to the hindquarters. Young horses, especially, have difficulty in maintaining the round frame in the walk to canter transition.

▶ RIDING AND TEACHING APPLICATIONS

1. Since the strain on the horse's back and hindquarter muscles is increased when he cannot use his head and neck to initiate the walk to canter, the movement should only be expected once the horse has developed sufficient strength in his hindquarters.

2. For a smooth and balanced transition, the rider has to prepare the horse by positioning him to take the correct lead. The horse's inside shoulder has to be ahead of his outside shoulder and his weight has to be on his outside legs. This position should guarantee the correct lead at canter. It is easier for the horse to do this with his natural outside neck bend because this places his inside shoulder ahead of the outside. In dressage competitions, however, an inside bend is required and therefore he has to have a soft inside bend. When introducing this positioning to the horse, the task is simplified if motivation is added by the horse's relative position towards other horses or the stable yard. The aid should be given at the precise moment of the walk sequence when the next step

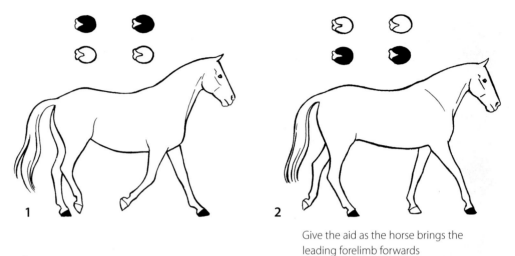

Figure 10.9. The walk
to canter sequence.

Give the aid as the horse brings the
leading forelimb forwards

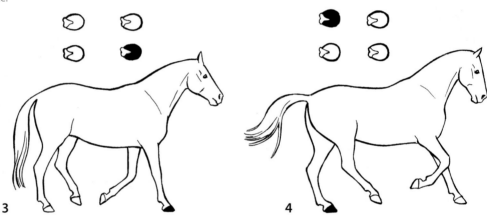

With the inside forelimb in stance the
next step is the trailing hind limb

The walk hind leg stance becomes
the first canter step

will be with the outside hind leg (which is the first canter step). Move
the horse's weight over to his outside side by pushing and tilting his
ribcage with your inside leg. When the horse has his weight on his outer
side, he will automatically be bent to the inside, but sponging on the
inside rein will ensure the yielding to the inside. Place your outside leg
behind the girth as an early-warning signal. Animate the walk to engage
his hindquarters and wake him up, with light tapping with your legs.
(Tapping produces tension in muscles). Maintain a positive contact on
the outside rein or bend your outside elbow slightly as you ask for the
canter. This will ensure that his weight is on his outside shoulder. Ask
for the canter with your inside leg in a slightly forward position, and ask
as the horse grounds his inside foreleg. His next step is his outside hind
leg and the first canter step. The reins should not be pushed forwards in

a

b

Photos 10.6a and b. The walk to canter transition. In (a) the horse is about to place his outside hind leg in the walk sequence. In (b) this same step becomes the first canter step. Note how the horse has lifted the head and neck to assist in lifting the forehand into the canter.

the transition or the horse will move forward into trot. Think of an upward movement rather than a forward movement.

3. It is important that the horse's shoulders are positioned towards the leading leg. If you look carefully, you will notice when his inside shoulder is slightly ahead of his outside shoulder. The aid should be given while the horse is in this position.

4. When the transition is performed as the horse is about to ground his outside hind leg, the transition will be clean. The horse will lift all three other legs off the ground, bounding into canter. The timing will be correct for a clean and balanced transition. If the rider is a split second late with the aid, the green horse will take the incorrect lead because he will then be in the wrong sequence of steps. The experienced horse will have to take extra, hurried walk steps until his legs are in the correct sequence. The transition will then be neither clear nor on the marker. It is important not to take the leg off the horse before you give the aid because that will slow down the timing.

5. Since the canter is an asymmetrical gait, it should be practised, with the correct bend, on both reins until the muscular development and ease of movement are equal.

6. Bad behaviour during canter, while none is shown in the trot, is often indicative of back pain/discomfort or hind leg muscle pain/discomfort.

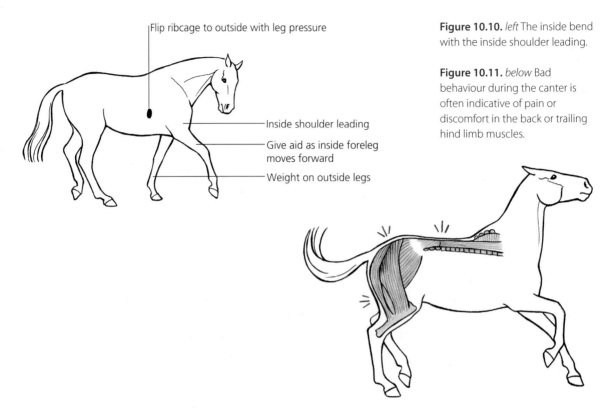

Flip ribcage to outside with leg pressure

Inside shoulder leading

Give aid as inside foreleg moves forward

Weight on outside legs

Figure 10.10. *left* The inside bend with the inside shoulder leading.

Figure 10.11. *below* Bad behaviour during the canter is often indicative of pain or discomfort in the back or trailing hind limb muscles.

Canter is the gait in which the force of gravity has the most effect on the horse's back and hind leg muscles. All the horse's back muscles and leg extensors have to work against this gravitational resistance. This strenuous muscle exercise highlights any sub-clinical muscle pain. Painful back muscles are not very noticeable at the trot.

When the horse misbehaves, swishes his tail or throws his head up when cantering on a particular rein, the problem is usually on the side of the trailing hind limb.

▶ JUDGING SIGNIFICANCE

1. The lifting of the horse's head in the walk to canter transitions is caused by natural muscle use and is not a result of resistance.

2. There are two causes of the walk to canter transition being unclear.
   a. The rider's timing is incorrect. This should be penalized under the 'effective use of aids' section of the test.
   b. The horse is ignoring the aid. This should be penalized under the 'submission and obedience' section.

3. A judge with a good eye can see before the actual transition, whether the horse will take the correct lead. Watch the horse's shoulder position. If

the outside shoulder is slightly ahead of the inside shoulder, the canter depart will be incorrect.

Biomechanics of trot to canter

Argue and Clayton[14] found that ridden horses use two types of leg sequence in the transition from trot to canter. In the first type the horse grounds the leading forelimb after the diagonal trot stance and then springs into the moment of suspension. When the horse initiates the transition with his hind limb Argue and Clayton found that he simply lifts the foreleg during the diagonal stance phase.[15] The remaining grounded hind leg pushes off and lifts the forehand into the first canter stride.

The type of transition the horse chooses depends on the exact moment the rider gives the aid, rather than on the level of engagement of the horse. The rider can elicit the preferred type of transition provided that the aid is given at precisely the correct moment and the horse reacts instantly. However, neither of the two sequences the horse uses has a negative effect on the canter transition. Riders generally do not concern themselves with developing one method in favour of the other because both methods lead to a smooth transition.

Natural trot to canter

In the natural trot to canter transition the horse initiates the transition by moving his head and neck forwards. He contracts his extensor muscles at the top of the base of his neck to initiate the lift of his shoulders. His head and neck are usually already high in the natural position.

The 'on the bit' trot to canter

In the 'on the bit' position the horse cannot lift his head and neck to move his centre of gravity back. He therefore uses the extensor muscles at the top of the base of his neck in the more strenuous isometric contraction (without shortening). This 'on the bit' position 'forces' him to place his hind legs more underneath his body to move his centre of gravity back. He places his weight on his outside legs, especially the outside shoulder, to free his inside legs for the transition.

---

14 C.K. Argue and H.M. Clayton, (1993b), 'A study of transitions between the trot and canter in dressage horses' (article in J.Equine Vet. Sci.13: 171–174) as quoted in W. Black and H.M. Clayton, *Equine Locomotion*, Harcourt Publishers Ltd. (London) 2001.

15 Ibid.

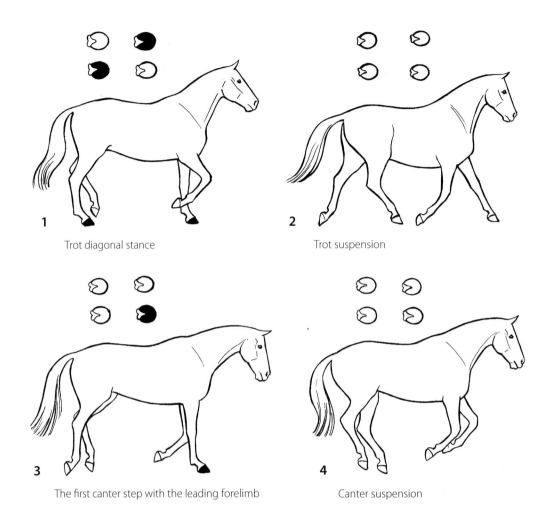

1 Trot diagonal stance

2 Trot suspension

3 The first canter step with the leading forelimb

4 Canter suspension

Figure 10.12a. Trot to canter type 1 – see text.

▶ RIDING AND TEACHING APPLICATIONS

1. The instruction for the second type of transition cited by Argue and Clayton should be given as the horse grounds his outside diagonal pair of legs (outside fore/inside hind) in the stance phase, or lifts his inside shoulder. The next step will be his outside hind leg, which will be the first step of the canter provided the horse is obedient and reacts instantly to the aid. This is automatic if the rider sits on the outside diagonal.

2. If the horse is prepared by sitting for a stride or two before the aid is given, he will pick up on this as a 'pre-aid' and be able to prepare his body for a clear and fluid transition.

3. There are two methods of teaching the young mounted horse to canter. These horses usually do not have the balance to canter in circles, therefore they should be cantered around the perimeter of the arena.

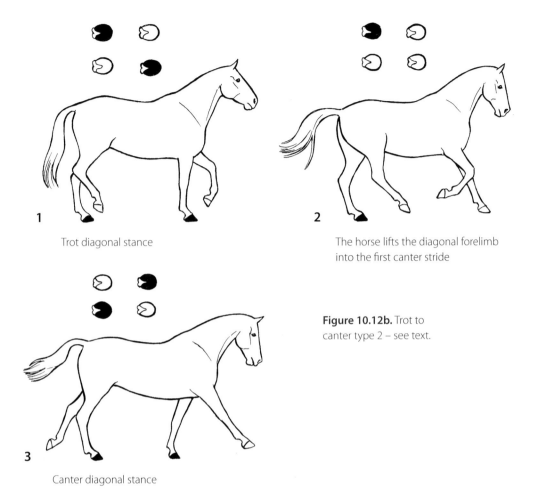

1

Trot diagonal stance

2

The horse lifts the diagonal forelimb into the first canter stride

3

Canter diagonal stance

Figure 10.12b. Trot to canter type 2 – see text.

a. The most natural method will help them to grasp the canter concept without confusion. Simply push the horse more forward in the corner furthest away from the entrance of the arena. You can use both legs to push him forwards until he breaks into the canter, but allow him to move his head and neck forwards. If he takes the incorrect lead, simply cross the arena. With this method the horse does not learn to take the correct lead, but his strength and endurance can be improved before insisting on the correct canter depart. Insisting on the correct lead could be confusing if the rider does not have the experience to position the horse correctly.

b. In the second method the rider has to position the horse and time the aids correctly with the stride sequence. The horse will then always take the correct lead from the first lesson on and will make an association between the specific aids and the correct lead. This will lead to faster learning. Position the horse by ensuring that his inside shoulder is leading. Retard the outside shoulder through bending your outside elbow and opening your arm away from the horse, thus moving his shoulder out. Flip his ribcage with your inside leg. Keep your outside leg back so that, should you need to move his hindquarters, this will assist in placing his inside shoulder in a forward position. Ensure that the horse has his weight on his outside legs. Weight on the inside foreleg will lead to an incorrect strike-off. Push him forwards in this position into the canter.

4. Once the horse understands the canter, the rider should half-halt into the canter transition to ensure the propulsion is in a vertical direction. This will ensure an immediate transition and prevent the faster trot and 'fall' into the canter.

5. When flipping the ribcage with your inside leg does not have the desired effect of placing the horse's weight on his outside shoulder, push the horse (with the same leg) into a few steps of leg-yield. This should place his weight on his outside legs.

6. In cases when everything you try simply does not seem to work, you may turn the horse's head to the outside with an opening rein and firm contact. This will move the horse's weight to his outside shoulder and bring his inside shoulder into a leading position. This is a temporary measure to teach the horse the concept of the correct lead and should be transformed as soon as possible to an inside bend.

Downward transitions from canter

The natural canter to trot

In the natural canter to trot the horse transforms the horizontal force of the canter into a vertical force by pushing his forelimbs into the ground. Argue and Clayton[16] identified two types of transitions from canter to trot. In the first type the stance phase of the diagonal pair of legs (the outside fore and inside hind) becomes the first trot stride. The horse then 'springs' from this diagonal stance onto the opposite diagonal pair of legs for the trot. In the second sequence from canter to trot, the horse initiates the change from the stance of the leading forelimb. The trailing hind limb is then placed on the ground to give the diagonal stance phase of the trot. In the first type of transition, the horse lifts his head and neck to push his centre of gravity back. In the second type of transition he drops his head and neck forward and down over the leading stance forelimb. The extensor pattern of his head

16 C.K. Argue and H.M. Clayton (1993b), 'A study of transitions between the trot and canter in dressage horses' (article in J. Equine Vet. Sci. 13: 171–174) as quoted in W. Back and H.M. Clayton, *Equine Locomotion* (London, Harcourt Publishers Ltd., 2001).

and neck assists in the braking by pushing his forelegs against the ground. He usually brakes with the leading foreleg of the canter stride, then brakes again with the other foreleg in the first diagonal trot stride.

The 'on the bit' canter to trot

The novice horse finds canter to trot in the 'on the bit' position somewhat unbalancing because he is not in the habit of using his hindquarters for balance. To transform the horizontal propulsion into a vertical force he has to move his centre of gravity back and 'push his forelegs into the ground', but the 'on the bit' position prevents the use of his head and neck in the push pattern. This disturbance of balance is manifested as 'falling into the trot', lifting his head and neck into the trot and running for the first few trot strides. The experienced horse, who is engaged and in collection, has developed superior power, balance and agility in his hindquarters to use them for braking. He will know the preamble to the downward

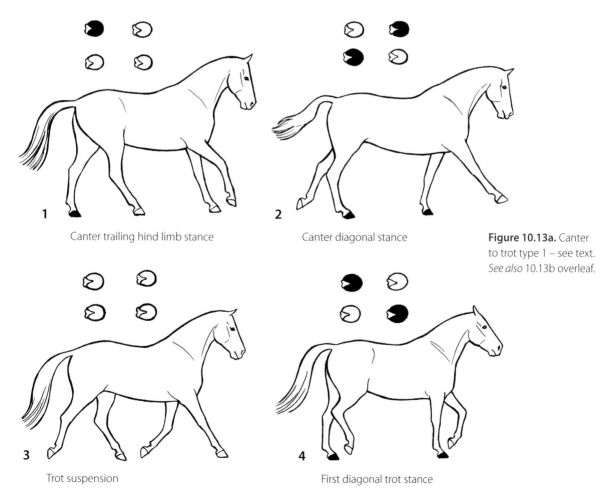

1   Canter trailing hind limb stance

2   Canter diagonal stance

Figure 10.13a. Canter to trot type 1 – see text. *See also* 10.13b overleaf.

3   Trot suspension

4   First diagonal trot stance

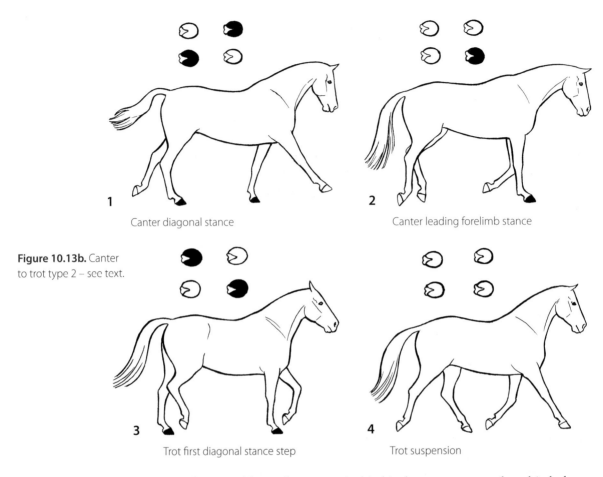

1   Canter diagonal stance

2   Canter leading forelimb stance

Figure 10.13b. Canter to trot type 2 – see text.

3   Trot first diagonal stance step

4   Trot suspension

transition and have the power in his hindquarters not to lose his balance into the transition. The aid should be applied during the moment of suspension to give the horse time to prepare for a balanced transition. He places his outside hind leg and then brakes with it together with the outside forelimb when the diagonal pair of legs takes the first trot step.

The natural canter to walk

The relaxed horse usually goes from canter to trot before he walks. In a heightened state of awareness he often goes straight from canter to walk or even straight into halt. He initiates the movement by lifting his head and neck in the push pattern to move his centre of gravity backwards. When braking with his hind limbs he drops his head and neck down.

The 'on the bit' canter to walk

Since the horse does not have the freedom of his head and neck to assist in this transition, he needs his hind legs in the weight-bearing and balanced position of engagement to do it with ease. The lifting of his head and neck, when he brakes with his forelimbs in the push pattern, is the most difficult part of the transition to change when training the young horse. When the aid is given during the moment of suspension the horse places his hind leg, which would also have been the next canter step, for the first walk step. When he learns this movement he tends to use his natural forelimb braking method. He usually weights the forehand too much and this leads to a few trot steps before the walk. This is also evident in the couple of jog-like steps he does with his hind legs into the walk while already walking with his forelegs. As soon as his weight is transferred backwards sufficiently, these hind leg jog-like steps will disappear. Then his fore and hind legs immediately move into the walk sequence. Some horses 'dive' down on the forehand because they are prevented from lifting the head and neck to move the centre of gravity backwards. These horses should be allowed to maintain a natural head and neck carriage through the transition until they are more engaged in the canter. Clear canter to walk transitions are usually only achieved by experienced dressage riders.

▶ RIDING AND TEACHING APPLICATIONS

1. Help the horse to balance in the downward transition from canter to trot by taking smaller, slower, more collected steps.

2. Maintain a round position with 'take and give' as an early warning signal and to encourage him to use his hindquarters to assist braking and balance. Maintain the sponging throughout the transition to explain to him that he is not to lift his head.

3. When teaching the young horse the canter to walk transition the rider should initially allow him to lift his head in the transition to enable him to maintain balance. Once the horse understands the canter to walk concept (he should not have any trot steps in between), he can start to learn the transition in a round frame. He should be given sufficient 'early warning signals' and engaging and balancing half-halts into the transition.

4. The aids for canter to trot and canter to walk should be given when the horse is in the moment of suspension. For canter to walk, give two or three collecting half-halts and with the third one close your knees, drop your heels and seat and breathe out into the walk steps. The three collecting half-halts help the horse to place his centre of gravity and weight backwards and thus engage his hindquarters. They are also an early-warning signal to prepare the horse for the transition and help to 'brace' the rider.

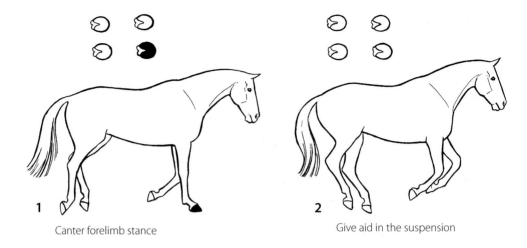

1. Canter forelimb stance

2. Give aid in the suspension

Figure 10.14.
Canter to walk.

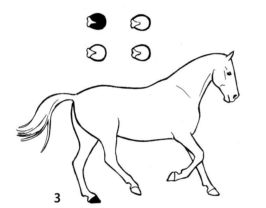

3. The horse places his hind limb, which becomes the first walk step

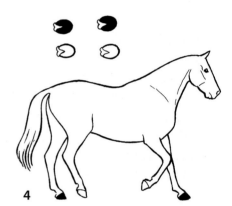

4. The next step is the ipsilateral forelimb

▶ JUDGING SIGNIFICANCE

1. During all the downward transitions from canter, the novice horse will attempt to use his head and neck for balance by lifting or hollowing it. This is not a sign of resistance, but a balance reaction. It usually means that the rider has not prepared the horse sufficiently and that the engagement is insufficient.

2. The maintenance of the horse's balance with a smooth, round frame through the simple change is more important than the rider's ability to do the simple change through precisely three walk steps.

3. Jogging-like steps often mean that the horse is not engaged enough through the transition.

Faults in the canter

The disunited canter

In the disunited canter the horse canters with the normal foreleg leading, but the opposite hind leg leading. This often occurs in nature as well as during training and is a regular occurrence in the lunge ring. Causes are:

1. In the lunge ring, going disunited is caused by two factors; loss of balance and/or motivation. It is extremely difficult for an inexperienced horse to canter in the small circle of the lunge ring, since in nature horses rarely canter in a circle. In the ring, the horse leads with his shoulders and keeps his head slightly to the outside to maintain balance (see Circles and Turns in Chapter 11). The trainer has to encourage him to move his head to the inside with 'take and give' on the lunge rein. If the horse does not yield to the rein pressure, or when his head is pulled into the circle, his balance will be affected. He thus swaps legs behind. He often also speeds up for a few strides as he turns to face the 'home' direction. This speeding up on a small circle leads to loss of balance with the consequent changing of his hind legs. He will now be cantering with his leading hind leg towards home and his leading foreleg towards the centre of the lunge ring.

2. The mounted horse usually changes legs behind when his neck remains rigid and unyielding to the 'take and give' of the rider's hands. His neck and spine muscles work as a unit and the pull on his rigid neck causes his hindquarters to swing out in the equine neck reaction. This causes

Photo 10.7. Horses often turn their necks to the outside of the lunge ring.

loss of balance. The horse then changes legs behind to maintain balance and thus becomes disunited. The problem is easily solved by teaching the horse to yield to the inside rein through 'take and give'. This yielding is all-important to ensure clean and straight flying changes.

Crookedness in the canter

In nature, the horse does not canter straight, but straightening him in this gait is one of the aims of dressage. There are two reasons for crookedness in the canter, both of which are natural to the horse.

1. The position of the fore and hind leading legs, coupled with a fairly rigid back, will position the horse naturally with his hindquarters to the inside. Both his shoulders and pelvis are positioned towards the side of the leading leg. This is probably a natural occurrence to prevent overreaching.

   Young horses are therefore naturally crooked in the canter, although generally very supple in all other work. They therefore have to be taught to canter straight. The first step is to ensure that all horses are equally supple on both sides. This is done through circle work, bending work and basic lateral work at the walk. Once the horse is supple, the canter has to be exercised in the shoulder-fore position. Riding in the shoulder-fore position in counter-canter around the entire arena is an easier straightening exercise for the rider than shoulder-fore in true canter, because the horse does not 'lean' onto the track. Leg-yield at canter and counter-canter exercises are all beneficial.

2. The second reason for crookedness in canter is connected to laterality. Natural 'sidedness' makes the horse favour bearing weight with the muscles of his dominant side because this is the stronger side. The non-dominant leg does not have the strength or the balancing ability of the dominant hind leg. Riders will notice that the horse favours the weaker leg even when standing in the stable. The horse will more readily take his weight on the stronger hind leg. When the weak leg is the trailing leg

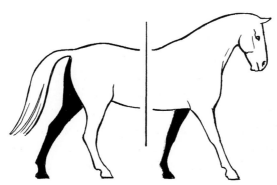

Figure 10.15. The inside leading shoulder and pelvis are both in a forward position during the canter.

on the outside during canter, the horse tries to avoid carrying weight on it by pushing his hindquarter weight to the stronger inside leg and against the rider's leg.

EXERCISE

(This is a balancing and strengthening exercise to improve the carrying capacity of the non-dominant hind leg.)

Lift your horse's stronger dominant hind leg and keep your shoulder close against it. Using your shoulder, slowly push him over towards the grounded leg and release again so that his weight moves towards you. 'Pull' his leg to your side a little and release it again so that his weight moves over his grounded leg again. Move his hindquarters slowly in all four directions for about three minutes. Push him slightly to the outside, then to the inside, then forwards and backwards. It is important that the movements are small and slow. Use this method to encourage the horse to make small circular motions on the grounded leg. This will develop the deep stabilizing muscles against the hip joint. After about two weeks of this daily exercise, you will notice a significant improvement in the weight- bearing capacity of the limb.

Photo 10.8.
Strengthening the hip stabilizers of the non-dominant 'weak' hind leg.

The four-beat canter

The four-beat canter is usually a rider-related problem. It is also common in retired trotters and American saddle horses. Causes are:

1. When the rider slows the horse down without simultaneously asking for impulsion, the diagonal pair of legs become dissociated. Because of the lack of impulsion, the action of the hind leg slows and grounds after what was the diagonal foreleg. (This has similarities with when forging in trot is caused by the forefoot impacting slightly before its 'diagonal' partner.)

2. The cause of the four-beat canter in trotters is somewhat different. In the trotter, the correct coordinated canter pattern is not exercised sufficiently during his racing career because canter strides are penalized in a trotting race and because of this he is discouraged from cantering during his formative years. Therefore, the muscles of the hindquarters and back, essential to the development of the canter, do not develop and strengthen sufficiently. The lack of exercise in the canter pattern and especially the lax ligaments in the hindquarters of trotters, disturb the horse's hind leg coordination. This causes the dissociation between the

diagonal legs. These horses do not learn to push for the suspension phase in the canter: some actually trot with their hind legs while cantering with their forelegs. Therefore they have to be taught to coordinate their hind legs correctly for the canter.

Both the causes of the four-beat canter are corrected by the same method – forward movement with impulsion in the canter. The rider should ask the horse for more 'jump' at every stride. First, the horse must learn to take big, ground-covering canter strides. The rider should ride him forwards with big bounding, but not fast strides, going large around the manège. The trotting horse also needs to do lots of canter on hacks and eventually hill work at the canter.

Only when the horse has enough strength and stability in his hindquarters, will he be ready to collect the canter. The rider achieves this by 'picking the horse up' with the legs wrapped round the horse's belly, with the seat muscles pinching up and stretching the rider's body straight at every stride. Think of riding the horse 'up in the air'. Once the horse does big, bounding steps, canter-trot-canter transitions and then canter-walk-canter transitions should be added.

The flat canter

There is a perception amongst some people that a horse's canter cannot be improved. This, however, is not entirely correct. A bad canter is never going to become an outstanding canter, but it can become quite adequate. The flat canter is often rider-induced. The rider simply does not ask the horse to 'jump' and the canter slows down without engagement of the hindquarters. This is the type of canter which usually becomes four-beat, and it should be corrected in the same manner as correcting a four-beat canter. Return to large canter strides with good impulsion before collecting it with appropriate half-halts and 'picking up' leg aids.

11

The Movements – Nature Versus Training

Biomechanically speaking, there is just about nothing natural for the horse in the manner in which we ride dressage movements. Yes, the horse will do most of the dressage movements in nature, but they are seldom performed in their complete form. In nature, the horse initiates every movement with his head and neck and he does them with his back in the extensor (hollow) pattern. Free horses seldom stay in the 'on the bit' position for longer than a few seconds and they do this only when they are showing off or when they 'prop' in the canter to walk or halt transition.

Horses have perfect balance at liberty because they have inner knowledge of the direction they take and of the gait they change to before they move, even though their reactions may be extremely fast in flight. The balance reaction to the change of direction or movement is automatic. This is not the case with the ridden horse. Once a rider is involved, the horse's balance is often compromised. Trained horses (and good riders) understand the preparation or preamble to the rider's requests, but many riders' interventions are ill-timed and lack adequate preparation. In the latter cases, the horse has no idea what the rider is going to ask of him and therefore cannot prepare for the next movement – which may well be the next step. In other words, many riders catch the horse by surprise most of the time. Therefore the horse's balance is disturbed at every turn, circle and transition. When his balance is challenged he will lift his head, or turn it in the opposite direction. Added to this, in ridden work we also impede the horse's natural balance mechanism by inhibiting his head and neck movements in the 'on the bit' position. We move his weight to his hindquarters and expect him to use them for balance, when the opposite is his natural way. The highly developed engagement, combined with the total flexor pattern in the individual dressage movements, is uncharacteristic of the natural horse. He carries more of his weight on his forehand and moves mostly in an extended frame. The natural horse does have enormous ability to use his body athletically in a variety of patterns, being able to do very complicated manoeuvres when at play and when having to move out of difficult spots. He *may* move in 'dressage' patterns of movement, but if he does so, it is usually only for a step or two. However, most of the horse's natural mechanisms for ambulation are modified when we ride dressage.

Gymnastic training (dressage and jumping) converts the horse into a super athlete. Correct schooling develops the bottom line flexor muscles, which strengthens his back, promotes engagement of the hindquarters and protects his weight-bearing front limbs against strain. It develops his musculature for the sole purpose of improving him for carrying the rider and doing the sport. However, he does not need to perform at such a high level in nature. He does not need this development to protect his body because he will be using his natural methods automatically and these are almost opposite to the movements of formal training. For example, he needs speedy acceleration for flight, but does not need sustained 'sitting' power.

This chapter aims to encourage riders to find appropriate, horse-friendly methods of teaching new movements to the horse. It should give riders more empathy when demanding controlled work and should remove some of the frustration when the horse *seems* to misunderstand. As explained in the Introduction, the term 'push' is used regularly to give the rider the idea of the effect on the horse. The rider has to influence the horse's balance reactions so that he can understand that he is to move over. This 'push' eventually becomes invisible light pressure.

Circles and Turns

The natural horse

Circular work does not come naturally to the horse because his rigid spine is designed to move in straight lines. Horses at liberty usually take the straightest route to their destination. A horse may move in large curves depending on the size of the paddock, or make sharp turns, but does not move in true circles naturally.

In nature, the horse usually initiates the circular shape by moving/leaning his shoulder into the bend, especially on his stiff side. He moves his head and neck to the outside in a balance reaction to move his centre of gravity over his base of support. He thus 'falls in' when he turns at liberty; he side-steps. At the walk, the horse turns his head in the direction of the movement and then takes the sideways step. However, the increased speed and small base of support at trot and canter could lead to disturbance of balance should the horse turn his head and neck first. Therefore, at trot, he carries his neck straight or slightly to the outside during turns. When he turns it to the inside, he moves his hindquarters to the opposite direction in a balance reaction. At canter, he mostly carries his head and neck in the opposite direction of the curve. This is why horses in nature do not develop well-shaped neck muscles. In nature the horse does not have a rider to tilt his ribcage to assist in the bend and elicit a balance reaction of the inside bend, therefore his head does not necessarily move in the direction of the circle.

Circles in the 'on the bit' position

In dressage, the horse has to move his head and neck slightly to the inside, in line with the circumference of the circle at walk, trot and canter. This will disturb his natural balance in the trot and canter if the rider does not ask correctly. When the rider asks for the bend via the reins, the horse yields his head and neck to the inside. In order to counteract this change of body schema, the horse has to move his centre of gravity to the opposite side. The horse's almost rigid spine restricts his ability to bend on circles, therefore his natural inclination is to move his shoulder into the turn (fall in). The horse has three methods of moving his centre of gravity in order to maintain balance in circular work when his head is bent to the inside.

Photo 11.1. The natural canter with the head turned away from the leading leg.

1. He can flip his ribcage over, but he does not seem to do this naturally and therefore needs the rider to 'request' it.

2. He can bring his hindquarters in line with his neck by stepping out with his hind legs.

3. He can pull his shoulder out of the circle ('hang out') when the circle is too small for him.

To prevent the hindquarters from stepping out, the rider has to tilt the horse's ribcage to the outside and ensure that the horse's neck has a yielding inside bend. If the rider does not counterbalance by pushing the ribcage sufficiently, the horse will attempt to maintain his balance by 'falling in' with his shoulder and turning his head and neck to the other side. To maintain the horse's shoulders on the correct size of circle, the rider has to move them in line with the circumference of the circle, and regulates this with the outside rein.

Contrary to popular belief, the horse does not necessarily trot in a circle simply by taking shorter steps with his inside legs than with his outside legs. This assumption has developed because riders tend to compare a horse's movement to that of a biped human, who does turn by taking shorter 'inside' steps, together with leg abduction. The process in the quadruped horse is, however, far more complicated, with many variables on which there seems to be limited scientific research. In the diagonal movement of the trot, the foreleg and opposite hind leg work automatically in unison in the diagonal pattern of movement: the diagonal hooves ground and lift simultaneously. Thus, hypothetically, a short step with the inside foreleg would mean that the outside hind takes a simultaneous shortened step: a long outside foreleg step will be coordinated with a long inside hind leg step. If the outside leg of the diagonal does not take the same length of stride as the opposite inside leg, the trot sequence will be lost. Alternatively, should the inside foreleg give a shorter step than the outside hind leg, but maintain the same time-frame, the horse will have to lift the foreleg higher to compensate for the shorter step. In both scenarios, the horse would be uneven in movement and the gait will not have a two-beat rhythm.

The fact is, however, that the horse does not walk, trot or canter in perfect circles. He adapts his movement to the circle by correcting it every few steps (not continuously). Since the horse's back does not bend sufficiently to maintain the curve of the circle his legs have to play a large

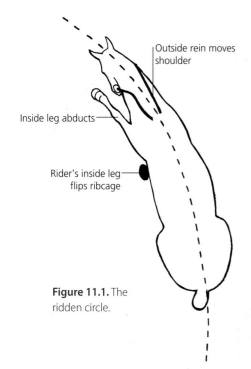

Outside rein moves shoulder

Inside leg abducts

Rider's inside leg flips ribcage

Figure 11.1. The ridden circle.

part in adapting his movement. His strides are essentially in straight lines, which he adjusts in the swing and/or suspension phase, from time to time, by stepping sideways a little. The horse's circles are thus made up of a series of straight lines corresponding to the size of each stride (see Figure 11.2a) and in trot and canter he turns while airborne. This negates the need to 'take shorter steps with his inside legs'. If he turned while

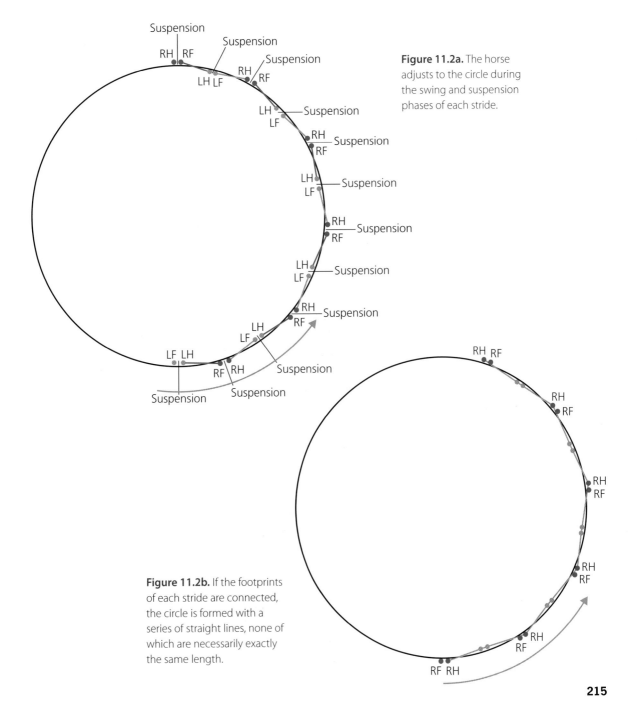

Figure 11.2a. The horse adjusts to the circle during the swing and suspension phases of each stride.

Figure 11.2b. If the footprints of each stride are connected, the circle is formed with a series of straight lines, none of which are necessarily exactly the same length.

his feet were in stance, they would have to swivel. (In walk, there is no period of suspension, but there are four individual steps and the gait sequence will not be lost if the individual steps are adapted to the rider's requirements.)

His shoulders and forelimbs guide the way and his hind limbs simply follow. At some strides he corrects his movement to align with the circular path by adducting his outside forelimb (bringing it closer under his body) and at other strides he corrects it by abducting his inside foreleg (opening it) a little. He does this according to the rider's rein instructions and other aids. In order to keep the hindquarters on the circular track the rider has to employ leg aids and simultaneously inhibit the 'equine neck reaction' by maintaining a yielding inside rein contact. Each stride length also seems to differ from the previous one as the horse adapts his stride to the circle.

Photo 11.2. The 'on the bit' circle with the rider moving the horse's shoulders into the circle. Note the large crossing (adduction) of the outside forelimb. Note that the horse leans his shoulder into the circle both in the natural and ridden curve.

EXPERIMENT

1. Draw a perfect 10 m or 12 m circle on a raked area of the arena by using a piece of cord tied to a pole in the centre of the circle.

2. Ride your horse on this line ensuring that he stays on it at every stride. You will immediately notice how important it is to keep his shoulders on this line. *Ride only one circle.* Ask a friend to keep an eye on only one fore or hind leg print.

3. Dismount and measure the distance from the hind leg print to the opposite foreleg print. Then continue to measure each full diagonal stride. You will notice that no two strides are the same length. You will also notice that the horse does not step evenly on both sides of the line.

It is the rider's skill which determines the shape of the circle. (Compare the often poorly formed circles of beginner riders to those of skilled riders).

Clearly, the distance travelled by the horse's inside legs has to be slightly shorter than that of his outside legs, but if the horse adjusts his body in straight lines during the suspension phase, this becomes negligible.

Added to this, the horse does not appear to have any concept of geometrical shapes. It is therefore doubtful that he has the ability to *plan* a perfectly sized circle, nor does he know in advance whether the circle is going to be 8, 10, 12, 20 m, or only a half circle during manège riding. The horse also does not automatically know what the rider is going to ask of him at the next stride, therefore, even if he could plan the circle, he would not know what size to make it unless the rider explained it to him every few steps. You can test this by letting go of the reins and taking your legs off the horse's sides. The horse may continue on a more or less circular shape for a few strides, but will not finish a figure of the required size. (A horse who is in the habit of being lunged may well continue on the circle, but this is a result of memory and submission, and not a consequence of planning.)

In contrast, man visualizes the circle. The human body immediately responds by preparing for the movement. The appropriate blood flow, nerve impulses, heat and muscle tone adapt in readiness to perform the movement. The thought alone produces these automatic responses. Since the horse cannot plan the circle, he does not visualize a whole circle from one suggestion (aid). Therefore his body does not react automatically to prepare for a specifically sized circle. He thus would not 'know' to take a consistently shorter step with his inside legs. He simply follows the rider's instructions as they maintain him on the circle. The horse's reactions to the size of the circles become easier the more they are repeated (memory and coordination).

The foreleg action on the circle

The small range of lateral movement in the horse's spine prevents a uniform bend around circles smaller than 12 m. As we know, simply turning his head and neck will not produce a correct circle. We have to convince the horse to move his shoulders in the circle or turn. The horse moves his shoulders into the circle, by abducting (stepping away from his body) his inside foreleg and adducting (stepping closer to his body) his outside foreleg (see photos 11.1 and 11.2 earlier this chapter). The rider moves the horse's shoulder by moving the outside rein towards the inside hip. This controls the size of the circle. The inside rein has to ask the horse to maintain the inside bend. If the circle is to be close to perfect, the rider will have to ask the horse to correct it by positioning his shoulders at almost every stride of the circle. When the horse is lunged without the barrier of a lunge ring, the abduction and adduction is very clear, because he does not correct himself at every step, nor does he correct the outside and inside legs with a consistent lateral step or angle: he usually corrects it when the lunge line becomes too tight. Horses who are lunged regularly become used to trotting in circles around a rider and adjust more surreptitiously. In these cases the side stepping will be more visible on a smaller circle.

However, when the rider asks for the 'correction' at every stride, this adduction/abduction is very small and not always visible to the naked eye.

The range of motion of this adduction/abduction is determined by the size of the circle. The bigger the circle, the smaller the abduction/adduction needed to ride it correctly. The sharper the turn, the bigger the sideways forelimb steps and the more visible they are to the observer. Observe how a horse does a walk pirouette. This is a magnification of how he moves in a circle with his forelegs.

The hind leg action on the circle

Visualize the horse's trunk as a large rigid barrel which the horse kicks forward at every stride. When the horse turns by moving his forelimbs to the side, his hind limbs have to move to the opposite side because the barrel cannot bend sufficiently. He then 'kicks' the barrel in the new direction. This is why it is difficult for the horse to maintain relative 'straightness' on a small circle. When the horse is in the lunge ring, with or without a lunge line attached, his hind legs do not track perfectly in the tracks of his forelegs at every stride: they usually step slightly to the outside at random intervals. The ridden horse is able to step perfectly into the tracks of his forelegs by abducting his inside hind leg and adducting his outside hind leg according to the rider's leg aids. His ability to rotate his hips allows him to point his inside hind hoof towards the circle as he abducts it (like a ballet dancer pointing sideways). The ability to step in line with his forefeet steps depends on him yielding his neck perfectly to the rider's inside hand, together with tilting his ribcage. This yielding prevents the horse's back muscles from becoming rigid and the hindquarters from swinging out (the equine neck reaction). The rider's legs push the horse's hindquarters and this motivates him to abduct and adduct his legs onto the circle.

EXERCISE

1. Lunge your horse in a lunge ring without lungeing gear. His neck is usually carried straight ahead or to the outside. Observe how he turns his head and neck to the outside while he moves his shoulder to the inside as he turns. This is noticeable especially on the 'stiff' side in trot and on both sides in canter. He usually only turns his neck to the inside when the pressure on the rein increases. When his neck turns in, he usually 'hangs out' with his shoulder. When his neck is yielding softly his hindquarters do not move out. When he resists the rein pressure his hindquarters move out.

2. Lunge your horse without side reins but with a lunge line in an open arena. Notice how you have to tug at the lunge line to bring his head in at certain parts of the circle because he does not generally trot with an inside bend. Notice how he moves his hindquarters out every time you 'pull' in his forehand. This is more evident when lungeing untrained horses and horses who are not lunged on a regular basis.

3. When mounted, ask the horse to turn immediately from the halt. You will notice that he takes a sideways step to do this. (See photo of natural pirouette on page 242.)

▶ RIDING AND TEACHING APPLICATIONS

1. The horse has to be prepared for the circle as well as for the size of the circle. The rider does this by asking for a slight inside bend a few strides before the actual turn. This will give the horse the opportunity to prepare and adjust his balance to initiate the circle or turn. Unless the rider explains to the horse that he is about to change direction and simply, without warning, turns his head into the circle or turn, he will lose balance. He will 'fall in' with his shoulder and move his head and neck to the opposite side. The rider will experience this as a stronger contact on the inside rein. The horse will also lift his head to maintain balance. Alternatively he may bend his neck, but lean out with his shoulder to maintain balance.

2. Since the horse cannot guess what size circle the rider would like him to do, the rider has to explain this throughout the entire circle more or less at each step, depending on the level of training. This is done with the outside rein, which moves the horse's shoulders in line with the particular size of circle, together with a vibrating inside rein to maintain the inside neck bend. This is the reason why the classicists tell us that 'the outside rein determines the size of the circle'.

3. Since the horse turns by leaning with his shoulders and side-stepping with his legs, it is the rider's responsibility to ask him to turn his head and neck in the direction of the turn and to push the horse's ribcage over and tilt it to enable him to redistribute his weight in order to maintain balance in this unnatural method of turning. This will prevent him from 'falling in' with bigger lateral steps.

4. The young/green horse's balance is improved when the rider maintains a fairly firm pressure with the inside leg, thus pushing his weight to his outside legs. This improved balance and weight distribution assists impulsion.

5. To prevent the horse from stepping out of the circle with his hind legs, the rider has to ensure that he yields perfectly to the inside rein in order to inhibit the equine neck reaction. Simply preventing the hindquarters from swinging out by using the outside leg behind the girth only solves the problem symptomatically. The maintenance of the 'curve throughout the horse's body', which is expected in dressage competition, is dependent on the correct yielding of the neck and the elasticity of the horse's hind leg abductor and adductor muscles.

6. Lateral work and stretch exercises improve the horse's ability to abduct and adduct his legs. These exercises thus improve his ability to step in his forehoof tracks during small circles.

7. The ground pole fan exercise is of little value in circle work. The horse simply finds the straightest line over the poles. He does not take higher, shorter steps with his inside legs, he simply steps closer to the poles with his inside legs at the narrow end and further away at the wider end, thereby giving steps of even length. He also steps out slightly with his hindquarters when the rider moves his shoulders into the curve.

8. The outside bend of the head and neck in circles and curves is patently clear during jumping competitions, especially at the lower levels. The horse moves his shoulder towards the fence, falling in, and the rider bends his neck to the outside in an attempt to counteract this. Correct this by teaching the horse to move away from your inside leg, thus tilting his ribcage.

Photo 11.3. The horse's 'natural' outside bend with the shoulder leaning into the curve towards the next fence. This is exacerbated if the rider tries to correct the bend with the outside rein, rather than the inside leg.

▶ JUDGING SIGNIFICANCE

1. When the horse steps out with his hind legs in the circle or turn, he has not yielded sufficiently to the rider's inside hand. He will thus have a false bend with a rigid spinal column.

2. When the horse lifts his head and neck into turns and circles, it is a sign that he has lost balance because the rider has not prepared him sufficiently into the turn.

3. If the horse has an outside bend in the circle or turn, the rider is not pushing his ribcage sufficiently with her inside leg to counter balance and the horse is not yielding to the 'take and give' on the inside rein.

4. When the horse appears to 'fall in' with his inside shoulder, the rider has not pushed the ribcage over sufficiently – and the rider has probably pulled the horse into the turn or circle with the inside rein.

5. When the rider pulls the horse into the circle with the inside rein, the bend is false. This is a common occurrence in dressage and can be

detected by the strong contact on the inside rein and the slight loop on the outside rein.

6. When the horse's outside shoulder 'pops out' of the turn or circle, the rider has not used enough outside rein to turn the horse's shoulders.

The biomechanics of 'falling in and leaning out on the shoulder

These terms refer to the horse's balance reactions when ridden in circles or turns. At specific points on the circle, the horse may 'push' his inside shoulder inward, or he may 'lean' out of the circle. He repeats this at the same spot on every recurrent circle. These actions are his natural methods of changing direction. In the ridden horse however, they can arise from disturbances to balance or from discomfort, but often they are the result of motivation. In such cases the horse pushes his shoulder towards the arena gate, the herd or the food/stable.

In biomechanical terms, when the horse is bent to the inside he has to carry more weight on his outside legs to prevent 'falling in'. He cannot have a true inside bend when his weight is on his inside shoulder. If he feels discomfort on these outside legs, he may try to avoid taking weight on them. He therefore moves his weight to the more comfortable inside leg, which changes the bend and pushes his shoulders in.

Photo 11.4. The horse's shoulder 'falling out' in the leg-yield exercise. The rider is pulling on the inside rein in an incorrect attempt to correct it.

EXPERIMENT

1. Go down on all fours. Bend your waist to one side. Notice how your weight distribution changes when more weight moves to your 'outside' leg and hand. This moves your centre of gravity to the centre of your base of support. Maintain the same bend, but lean on your 'inside' hand and leg. Your centre of gravity will not be over your base of support. Your incorrect weight distribution will soon tire your muscles, which are now contracting against gravitational resistance.

2. Stand at the ribcage of a mounted horse. Slowly push against the rider's leg. Notice how the horse bends his neck to the inside and lifts his weight off his inside legs. The rider will also feel the horse moving his weight to his outside legs with this inside bend.

When the horse moves his weight from his outside shoulder onto the inside shoulder, his bend changes and he 'falls in'. He either straightens his neck or turns it to the outside. This new bend may not be visible, but the contact will become firmer on the inside rein, proving that the bend has changed. He will then be contracting the incorrect muscles and his bend will effectively be to the outside at that particular part of the circle. He will abduct (move out) his inside foreleg, which will make the circle smaller. This 'falling' in on the inside shoulder feels as though the horse is pushing against the rider's inside leg.

When the horse leans/pushes/hangs out of the circle or 'pops' his shoulder out, he maintains the inside bend and weight distribution. However, he places too much weight on the outside leg, leans over the shoulder and abducts his outside leg and shoulder in an attempt to move in that direction. He does this usually towards the entrance of the manège, towards home or the other horses. He thus enlarges the circle with his outside foreleg.

▶ RIDING AND TEACHING APPLICATIONS

1. The horse 'falls in' with his shoulder on his 'stiff' side, when he does not want to take extra weight on his outside foreleg or when he is motivated by outside factors, such as other horses. When he 'falls in' without any obvious outside reason or stiffness, the cause may be discomfort in the outside foreleg, often in the shoulder muscles. A good physiotherapist can usually feel stiffness in the shoulder muscles. The discomfort can also be in his foot, even without the presence of lameness: he simply avoids weighting this foot. A veterinary or farriery check should solve the problem.

2. The horse has to move his weight onto the outside shoulder and outside hindquarter in order to lift his inside legs for the canter depart. If his weight is on his inside shoulder, he will take the incorrect lead in canter. Falling in on the shoulder is corrected by pushing the horse over with the inside leg (it helps to place the inside leg slightly forwards), leading the shoulder over by opening the outside rein, 'take and give' on the inside rein and giving a light tap on the inside shoulder if necessary. If you touch him with the whip on his inside shoulder he will transfer his weight to his outside shoulder immediately.

3. Falling out is a little easier to remedy. Simply tighten the outside contact and move your hand closer to the horse's withers and towards your inside hip. In persistent cases you may have to move your hand over the withers until the horse is obedient to the outside rein. A light tap on the outside shoulder, together with a firm outside rein, will teach the horse to align his shoulder. It usually takes only three repetitions of this light tap for the horse to learn to respond to the tightening outside rein alone.

4. Young horses often lean out of the circle excessively when learning to canter in a circle. This is because it is so unnatural and unbalancing for them to canter in a 20 m circle. They usually lean out on the open side of the circle towards the gate. Correct this by making a sharp turn before the horse starts to lean out. For example, if the circle is at E in the arena and the horse leans out at L, make a sharp turn before the centre line and turn the horse towards R or M. It is important to look at and aim for the marker. By doing this, he will not be able to lean out. Within two to three repetitions he will give up his attempts to lean out and will do the circle correctly.

5. In order to elicit straight flying changes, the horse has to transfer his weight to the new outside shoulder one stride before the change. This 'frees' the shoulder of the new leading leg. This is the reason why the horse should take one straight stride before the direction change in the canter zigzag. (See also Flying Changes, later this chapter.)

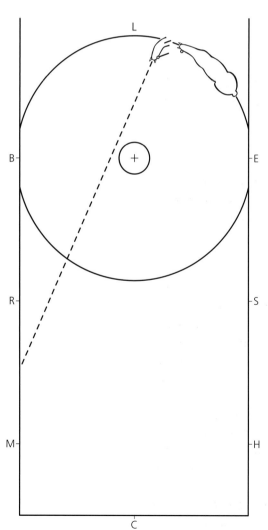

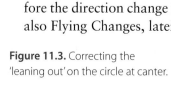

Figure 11.3. Correcting the 'leaning out' on the circle at canter.

The biomechanics of the hindquarters 'falling in'

When the horse places too much weight on his inside hind leg and abducts it, his hindquarters 'fall in'. It will feel as though the horse is pushing against the rider's inside leg. This is generally caused by the horse's natural crookedness. When this 'pushing in' is an active resistance, it is usually a sign of discomfort. The horse pushes his weight from the uncomfortable outside hind leg to the inside hind leg. The problem is amplified during the canter. There is a common misconception that the horse is not engaging his inside leg when he brings his hindquarters in. The fact, however, is that he is reluctant to place weight on his outside hind leg and engage it.

▶ RIDING AND TEACHING APPLICATIONS

Hindquarters falling in indicate one of three problems:

1. The horse is not supple enough: the rider should do more suppling and stretching exercises such as shoulder-in.

2. The horse is crooked as a consequence of the natural canter footfalls. This is corrected with suppling exercises and the shoulder-in at the trot and canter. Straighten the horse through the shoulder with the outside rein moving the shoulder in: the inside leg pushes the horse's body onto the track.

3. The horse is experiencing discomfort either in his outside hind leg or outside back muscles, and is therefore reluctant to weight his outside hind leg. He should be checked by a veterinarian and physiotherapist.

The biomechanics of the tilted head

As mentioned earlier, the most common cause of the tilted head is the motivational tilt. In this case the horse is positioned with an inside bend, but wishes to look to the outside. He bends his neck correctly at its base, but tilts his head, from the second vertebra, to the outside to see his friends, to point towards the entrance of the arena or to point towards the stable. He usually does this with regular monotony at the same spot, during the schooling session.

The second cause is inadequate rider technique. The rider simply pulls the horse with the inside rein around corners, around circles and in the shoulder-in (the false bend), but the horse pulls against this with his outside neck muscles. The consequence is an outside neck bend with an inside head/nose tilt.

The horse may also tilt his head when his balance is compromised during circles and turns. The rider asks the horse to bend his neck, but the horse simply 'falls in' on his shoulder. The rider then takes more contact on the outside rein in an attempt to prevent the shoulder from 'falling in'. This action takes the horse's nose out. In this case the bend and the tilt are to the outside. The horse swivels his head to the outside.

▶ RIDING AND TEACHING APPLICATIONS

Photo 11.5a. *below left* The motivational tilt. This tilt is to the outside towards the entrance of the arena which is on the horse's right.

Photo 11.5b. *below right* The tilt, caused by pulling on the inside rein, is to the inside. It is actually a form of the false bend.

1. Correct the motivational tilt by positioning the horse's nose to the inside with your inside rein. You may have to open your inside arm or lift it to explain to the horse that he should point his nose in the correct direction. He can only correct it if he understands what to do. Maintain strong inside leg pressure to flip the ribcage.

2. Correct the riding technique by using 'take and give' or vibrating inside rein aids together with the inside leg pushing to tilt the ribcage. This will ensure that the horse bends his own neck.

3. Correct the horse's balance by pushing his shoulder to the outside. He should be carrying his weight on his outside shoulder during turns and circles. Teach him to move his shoulder away from your inside leg pressure. You may tap him lightly on the shoulder with the whip while simultaneously pushing with your inside leg in a slightly forward position. The horse will make the connection after three repetitions and move his shoulder out from inside leg pressure alone. Once the correct weight carriage is established, turn the horse by means of 'take and give' on the inside rein, together with inside leg pressure on the girth.

▶ JUDGING SIGNIFICANCE

1. An inside tilted head means that the horse has an incorrect bend.

2. This fault should also be considered under the 'rider position and correct use of aids' section of the test.

3. The motivational outside tilt is usually caused by a lack of submission/ concentration.

The Rein-back

The natural 'rein-back' (backward stepping)

In general, horses do not take many backward steps naturally. They usually move back two or three steps to manoeuvre out of a difficult position; they then turn and move in the preferred direction. These few steps are often dissociated and not in a diagonal sequence. A few horses may step back a little distance to reach an opponent for kicking. The horse halts with his weight on his forelimbs. The backward movement is slightly more demanding than moving forwards because the balance control for moving the centre of gravity (i.e. the neck) is in front. He initiates the backward stepping by leaning his hindquarters back and lifting his head and neck. These two actions move his centre of gravity back and they lift the weight off his forelimbs to free them for taking the backward steps. The lifting of the neck has a natural hollowing effect on the back because of the natural extensor movement pattern. He then moves a hind leg, followed almost simultaneously with the diagonal foreleg. He plants the diagonal legs simultaneously. After a few steps, the diagonal movement usually becomes dissociated because his foreleg steps slow down and the movement starts to resemble a four-beat backwards walk sequence. This is related to the fact that he carries more weight on his forehand and is thus slower to lift his forelegs. Balance is more difficult on the small two-legged diagonal base when movement is slow. Both fore and hind limbs have a braking action in the rein-back.

Rein-back in the 'on the bit' position

The rein-back may be a little difficult for some horses, especially in the 'on the bit' position, in which it is an unnatural 'man made' pattern of movement with flexion of the forehand yet extension of the back, hips and hind legs. It is probably the movement Novice and Elementary level riders lose the most marks on in a dressage competition. Because the horse's forehand has to lighten to enable him to do a correct rein-back it is really an advanced dressage movement.

It is not easy for the horse to use his head and neck to 'lift' his weight off his shoulders when his neck movements are inhibited in the 'on the bit' position. Although he can move his rump back, that alone does not move his centre of gravity back sufficiently. Thus he has to move backwards with his legs only and it is very difficult to take large steps without the ability to move the centre of gravity back. This is probably the reason why most horses shuffle backwards before perfecting this movement. Since the movement is an extensor pattern with the back and hind leg extensors moving the legs backwards, the muscle action is not the same as in engagement. The forelimbs are converted into the engine while the hind limbs become the 'struts' for the body to move over. The forelimbs push against

Photo 11.6. The natural rein-back. Note the lifting of the neck and the hindquarters leaning back.

resistance (the ground) to move the horse's body over his hind limbs. In engagement, the quadriceps femoris muscles extend the stifles while the hamstrings extend the hip joint to push against the ground. In rein-back, the quadriceps femoris muscles flex the hip joints while the hamstrings flex the stifles to pull the horse's body over the hind limbs. Although the same muscles are in action in each case, they are used and strengthen differently.

The process of 'on the bit' rein-back does, however, place the horse's hind legs more underneath his body and condition the correct muscles, which is essential for the engagement of the hindquarters. Forward-going horses seem to find this movement especially difficult. Horses who place too much weight on their forelegs in the halt find it difficult to reposition their weight for the rein-back.

▶ RIDING AND TEACHING APPLICATIONS

1. The horse naturally carries more weight on his forelegs when he halts. He therefore has to learn to place his weight backwards before taking the first step of rein-back. If his weight is on his forelegs he will do one of the following.
    a. Drag his front feet.
    b. Hollow his neck.
    c. Rein-back in a walk sequence. When a horse does this, his front legs move slower than his hind legs and this is the cause of the lost sequence.
    d. Shuffle backwards in little steps.

EXERCISE 1

Get down on your hands and knees. 'Walk' backwards. Notice how much easier it is on your supporting hand when you move your buttocks back a little to lighten the weight off your shoulders.

EXERCISE 2

Ask a friend to stand in front of you and give her a sudden shove backwards without warning. The natural response of a person shoved in this way will be to hollow their back, lift their arms and take backward steps. Now do the same experiment with your horse by shoving him backwards against his chest. You will notice that he lifts his head and neck, then leans back before he moves backwards.

2. Correct rein-back problems by keeping the horse's weight off his shoulders into the halt. Use a few collecting half-halts into the halt. Do not allow him to 'settle' into the halt. Once he has 'settled', his weight will

be firmly on his shoulders. Ask for the rein-back while maintaining a light contact. Do not pull the horse back. If you do so he will then pull against your hands and this places more weight on his forehand/ shoulders.

3. Once the horse can piaffe, his rein-back will improve through the development of his balance on a small base of support and the superior engagement of his hindquarters.

4. The rein-back removes the horse's forward impulsion, but it places the hindquarters more underneath the horse and activates the hip flexor muscles, thereby assisting the process of engagement. It is the transition from rein-back to trot that increases impulsion and engagement and develops the appropriate parts of the muscles.

▶ JUDGING SIGNIFICANCE

The halt period before the rein-back, as requested in the dressage tests, places the horse's weight on his forelimbs. If this period is too long, it has a negative effect on the rein-back. The horse may then learn to 'walk' back, pace back, drag his forelegs or hollow in his neck to move his centre of gravity back in order to manage the movement. At lower-level dressage tests, the horse should not be expected to halt for too long before asking for the rein-back. Once the horse has figured out how to manoeuvre his weight with ease, he should be able to do it under most conditions.

Lateral Movements

The horse is not designed to take large lateral steps at speed. Because of the absence of collarbones his fore- and hind limb adductor muscles are specifically adapted to stabilize the limbs onto the body to prevent splaying. Therefore, in nature, the horse takes relatively small lateral steps and only a few at a time, usually to manoeuvre out of small spaces, to turn or when playing. At the slower gait of walk, the limbs need less stabilizing than at the faster gaits. Therefore, at walk, he is able to take larger lateral steps.

Biomechanically, lateral movement is initiated by the same principle as forward movement. The horse moves his centre of gravity beyond the perimeter of his base of support and then 'falls' to take the step. He does this by moving his shoulder in the direction of the movement. At the faster gaits of trot and canter he generally moves it to the opposite side to control his balance. At the walk, however, he may move his head in either direction depending on his motivation.

The horse initiates the lateral hind leg movement, such as the turn on the forehand, by leaning his rump sideways until his centre of gravity moves sufficiently for him to take a step with his opposite hind leg.

Balanced lateral work in dressage depends on the horse's ability to maintain the bend while adjusting his weight from his outside legs to his inside legs and vice versa. When his balance is disturbed to the side, he regains it by moving his neck to the opposite side to pull him out of the 'fall'. This is the difficulty in many of the lateral movements.

The turn on the forehand

The natural turn on the forehand

In nature the horse will do this movement for one or two steps only, but he uses the same biomechanical technique as he does in the mounted exercise. He leans over with his rump until the bulk of his hindquarter weight is placed over his outside hind leg. He then moves his inside leg closer to the outside leg, or crosses it. His weight then moves to his inside leg to allow him to take the lateral step with his outside leg. This process is repeated at every step. The horse can usually move his hindquarters over better on one side than the other. This is a consequence of his natural dominance/laterality and the consequent weaker balance on the non-dominant hind leg. When his stability is weak on the outside leg, the crossing over of the inside leg must be shorter and faster. His head and neck usually stay in the normal straight position in the exercise because the balance of his forehand is not disturbed.

The mounted turn on the forehand

This movement is usually performed early in training and is not a competition movement. Its sole purpose is to teach the horse to yield to the rider's pushing leg. It is therefore not necessary to perform it in the 'on the bit' position. When the mounted movement is performed, the rider tends to pull on the inside rein on the same side as the pushing leg. This pulling on the inside rein causes tightness through the horse's entire spine from his neck backwards and forces him to step sideways with his hindquarters (the equine neck reaction). Although this is effective, it does not teach the horse to move away from the rider's leg, but teaches him to react to the rider's hand. This is the reason that there should be no pull on the inside rein.

▶ RIDING AND TEACHING APPLICATIONS

1. Riders often do not realize that when they push the horse's hindquarters laterally with one leg, their other leg inadvertently 'tries to help' in an

associated movement. This gives the horse two opposing messages. When doing this movement, the rider's passive leg should initially be moved off the horse to ensure that the horse gets one instruction alone. This may not look good initially, but as soon as the rider learns to dissociate the movement of the two legs, the passive leg can be replaced.

2. Riders can prevent the associated pull on the rein on the side of the active leg by keeping their hands close together when performing this exercise. It helps to keep the knuckles touching throughout the exercise. This will prevent the inside hand from pulling and will teach the horse to move away from the leg pressure alone.

3. This is the only movement where stepping back as an evasion is acceptable because the horse is learning the concept of moving away from the rider's leg. Horses usually attempt to evade this movement by walking forwards out of it. They do this especially at the end of the exercise when they simply walk straight to the track before the rider has realized that the horse is 'cheating'. This forward evasion soon becomes a habit. If the forward evasion is prevented by two-handed half-halts, the horse may try to evade the lateral steps by taking some backward steps. These are seldom towards the track (i.e. they come at other phases of the turn).

Photo 11.7. The turn on the forehand. The rider's inside leg is off the horse to ensure that the horse receives a single instruction only. It should be replaced passively once the rider's coordination has improved. This photo shows how the horse leans his rump laterally to move his centre of gravity.

Photo 11.8. The turn on the forehand. The rider's knuckles of both hands should touch to ensure that there is no pull on the rein on the side of the active leg.

If the rider continues to push the horse laterally towards the track, even while he is taking backward steps, he soon learns that he cannot evade the lateral steps. He thus grasps the concept more quickly, after which he never tries to back out of the movement again. The horse generally learns this movement in two sessions, after which it never needs to be practised again. From this exercise, the training moves on to more useful lateral exercises such as leg-yielding and shoulder-in, in which backward movement is discouraged with bilateral leg aids.

Leg-yielding

Although this is the natural lateral pattern of movement of the horse, it is not seen in its whole form very often in nature. The horse either moves his shoulders laterally, or he moves his hindquarters laterally. He initiates the movement by pushing over his shoulder to move his centre of gravity. He bends his neck in the opposite direction in order to keep his centre of gravity over his base of support and maintain balance. When he moves his hindquarters over, he leans over with his rump first to move his centre of gravity, then takes the step.

In dressage we insist that the horse maintains a straight neck and stays on the bit. This position inhibits his balance reactions. It is more difficult for the horse to move laterally when he cannot push his weight over his shoulder or move his neck to the opposite side from the movement.

Photo 11.9a. *above left* The leg-yield with a neck bend is the natural method for the horse.

Photo 11.9b. *above right* The leg-yield with a straight neck is more difficult for the horse to perform.

▶ RIDING AND TEACHING APPLICATIONS

1. When the horse pushes his shoulder out, he has placed too much weight on his outside shoulder. Consequently, he will have too much neck bend and his hindquarters will trail. Riders usually attempt to correct this by pulling on the inside rein and pushing more with the inside leg, but this only leads to more neck bend. Correct the problem by 'retarding' the horse's shoulder movement by taking a firm outside rein, and push it closer to the horse's neck in the direction of your opposite hip. If this is not effective enough, move your hand over the horse's spine. Crossing the hand over the withers at this stage has no negative biomechanical consequences – it is only a question of aesthetics. What is important is that the horse understands your instructions. This action negates the need to push hard with the inside leg behind the girth. It will encourage him to distribute his weight more evenly over both shoulders and straighten his neck. Continue to push the horse's hindquarters over at every stride.

2. Pulling the outside rein closer to the withers straightens the horse's spine and brings his hindquarters in line with his neck and shoulders. When

the horse loses the angle, all the rider has to do is to tighten the outside rein while maintaining the soft inside bend and the horse's hindquarters will step sideways and increase the angle. This is an automatic reaction and again negates the need to push hard with the inside leg behind the girth.

3. A rider wishing to look back to ascertain whether the horse's hindquarters are trailing or leading should preferably do so over the inside shoulder. This not only gives the rider visual feedback to correlate with the correct 'feel' of the angle, but the rider will immediately and automatically correct the angle. Looking over the outside shoulder does not have this effect. Looking over the rider's outside shoulder could give an erroneous perception of the angle of the movement.

4. Teach the horse the leg-yield with his head facing the fence. This ensures that the rider's communication is effective. When leg-yielding is performed across the diagonal the rider is often 'fooled' into thinking that the horse is moving laterally when he is actually simply moving straight across the diagonal. The horse does then not learn what is required.

5. Use this movement to correct the bend during half-pass. When the horse loses the bend in half-pass, move him to the opposite direction for a few

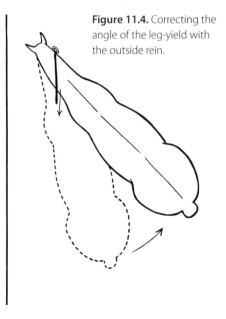

Figure 11.4. Correcting the angle of the leg-yield with the outside rein.

Photo 11.10a. The pony's shoulder is 'falling in' in the leg-yield.

Photo 11.10b. The act of looking over the inside shoulder gives the rider the correct feedback of the horse's angle.

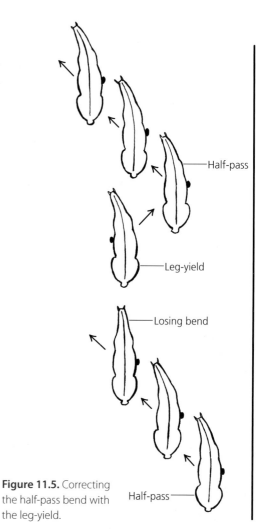

Half-pass

Leg-yield

Losing bend

Half-pass

Figure 11.5. Correcting the half-pass bend with the leg-yield.

steps of leg-yield. This will re-establish the correct balance and bend. Once the bend is re-established, move him back to the half-pass again.

6. The opening forelimb and crossing hind limb step can be enlarged if the rider's leg is used as the horse's inside foreleg grounds. The crossing forelimb and opening hind limb step can be enlarged by using the leg aid as the horse grounds his outside forelimb. This principle applies to all lateral work.

7. The horse's muscles condition during the stance phases of a movement because they have to push against resistance (the ground) to make the limb or body move. The swing phases allow the muscles to stretch. Therefore, in leg-yielding, the adductors strengthen when the outside limbs are in stance, 'pulling' the body over. The abductors strengthen when the inside limbs are in stance 'pushing' the body over.

▶ JUDGING SIGNIFICANCE

1. This movement should not be included in dressage tests as it is difficult to define the exact features of the movement. It is a training movement to teach the horse to yield to the rider's leg. Once the horse can yield sufficiently the movement is replaced by the half-pass or shoulder-in and is only used as a corrective measure.

2. The important part of this movement is the yielding to the rider's leg. Therefore, the rider should not pull on the inside rein. Too much inside bend is a sign that the rider is pulling on the inside rein.

3. The shoulder 'popping out' and the horse losing angle are signs that the rider does not have enough outside contact.

Shoulder-in

The shoulder-in, practised on three/four tracks, has the same biomechanical elements as leg-yielding in terms of natural balance mechanisms. The bend in both movements, as in nature, is in the direction opposite to the movement and thus does not push the horse out of balance. Although shoulder-in is a 'man-made' pattern of movement and not completely natural for the horse, its close connection to the leg-yield ensures that it is fairly easy for horses to perform.

The lateral flexion pattern is consistent throughout the body, but the horse is expected to move his hind legs in a straight line. Since the horse's spine has extremely limited lateral flexibility, this may well be an optical illusion. The pressure from the rider's inside leg tilts the ribcage to give an impression of an inside bend. The outside forelimb abducts to open while the inside forelimb adducts to cross over during their respective swing phases. The hind limbs are brought closer together through the adduction of the inside hind limb, which brings it more underneath the horse's abdomen. As soon as the angle becomes too big, the inside hind leg moves across the horse's centre line and the movement becomes a leg-yield.

Although the movement is fairly uncomplicated for the horse, the rider has to learn complicated coordination patterns to elicit this movement from the horse. If the horse maintains a rigid neck in this movement, his hindquarters will move in line with his neck. That is to say, they will swing out and the bend will then be lost. If the rider pulls on the inside rein, the horse will resist, his neck will tighten and also lead to the 'equine neck reaction'. When the horse loses balance, he will lift his head and neck 'off the bit'.

Photo 11.11a. *top left* The shoulder-in controlled by the outside rein.

Photo 11.11b. *top right* The rider communicating incorrectly by pulling the horse's shoulder in with her inside rein.

Photo 11.11c. *left* The shoulder 'falling out' is another fault caused by the pulling inside rein

▶ RIDING AND TEACHING APPLICATIONS

1. In the shoulder-in the shoulder movement is controlled by the outside rein. If the rider attempts to bring the shoulder to the inside by pulling on the inside rein, it will have the opposite effect: the horse will bend his neck to the inside excessively, but will 'pull' his shoulder to the outside by abducting his outside foreleg. Correct the excessive abduction of the outside shoulder and foreleg by taking a stronger contact on the outside rein. Move the shoulder by taking the outside hand towards the inside hand or towards the inside hip.

2. The tightening of the neck, and consequently the entire spine, which leads to the hindquarters swinging out, should be inhibited throughout the movement with 'take and yield' on the inside rein or on both reins if necessary. The horse will yield his neck and his quarters will immediately cease swinging out.

3. A conservative four-track shoulder-in has more gymnastic value than the three-track shoulder-in in the training of the horse. However, when too large an angle is asked for, it has little bend and becomes a leg-yield.

4. It is usually the rider, not the horse, who struggles with this movement. An experienced rider can elicit a shoulder-in from any horse at the first attempt.

5. When riders first learn this movement the horse often loses impulsion. This is because the rider is struggling to coordinate limb movements and apply the aids correctly and thus unwittingly blocks forward movement. This blocking can originate in any part of the rider's body but is most often caused by a difficulty in dissociating the movements of the inside arm from the inside pushing leg: the rider inadvertently continues to pull with this arm.

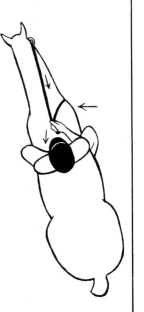

Figure 11.6. Controlling the shoulder movement in the shoulder-in. Move the outside hand towards the hip.

▶ JUDGING SIGNIFICANCE

1. When the horse's hindquarters swing out, he will not be yielding correctly to the inside rein. The horse's spine will be rigid and the bend will be insufficient.

2. When the horse's outside shoulder 'pops out', the rider does not have enough contact on the outside rein. This is usually apparent when the horse has excessive bend in his neck.

3. Slowing down is usually an indication that the rider is blocking the forward movement in some fashion.

4. A four-track shoulder-in has better suppling and strengthening qualities than a three-track shoulder-in, provided the horse's inside hind leg does not cross the midline of his body.

Half-pass, travers and renvers

The half-pass, travers and renvers are 'man-made' patterns of movement which are not natural to the horse. They are the movements that, especially during canter, place the most stress on the horse's leg and sacro-iliac joints. During travers, renvers, half-pass and the pirouette, the horse has to maintain a bend which is the opposite of his natural inclination. Moving in the same direction as the bend interferes with the horse's natural balance reactions because the position of his head and neck moves his centre of gravity laterally beyond the perimeter of his base of support. He therefore moves too much weight onto his leading inside shoulder, 'falling' onto it and speeding up to maintain balance. (This is similar to 'running' at the trot when the horse's weight is on his forehand.) Too much weight on his inside shoulder also changes the bend. The horse therefore may move his head to the opposite (natural) side, tighten his neck muscles in co-contraction or simply tighten the opposite neck muscles in an effort to regain equilibrium and bring his centre of gravity within the perimeter of his base of support. His natural balance reaction is to change the bend of the half-pass, travers, renvers and pirouette either with his neck or alternatively by swinging his hindquarters in the opposite direction. This latter reaction is, however, prevented by the rider's outside leg. To correct the bend, the weight distribution and the balance, the rider has to 'flip' the horse's ribcage over. The emphasis on moving forwards during the training of these movements assists the horse in maintaining his balance, bend and the angle of the crossing of his legs.

During all lateral movements, the horse conditions muscles which he generally does not strengthen naturally. Horses who do not do lateral movements have hollow areas on the sides of their hindquarters in the area of the biceps femoris muscles and thus find these movements more difficult to perform. These areas bulk out as soon as horses do regular lateral movements.

▶ RIDING AND TEACHING APPLICATIONS

1. The half-pass, travers and renvers are not only difficult movements for the horse to perform, but riders need superior motor coordination and balance to master them. During these movements each of the rider's limbs has to explain a different task to the horse. The rider's inside hand, with 'take and give', explains that the horse should bend to the

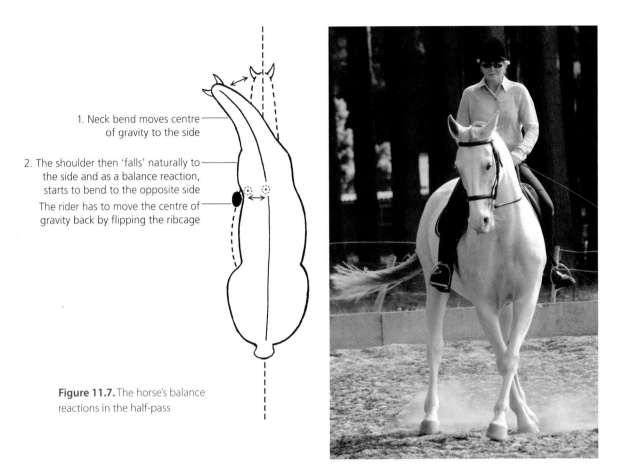

1. Neck bend moves centre of gravity to the side

2. The shoulder then 'falls' naturally to the side and as a balance reaction, starts to bend to the opposite side

The rider has to move the centre of gravity back by flipping the ribcage

Figure 11.7. The horse's balance reactions in the half-pass

Photo 11.12. The half-pass.

inside. The outside hand moves the horse's shoulder over and controls the extent of the shoulder movement. The fingers of both hands ensure that the horse does not lift his head. The rider's inside leg not only flips the ribcage over for the bend, but also maintains the impulsion. The rider's outside leg pushes the horse behind the girth to move his hindquarters over. Added to all this, the rider has to ensure that the horse maintains his balance. Learn them by chunking the movements into their basic building blocks.

2. To ensure that the forehand leads the movement, first point the horse's nose and shoulders at the marker (and keep this association throughout the movement) and then move his hindquarters over.

3. When the horse moves his shoulders over too fast, retard them by moving both hands to the outside.

4. Take time practising them at the walk to help the horse find his equilibrium and understand each movement.

▶ JUDGING SIGNIFICANCE

1. When the horse loses balance and moves over too fast, the rider's inside leg is not effective enough.

2. There are three reasons why the hindquarters may lead the movement:
   a. The rider's outside leg is pushing too much.
   b. The rider's inside leg lacks effectiveness.
   c. The rider is not moving the horse's shoulders over.

3. When the hindquarters trail, the rider's outside leg is not effective.

The walk pirouette

The natural walk pirouette

Photo 11.13. A Horse performing the natural pirouette: The hind legs do not move.

In nature, the horse usually bends his head and neck in the direction of the movement, but he *may* bend them to the outside depending on his need. This is followed by his shoulder moving over. Since there is no forward movement, his balance is slightly compromised. He therefore does one or two steps in pirouette with his forelegs to manoeuvre out of a tight spot. He generally swivels his hind legs for two or three steps and then steps out wide to bring them in line with his spine. He then starts to take forward steps, or simply halts.

The 'on the bit' walk pirouette

The pirouette is a difficult movement for the horse. It is another 'man-made' pattern of movement which inhibits the horse's natural inclination to move his hind legs out in line with his spine when turning. In mounted training, he has to move his head and neck in the same direction as the movement. This moves his centre of gravity to the inside and places more weight on his inside foreleg. This head and neck position works against his natural balance mechanism of moving laterally. His natural inclination is to bend head and neck in the opposite direction from the movement in order to maintain balance.

He is also required to 'march' with his hind legs, which is against his natural reaction to swivel or step wide when there is no forward movement. In the ridden pirouette the horse carries more weight on his inside hind leg. This can easily lead to swivelling and only the rider's superior communication techniques can prevent this. The horse steps wide to broaden his base of support, to bring his spine in line with his head and neck and to move the weight off his inside hind leg. The horse has an inclination to slow down the rhythm to change the direction from forward to lateral marching in one place.

▶ RIDING AND TEACHING APPLICATIONS

1. When the horse tightens his neck, or lifts it, his hindquarters will become 'stuck'. Prevent the sticking hindquarters with continuous vibration on the inside rein. When he yields correctly to the inside rein, he should lift his hind legs at every step.

2. When the horse is allowed to place too much weight on his inside hind leg, it will 'stick' and swivel. The rider's inside leg should prevent this by pushing the horse's ribcage, and thus the weight in his hindquarters, to the outside.

3. Prevent the hindquarters from swinging out on the stiff side with stronger outside leg pressure behind the girth, 'take and give' on the inside rein and slightly forward movement.

Photo 11.14. The walk pirouette.

4. When the horse is allowed to place too much weight on his inside foreleg, he will lose the bend. His hindquarters will step wide and out.

5. In order to maintain the correct inside bend, the rider has to maintain inside leg pressure on the girth together with continuous vibration on the inside rein.

6. Most horses use different techniques for the right and left rein pirouettes. This, again, seems to be as a result of insufficient balancing ability on the weaker, non-dominant hind leg. Usually on the 'soft' side, the rider has to initiate the movement with an opening inside rein to lead the shoulders. On the stiff side, however, the rider has to have a strong pushing outside leg from the onset or the horse will step out to avoid bending. On this side, the horse tends to push his hindquarters out because his lateral neck and back muscles are slightly tighter. This moving of the hindquarters is also a consequence of the natural abduction (stepping out) pattern of the outside leg.

▶ JUDGING SIGNIFICANCE

1. This is one of the most difficult movements for the horse, as well as the rider, to perform correctly. It is requested quite early in the training of the horse, but it is also performed at FEI level. It should be scored according to the level of the test. An inexperienced horse should not be expected to do this movement on one spot. Expecting this at the lower levels can only lead to problems later on.

2. Sticking hindquarters are a sign that the horse is not yielding to the reins. He is tightening the top line muscles of his neck, thus hollowing.

3. The horse will swing out his hindquarters when he is not yielding to soft inside rein pressure.

The canter pirouette

The natural canter pirouette

The natural canter pirouette is usually a quarter turn on a half rear. It is a swivel on grounded hind legs, which the horse uses to change direction when playing. Although his head may be in the 'on the bit' position, his back is hollowed to lift his forehand. In the natural canter pirouette, the horse's head is usually turned to the *outside*.

The dressage canter pirouette

Of all the dressage movements, this is probably the most taxing on the horse's musculo-skeletal system. He has to lift his forehand with his top line muscles, while his bottom line muscles have to maintain the flexor pattern. The horse's gluteal muscles and the lumbar section of his longissimus muscles thus carry the brunt of this force and therefore have to be powerful. The forward propulsion in the hind legs is changed into a braking activity. This affects the horse's balance mechanisms: he loses the assistance of forward momentum to maintain balance. A consequence of this is that the canter footfall sequence is altered.[1] The slow speed necessitates a bigger base of support; the horse keeps his hind legs in stance for longer; the diagonal support phase is entirely dissociated, there is no suspension phase and therefore cadence is reduced.[2] To explore this further: his single hind leg stance phase is shortened; his second hind leg is grounded speedily to add a double hind leg stance phase to broaden the base of support while his forehand is moved laterally; his trailing foreleg then grounds, closely followed by his leading foreleg. His hind legs lift, one at a time, as the trailing forelimb grounds.

▶ RIDING AND TEACHING APPLICATIONS

1. It is very important that this movement is only attempted once the horse has developed sufficient power in his hindquarters. If it is started too early, he will not be able to hold the single hind leg stance.

2. The horse should learn to canter in one place before commencing with the actual pirouette. This improves his balance as well as the power of his hindquarters.

3. When the movement slows down too much, especially at the beginning of training, the dissociation is increased. Both hind legs will then ground simultaneously.

4. When the 'circle' is ridden too small early in training, both hind legs will ground simultaneously.

5. It is important that the horse yields to the inside rein and maintains the bend. When the bend is lost the horse is more likely to swivel. If the rider's outside shoulder is held back, the horse is less likely to lose this bend.

---

1 H.M. Clayton, 'Performance in equestrian sports', in W. Back and H.M. Clayton, *Equine Locomotion* (London, Harcourt Publishers Ltd., 2001).

2 Ibid.

6. When the horse does not yield to the inside rein, he will have too much weight on his inside shoulder. He will move his hindquarters out or both hind legs will ground simultaneously to maintain balance.

7. In the canter, the horse uses momentum to maintain balance. Therefore, in the canter pirouette, he may move his shoulders over too fast and over-rotate. This can be counteracted by the rider's outside shoulder being kept well back and the inside leg well forward. The yielding inside bend of the horse's neck assists this.

▶ JUDGING SIGNIFICANCE

1. It is important that judges understand the dissociation of the sequence in order to have a clear picture of the correct sequence of this movement.

2. The horse slows down naturally to maintain balance and the correct gait sequence.

The Piaffe

This type of movement is not natural to the horse and is performed very rarely in nature. The piaffe is a diagonal movement, giving the impression of remaining in place (although there is usually a little forward movement). One diagonal pair of legs ground as the other diagonal pair lift. The hind limbs show considerable braking activity to avoid forward movement of the body.[3] The propulsion is vertical. Therefore the horse's weight should be distributed equally between the fore and hind legs. His hind limbs thus have to move well underneath his body, decreasing the size of his base of support, and his head and neck carriage becomes high. This small base of support, combined with a high centre of gravity and the absence of forward movement, challenges the horse's equilibrium. It turns him into an upside-down pyramid, which is a position of unstable equilibrium. The horse therefore always has at least one foot in stance, which means that the movement has no true moment of suspension. The apparent suspension is an optical illusion created by the slow flexion and extension of the fetlock, stifle and hip joints resulting in the synchronized rising and sinking of the horse's torso and the momentary pause of the hooves in the swing phase. Horses often leap forwards to maintain balance when learning the piaffe. Long-backed horses especially find this position difficult to maintain, as it is demanding on their equilibrium. The maintenance

---

3 E. Barrey and S. Biau, 'Locomotion of dressage horses' (paper presented at conference on Equine Sports Medicine and Science, 2002).

of balance and the braking activity of the hind legs in this movement can be compared with pushing back on the pedals of a bicycle in order to keep it motionless without falling over.

The piaffe is the ultimate position of collection in competition dressage and is biomechanically opposite from the passage. Some extravagant-moving horses prefer the more forward passage to the stationary piaffe. These horses need careful and tactful riding and may take longer to find enough stability to perfect the movement. Many horses, however, find this movement relatively easy to learn, but the so-called 'lazy' horses do not perform it readily.

Research has shown that the ground reaction force is low in the piaffe.[4] The contraction of the quadriceps muscles, pushing the feet against the ground and straightening the stifles, is slow. This means that momentum does not assist the muscles as they push and simultaneously balance the horse's body in a vertical direction. The quadriceps muscles contract in eccentric contraction to flex the stifles against gravity as the leg joints 'fold'. They then change into concentric contraction to straighten the stifles by pushing the body up against the ground. During this changeover, each stifle has to be stabilized by all the muscles and ligaments around it. This sustained muscle action, especially the quick changeover from eccentric to concentric contraction and stabilizing of the stifle is extremely strenuous, tiring and unnatural for horses. During eccentric contraction the muscles are used as brakes, not as motors. Unaccustomed eccentric contraction (too strenuous, too long, or too many repetitions) leads to *delayed onset muscle soreness* (DOMS) which is accompanied by microscopic muscle damage scattered throughout the muscles. Well-conditioned quadriceps muscles are thus absolutely essential for this movement. These should be developed gradually through strength and engagement exercises.

In piaffe, the horse hardly moves forwards and therefore he does not have to stretch his head and neck in order to take a step. By the time the horse learns the piaffe he should be quite comfortable in the 'on the bit' position. The piaffe is a flexor pattern movement and therefore the horse should be light in hand. Strong contact means that the horse is in the extensor pattern and thus may lose rhythm, coordination, the movement sequence and, especially, engagement.

The horse naturally engages and brings his hindquarters relatively far underneath his body to do this movement. He does this to place his quadriceps femoris muscles at the correct angle for vertical propulsion. The exact position of the horse's hindquarters depends on his conformation and the direction of the force.

---

4 H.M. Clayton, 'Performance in equestrian sports', in W. Back and H.M. Clayton, *Equine Locomotion* (London, Harcourt Publishers Ltd., 2001).

Photo 11.15. The piaffe.

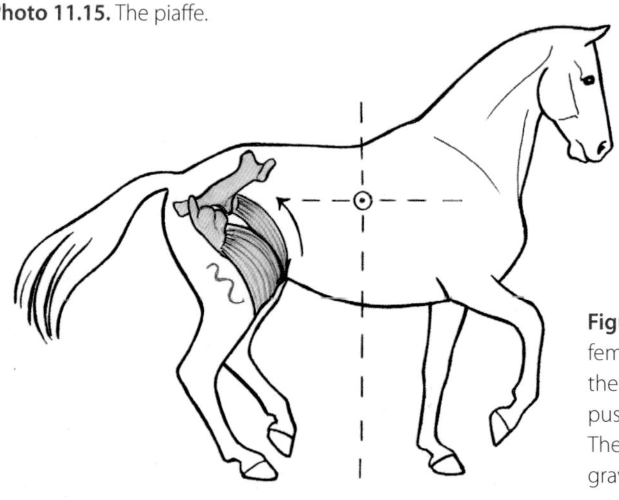

Figure 11.8. The quadriceps femoris muscles straighten the stifle when the hoof pushes against the ground. They then flex it against the gravitational resistance.

▶ RIDING AND TEACHING APPLICATIONS

1. The piaffe is a movement which improves all other movements because of its engaging effect on the horse's hindquarters. It squares up the halt, improves the rein-back and corrects the medium and extended trots. It engages the hindquarters in readiness for all the collected work.

2. Half-steps can be practised with novice horses because the lack of ground reaction force means that doing so does not place too much strain on their muscles. Horses do, however, need adequate development of their quadriceps muscles before starting this movement in place. The half-steps help to develop these muscles.

3. Since some horses find it difficult to balance in the piaffe, riders need to take great care not to pressurize them into the 'stationary' position.

4. The quality of the piaffe is improved by shortening the overlap of the hooves in stance and improving positive diagonal advanced hoof placement.

▶ JUDGING SIGNIFICANCE

Each horse will have his own particular 'shape' in this movement depending on the optimum angle for the most effective use of his quadriceps femoris muscles. This depends largely on conformation and muscular anatomy. The visual picture may well be important, but the rhythm, balance, cadence and lightness should take preference when judging the movement.

The Passage

The natural passage

In contrast to the piaffe, horses passage regularly in nature, but they do this with a hollow and tight neck and back and with their tails lifted – the extensor pattern. They often push with a wide hind leg stance and trailing hind legs. They are usually in a state of heightened alertness and in the tense fright/flight mode when they passage in nature. This adrenalin gives them the extra lift to spring from one stride to the other. Clearly, huge power is not necessary for passage in the free frame because foals do it regularly when excited. The horse uses his elastic recoil ability to convert his energy in a vertical direction to bounce from one diagonal pair of legs to the other, like jumping on a trampoline.

Photo 11.16. The natural, hollow passage.

The 'on the bit' passage

The classical passage is ridden in a round flexor frame, the opposite of the natural passage. Therefore, it should only be taught once the flexor muscles have been well conditioned in the 'on the bit position'. This is the 'Irish step-dancing' of the dressage world. The forelimbs elevate the forehand, while the hind limbs provide both upward and forward propulsion.[5]

5 E. Barrey and S. Biau, 'Locomotion of dressage horses' (paper presented at conference on Equine Sports Medicine and Science, 2002).

The hind limbs also have a braking activity to moderate the forward movement of the body. Positive advanced diagonal hoof placement is significant, especially in the more successful competitors.[6] Since the movement is dependent on elastic recoil and is not significantly ground-covering, there is not a need for large changes in the centre of gravity.

The passage does not appear to be a particularly difficult movement for horses. They regularly use it as an evasion so as not to collect and engage the hindquarters. They then move into a 'passagy' trot. Horses seem to 'play' with their elastic recoil to produce passage.

▶ RIDING AND TEACHING APPLICATIONS

1. The passage usually develops as a natural consequence from the piaffe. Therefore, teach the horse the more difficult movement of piaffe first. Elevated forward steps out of the piaffe then slowly develop into passage steps. This method of teaching the piaffe first is very important with horses who show a natural passage during moments of excitement or who 'offer' passage when asked for a half-halt. With these horses, teaching the passage first could lead to difficulties in teaching the piaffe. The wisdom of teaching the piaffe first will become very obvious to anyone who has taught passage first, but then found that their horse shows a marked propensity to passage, but a profound disinclination to piaffe.

2. During the training of the passage, the horse may take a larger step with one diagonal. This is usually caused by weaker balance of the non-dominant hind leg, which the horse grounds quicker. The larger step demonstrates the horse's innate ability. Therefore the rider should do exercises to develop the weaker hind leg.

3. The transition from piaffe to passage is relatively easy because of the elastic recoil and vertical propulsion in the piaffe. The gluteal muscles necessary for the transition are usually well-developed by this stage.

4. Transitions between medium trot and passage help to improve the quality of the passage.

▶ JUDGING SIGNIFICANCE

1. The passage to piaffe transition is extremely difficult. The passage is essentially a movement of extension and the piaffe is a movement of extreme collection. The balance adjustment from the large airborne

---

6 H.M. Clayton, 'Performance in Equestrian Sports', in W. Back and H.M. Clayton, *Equine Locomotion* (London, Harcourt Publishers Ltd., 2001).

Photo 11.17. The dressage passage.

movement of passage to the small base of support of the piaffe is the major difficulty horses experience in this transition.

2. The transition from piaffe to passage is dependent on muscle power to change from the pushing power of the quadriceps femoris muscles to the coordinated power of the muscles producing elastic recoil. By the time the horse can perform these two movements, this power is usually sufficiently developed.

3. Each horse has his own style of passage, which no amount of training is going to change significantly. Thus the beauty of the movement is in the eye of the beholder.

4. Be aware of the passagy trot. This is usually a sign that the horse is 'faking' engagement.

5. One or two passagy trot steps in the transition from extended trot to collected trot is often a sign that the horse has superior power in his stride so that the half-halt produces vertical velocity.

The Flying Change and the Counter-canter

Flying changes are completely natural for the horse to perform. Horses perform them regularly from birth when they canter and change direction. In nature however, the horse does not often do clean changes. He usually canters a few strides in counter-canter with his head to the outside and when he becomes too unbalanced he changes legs in front and then, after a few strides, changes the lead behind. When a curved path of progression is not deep, he may continue at a leisurely counter-canter. In nature, the horse turns his head and neck to the opposite side of the change.

The flying change is a movement of extension in which the horse stretches his head and neck.

In dressage, the horse is required to change the lead during the moment of suspension simultaneously in his fore and hind legs. He thus needs long air time for the change. He is also required to change in a collected flexion frame. This is a hindrance and leads to croup-high changes, or changes that are not clean. Freedom of his neck and a slightly longer frame during the change are necessary for clean changes since he has to be in control of his balance mechanisms. He then lands in the correct canter sequence on his trailing hind leg.

▶ RIDING AND TEACHING APPLICATIONS

1. The flying change is easy for the horse, but seems to be a difficulty for many riders. The rider's timing has to be correct to elicit a clean flying change from the horse. As soon as the rider's timing is correct, the horse will usually do the change correctly.

EXERCISE

Canter on your own legs in a large circle. Change rein and note how the counter-canter feels uncomfortable. The horse experiences the same uncomfortable sensation and will thus do a flying change to avoid discomfort.

2. Since this is a natural movement which the horse performs from birth, the rider does not have to wait until the horse's training is advanced before teaching it. The counter-canter, however, is a more complicated athletic movement for the horse. To ensure that the horse understands the counter-canter, it is good practice to teach this movement before the flying change. Inexperienced riders may have difficulty in teaching the counter- canter if they teach the horse the flying change first.

3. To ensure clean changes it is very important that the rider allows the horse to stretch his neck forwards in the initial training of the flying change. This slight forward stretch will ensure changes which are 'through', clean and smooth.

4. If there is a lateral restriction in the horse's neck, the change will not be clean because of the 'equine neck reaction' which tightens the spine.

Ensure that the horse yields his neck perfectly to both sides, especially in the counter-canter, before attempting flying changes.

5. The horse has to move his weight over to his new outside shoulder before the change is asked for. This is the same principle as for the canter depart. The new inside bend should be requested a stride before the change to ensure that the horse can jump through and the change is clean. By the time the horse can do sequence changes with ease, this clear change of bend is not usually required.

6. During the initial training the rider may have to make a definite balance disturbance into the change by 'swinging' the horse's forehand to the new side. This is to ensure that the horse understands the concept.

7. If the suspension period is not long enough, the horse may not have enough air time to coordinate his diagonal pair of legs in sequence. The diagonal hind leg may thus be marginally late (almost like a four-beat canter). Should this become a problem, resolve it by allowing the horse a longer stride.

▶ JUDGING SIGNIFICANCE

1. Changes which are not clean are often a sign that the horse is not yielding sufficiently to the new inside rein and is weighting his new inside shoulder.

2. Changes which are not 'through' are often a sign that the rider's contact is too strong.

3. Croup-high changes are often a sign that the rider is not yielding the hands and arms sufficiently.

4. The horse is late behind when his trailing hind limb changes at the end of the sequence instead of leading the sequence.

5. The horse may lose the canter sequence slightly when the diagonal stance phase is dissociated and the diagonal hind limb is grounded slightly after the diagonal forelimb (four-beat canter). This is a 'smaller' fault than being late with the trailing hind limb.

6. Swinging hindquarters in the changes usually mean that the horse's neck is rigid and he is not yielding to inside rein pressure (the equine neck reaction).

The Biomechanics of Jumping

Dressage horses are the 'rhythmic gymnasts' of the equine world. They specialize in flexibility. The jumping horses are the 'artistic gymnasts'. These gymnasts specialize in tumbling and jumping exercises. They need a combination of superior power, agility, suppleness and balance. They also need to know how to save energy when jumping, that is, they should not over-jump. Horses with good jumping technique only miss the poles by a few centimetres. Barrey and Galloux found that horses with poor jumping technique used greater forelimb braking force to compensate for weak hind limbs.[7] Each horse has his own individual technique which he repeats over every jump. A horse with a poor technique uses more energy to lift his dragging legs over the fence. This jumping technique seems to be a physically heritable ability passed on from generation to generation, although recent research has shown that conformation, by itself, is a bad predictor of jumping ability. A weak rider's influence can have a negative effect on a talented horse, but a horse with inadequate jumping technique cannot develop into a brilliant jumper despite the skills of a superior rider. This same principle seems to apply to the technique of dressage horses' movement.

The natural jump

During the natural jump, the horse perceives the fence on the approach. He then assesses the height and the distance with his automatic visual motor coordination skills. He automatically judges the effort needed to clear the fence and adjusts his stride to reach the fence in the correct place to clear it. He uses his neck in a perfect bascule to move his centre of gravity and to lift his forehand in the correct angle to clear the fence. He is not restricted by an outside force such as the rider's hands 'holding him into the fence' and he does not knock the fence. In fact, the horse who is in danger of knocking the fence won't even attempt to jump it unless he is in fright/flight mode.

Biomechanical analysis of the jump

The ground reaction force is all-important in jumping. Once in the air there is no resistance for the muscles to push against and therefore nothing can change or be changed. The push of the horse's hind limbs against the

---

7 H.M. Clayton, 'Performance in Equestrian Sports', in W. Back and H.M. Clayton, *Equine Locomotion* (London, Harcourt Publishers Ltd., 2001).

ground at take off thus produces the power and energy necessary to clear the height. The head, neck and forelimbs create the vertical lift and determine the flight path.

The take-off

The horse starts to prepare his body for the jump, the stride before take off. This final canter stride is shorter and four-beat.[8] At the take-off stride the horse lowers his head and neck forward and down. His withers drops between his shoulder blades and his foreleg fetlocks touch the ground in extension. He goes down in preparation to push up and take off. This procedure creates leverage around the joints for elastic recoil and optimal muscle contraction to project the horse upwards. This forelimb braking action changes the horizontal force into a vertical upward force, lifting the shoulders. It is somewhat like the action of a jack-in-the-box. Interference at this point can lead to poor execution of the jump.

The horse grounds both hind legs well underneath his body for the take-off. He lowers and flexes his hind legs to balance and gather for the powerful upward push. His head and neck extensors, back extensors and gluteal muscles, in that order, then all contract to lift his entire forehand off the ground against the force of gravity. He then stretches his neck forwards and straightens his stifles, hocks and hips to thrust his body forward and up over the fence. This spring-like stretch of the head, neck, body and hind legs produces the power to jump high. The horse thus needs extremely strong muscles in his hindquarters and back for this lift at take-off.

The flight

This is followed by the flight pattern, during which the horse has to stretch his neck forwards and round in order to round his body over the fence. This flexor pattern of the head and neck encourages the horse to fold his forelimbs to prevent knocks. It is unnatural to fold the forelegs sufficiently when the horse is hollow in the extensor pattern over the fence. The horse's lumbo-sacral joint is, however, in extension and assists the horse in 'kicking' his hind legs back out of the way of the obstacle.

The landing

As the horse starts to descend, his body automatically prepares for a balanced landing. His neck lifts to move the centre of gravity back. His forelegs

---

8 H.M. Clayton, 'Performance in equestrian sports', in W. Back and H.M. Clayton, *Equine Locomotion* (London, Harcourt Publishers Ltd., 2001).

a

b

c

d

e

f

extend to brace and balance in the landing. He lands on his trailing foreleg and this is followed closely by the leading foreleg. Since the horse lands with all his weight on his forelegs, this leads to enormous stretch of the fetlocks during the landing. He lifts his head and neck and uses his back extensor muscles again to lift his forehand and to rebalance him in the recovery. The recoil from the huge ground reaction force lifts the forelegs into the suspension phase before the trailing hind leg touches the ground for the first canter step. This momentum is to ensure that his balance is maintained when his hind legs hit the ground with forward velocity. His back, hips and hind legs move into full flexion to ensure immediate hind limb engagement during landing. The leading hind leg is grounded immediately after the trailing leg to re-establish forward momentum and assist his balance to take the next canter stride away from the fence.

▶ RIDING AND TEACHING APPLICATIONS

1. The horse's head and neck initiate the jump, raise him over the fence and determine the flight path. He balances himself with his head and neck at the take-off, during the flight, at the landing and at the move-off. The horse therefore needs freedom of his neck throughout the sequence. Restriction of his head and neck in any part of the jump may have a negative effect on his balance and ability to clear fences. The rider's arms should thus yield towards the horse's mouth and not attempt to 'hold' him into the jump. (Human high-jump athletes use their arms in a similar fashion to the horse using his neck.)

2. The quality of the jump is dependent on the quality of the approach and the take-off. The quality of the approach and the take-off are dependent on the horse's balance and ability to engage his hindquarters. This is entirely the rider's responsibility. It has been found that 'most jumping errors are a result of inappropriate 'aids' from the rider'[9] and that horses show less tendency to over-jump with a good rider.[10] Thus poor rider-horse communication, poor body use and rider interference have negative effects on a horse's jumping ability.

3. In the approach, the horse also needs freedom of his neck to lift and lower his head in order to see the fence and judge the distance and the height. When a horse is 'held' into the jump, he will be pulling with his extensor muscles and will have too much weight on his forehand. This

Photo sequence 11.18.
photos on opposite page
The jump sequence with the horse in self-balance.
a. The take-off, showing lowering of the horse's head, and fetlocks touching the ground. The hind legs are grounded well under the body.
b. The forehand is lifted off the ground while the hind limbs are lowered and flexed.
c. The flight pattern showing a bascule and flexed forelimbs.
d. Landing on the trailing foreleg.
e. Followed closely by the leading foreleg.
f. The forelimbs lift before the hind limbs are grounded.

9 H.M. Clayton, 'Performance in equestrian sports', in W. Back and H.M. Clayton, *Equine Locomotion* (London, Harcourt Publishers Ltd., 2001).

10 W. Back and H.M. Clayton, *Equine Locomotion* (London, Harcourt Publishers Ltd., 2001).

will prevent engagement of his hindquarters into the take-off. This 'holding' into the jump is totally preposterous. How can a mere rider attempt to balance a 600 kg (1323 lb) horse into the jump by holding the reins? *Imagine human high-jump athletes attempting to jump at the Olympics with ropes tied around their body, holding them back. They would never make the height.*

This 'holding in' interferes with the horse's visual motor coordination ability and balance mechanisms, thereby preventing him from co-ordinating his body to the height and distance of the fence. The horse then has difficulty in judging and adjusting his stride to reach the correct take-off point. It also affects his ability to manoeuvre himself 'out of trouble'. Such holding often leads to knocking a foreleg and may even cause back injury. Barrey and Galloux found that 87 per cent of jumping faults are caused by forelimb error.[11] Therefore, riders should use effective half-halts, followed by softening of the reins, to balance the horse and allow him to jump with self-carriage.

4. Horses who jump hollow, in the extension pattern, when they do not have the freedom to bascule, often show a tendency to knock poles. They may not make the distance over a big spread, which could cause serious injury.

5. The horse's canter needs to be engaged and elastic for jumping, which allows him to adjust his stride with ease in the approach. A light contact is essential for this.

6. It has been shown that the forces required to jump small fences (± the horse's elbow height) are not significantly more than to take an ordinary canter stride. The horse does not have to lift his centre of gravity significantly at these heights. Horses do, however, need great strength to project their centre of mass over high fences.

7. If a change of direction is to follow a jump, the lead has to be changed in flight before landing to ensure optimum balance.

8. It is essential that the ground after the jump is of good quality to increase shock absorption for the forelimbs which carry the weight of the horse at landing.

---

11 H.M. Clayton, 'Performance in Equestrian sports', in W. Back and H.M. Clayton, *Equine Locomotion* (London, Harcourt Publishers Ltd., 2001).

Conclusion

The horse was well-designed to meet mankind's needs through the centuries. He is one of the most adaptable of all animals and has been used extensively for all kinds of transport, for heavy work and, in essence, as the 'engine' for many machines. These days, the majority of horses are used solely for sports riding and leisure time activities. As such, they are trained for the sole purpose of pleasing us riders. We therefore have a duty to be ethical and kind in our training and we have a responsibility to ride our horses in an empathetic manner.

The first steps in the training format of the horse are to establish *rhythm* and *balance*. For many years, I did not realize the impact that these most important factors had on the horse throughout his training. It was only when I started thinking about such phrases as 'popping the shoulder', 'ride from the inside leg to the outside rein', 'take contact on the outside rein', 'leaning out of the circle', 'falling into the circle', 'running', 'hollowing in the transition', 'resisting', 'leaning on the rider's hands', 'heavy in the hands', 'incorrect bend' and many more, that I began to realize that the ridden horse's major problems are twofold – rider interference and lack of communication skills. Horses do what horses do. If we want them to do what we desire, we have the responsibility to get the message across with a method which will not cause disturbance of balance and which the horse can understand immediately.

In fact, the more I researched into and observed horses, the more I realized that the way we tend to ride compromises horses' natural balance reactions. I came to appreciate that most of the horse's 'arguments' are caused by this difficulty, compounded by the common training practice of giving two opposing messages – one to go and a simultaneous one to stop.

When I explained the balance adjustments a horse has to make in the 'on the bit' position, a pupil of mine responded with the comment: 'They are truly amazing animals. They manage to look perfectly graceful and perfectly balanced in spite of the rider.' This tribute to the horse notwithstanding, this book has attempted to explain the amount of assistance the horse needs from the rider to ensure that he maintains this perfect balance and grace in his ridden work. We owe it to the horse to help him prepare for every movement so that he does not lose his equilibrium and 'fall in', 'push out', raise his head in 'resistance' or become heavy in the hands.

Too often, however, we expect far too much from an animal who owes us nothing. Phrases such as 'resistance' suggest that we expect horses to understand our often inadequate communication skills. This may even lead to abuse from spurs, whip and bit. Some horses are even sold on because they don't submit to a particular owner, yet become perfectly amenable with a new rider who has better communication skills. Years ago, Alfred North Whitehead (1861–1947) made the point that a major problem with humans is that we try to match the world to our perceptions rather than adjusting our perceptions according to the world. The horse has had to fit in with our inadequate perceptions and moderate communication skills for millennia. It is now time for us to change our perceptions. We have to realize that our horses' sometimes unwanted reactions are simply *what horses do*, because they are horses, and they do not want to be uncomfortable or unbalanced. It is our duty to understand these reactions, to control our own bodies and communicate our instructions clearly and with good timing. In other words, we should communicate in a manner which the horse can understand with ease, so that it is easier and more pleasant for our horses to comply. If we can achieve this, many schooling problems will become simply avoidable, because correct communication leads to instant learning, even with a 'difficult' horse.

Glossary

Abduction: refers to the lateral movement of a limb sideways, or partially sideways, away from the body.

Adduction: refers to the lateral movement of a limb sideways or partially sideways towards the centre of the body and includes continuing beyond the midline of the body.

End range: movement has a mid-range and two ends. Generally, most movement falls within the mid-range because this is where movement is at its most comfortable. For example when we walk we do not take the largest possible steps because that would be too tiring, we stick to the mid-range of movement. The end ranges are the limits to which a joint can stretch and therefore the muscles have to stretch to reach these limits. Using the walk as an example, the furthest the leg can protract is the one end range and the furthest it can retract is the other end range of movement.

Gravitational resistance to muscle action: muscles only strengthen when they resist some form of force. Gravity forms a strong resistance against which muscles contract.

Ground reaction force (GRF): according to Newton, for every action there is an equal and opposite reaction. Since there is always an interaction between a body and the ground upon which it is positioned, the body's reaction to the ground is always accompanied by a reaction from it. This is called the ground reaction force (GRF): it reflects the upward acceleration of the body. We use this external force as propulsion to initiate and control movement.

Inertia: according to Newton, every body continues in its present state of rest/movement until a force acts on it. Inertia is the state of rest or its present state of movement. Force or resistance is needed to change this state or to change velocity.

Proprioception: The automatic knowledge of the exact position of each body part.

Tensegrity: A word derived from 'tension' and 'integrity', referring to structures that maintain their integrity due primarily to a balance between structure and continuous tensile forces (e.g. muscle and bone). The mechanics of this are: load one corner of the structure, and the whole structure will give to accommodate the load; load it too much and the structure will break at some weak point removed from the area of applied strain (i.e. not necessarily anywhere near where the load was placed), because the structure distributes the strain along the lines of tension.

Index